THE ESTATE
PLANNING GUIDE

THE ESTATE PLANNING GUIDE

Martin M. Shenkman, CPA, MBA, JD

John Wiley and Sons, Inc.
New York • Chichester • Brisbane • Toronto • Singapore

Library of Congress Cataloging-in-Publication Data

Shenkman, Martin M.
  [Estate planning guide]
  Martin Shenkman's estate planning guide.
    p. cm.
  Includes index.
  ISBN 0-471-54203-2 (alk. paper) : $39.95 (est.), — ISBN
0-471-53496-X (pbk. : alk. paper) : $19.95 (est.)

  1. Inheritance and transfer tax—Law and legislation—United
States. 2. Gifts—Taxation—Law and legislation—United States.
3. Estate planning—United States. I. Title. II. Title: Estate
planning guide.
KF6572.S59 1991
343.7305′3—dc20
[347.30353]   91-14341

Printed in the United States of America

10 9 8 7 6 5 4 3 2 1

In memory of my grandparents Sam Shenkman, Rose Goldberg, and Rezsin Wolf, whose love will always be among my most cherished assets, and whose memories will be one of the most important legacies I pass on to my children.

PREFACE

Estate planning—you've acquired a substantial estate, but if you don't take the necessary steps to plan for the management and disposition of that estate, the businesses and investments you've spent a lifetime building may not be used in the manner you want.

Without a properly prepared *inter vivos* (living) trust and living will (medical directive power of attorney), you cannot be certain that you will be cared for in the manner you want in the case of debilitating illness. In the case of either severe illness or death, if you and those you work with haven't prepared appropriate powers of attorney and partnership or shareholders' agreements, including workable buy-out provisions, significant disruptions may occur in your business and financial affairs.

Similarly, without a proper will and thoughtfully prepared trust arrangements, your wealth may not best serve your children and other heirs. A special child may not receive the care you wish; another child, too young or immature to realize the magnitude of his or her error, could squander a substantial fortune. With the exception of those documents relating to medical matters, if all of the above-mentioned instruments are not crafted with the greatest attention to the complex tax laws affecting wealth and estates, your biggest beneficiary easily could be Uncle Sam.

The Estate Planning Guide is designed to help taxpayers who have been successful in their business and investment affairs, and the insurance agents, accountants, lawyers, and financial planners who serve them, use the key concepts needed to address each of the above planning areas.

A varied approach is taken, employing background discussion, detailed analysis of specific topics, financial calculations, sample forms and agreements, estate tax projections, and sample tax returns. The process of estate planning may seem intimidating, but it is less daunting than the risk of having your hard-earned wealth dissipated, or the fear involved in not adequately protecting yourself and your greatest asset, your family.

MARTIN M. SHENKMAN

Teaneck, New Jersey
August 1991

ACKNOWLEDGMENTS

I would like to thank a number of people who were of considerable assistance in the preparation of this book. Michael Hamilton of John Wiley & Sons, whose support and encouragement were outstanding, as usual; Saul Gerstenfeld, for his review of the manuscript; Rabbi Aryeh Weil of Congregation Bnai Yeshurun, Teaneck, New Jersey, for his assistance in preparing the discussion of Jewish laws, as they affect estate planning; James B. Boskey, Esquire, professor of law at Seton Hall Law School, Newark, New Jersey, for his preparation of the discussion of Islamic laws in relation to estate planning; Monsignor Harold Darcy, Esquire, chaplain of Seton Hall Law School, Newark, New Jersey, for his preparation of the discussion of Catholic viewpoints on living wills; Carl Weinstein, partner with the New York City accounting firm Diamond, Kerbis & Weinstein, for his preparation of the sample tax return and hypothetical case study for the "kiddie tax"; David Kahn and Jeffrey Grossman, partners with the New York City office of the accounting firm Goldstein Golub Kessler & Company, P.C., for their preparation of the sample tax returns and hypothetical case studies for the chapters on the estate and gift taxes; David McFarland, marketing manager for BNA Software, a division of the Bureau of National Affairs, Inc., Washington, DC, for providing the Estate Tax Spreadsheet used in the estate planning example for a family business, and Joseph Donovan, estate tax managing editor for BNA Software for his assistance in discussing the program and formulating that example; Gregory Kolojeski of Brentmark Software, a division of Commerce Clearing House, Chicago, Illinois, for providing the Charitable Financial Planner software and for his assistance in discussing the program's use in planning for charitable giving; Jackie Schlanger for lending me his information on estate planning for children with developmental disabilities (materials were prepared by the Association for Retarded Citizens, headquartered in Arlington, Texas); Mark Hopkins, editor of *Shopping Centers Today*, for suggesting the title to Part II of this book; Laurence Celniker, an insurance agent with Northwestern Mutual Life/Baird, Parsippany, New Jersey, who prepared the projections for the insurance funded example in the discussion of the estate tax; Mary Meyer, associate director of public education with Concern for Dying, New York City, for her assistance with comments on the living will; and Israel Polak and Rabbi Willig for their time, discussions, and insights concerning

Jewish law and estate planning. Any errors in the text are solely my responsibility and not that of any of the parties acknowledged above.

Most of all, thanks to my wonderful wife Shelly and my two sons, Yoni and Dov, for their tolerance and love.

M.M.S.

CONTENTS

PART THREE
PLANNING FOR SPECIAL
PEOPLE/BENEFICIARIES

PART FOUR
PLANNING FOR SPECIFIC ASSETS

THE ESTATE PLANNING GUIDE

INTRODUCTION—
WHAT'S INVOLVED IN
ESTATE PLANNING

More than $5 trillion in assets are owned by Americans over age 65. A phenomenal amount of wealth. Much of it is due to the appreciation of real estate, such as homes; other parts are accounted for by stock appreciation and by the value of closely held businesses.

In its broadest definition, estate planning is the process of (1) creating, (2) managing, (3) planning for, and (4) eventually passing on this wealth. If you're reading this book, you, your family, or your clients probably have already achieved the first two steps, creating and managing wealth. Everyone must be concerned with estate planning, particularly those who have accumulated more than $600,000 in assets, because up to that amount can avoid the estate tax. This book will focus on the latter two components: planning for your wealth, and for its eventual transfer to your heirs.

Tax planning is often the first issue raised when it comes to estate planning. Clients want to know: "How do I keep Uncle Sam from getting so much?" Taxes are vitally important, because careless planning can create tremendous tax burdens. A major goal of this book is to show you the methods of minimizing estate taxes and provide you with many of the necessary tools.

Saving taxes, however, must never be your primary goal. First and foremost, you must protect yourself and your family. You should carefully and thoughtfully identify your personal life goals, taking into account your own needs and your family's needs. Discuss these matters with those closest to you. Revise them as many times as necessary. To help you with these issues, there are chapters addressing divorce, special children, charities, and more.

Religious considerations are also important, and too often they are overlooked. It is a fact that many people who profess religious indifference while they are young and healthy often change, sometimes substantially, when faced with the prospect of their own death, or the death of a close family member. Clergy are never mentioned as part of an estate planning team, but they can be of real assistance. Although this book can do little more than raise the topic, providing just a brief glance at some of the religious implications of living wills and estate plans, this information may encourage you to discuss your ideas and feelings with your clergy.

Only after the personal, family, and religious matters have been addressed do the cold financial and tax issues deserve attention. On the other hand, never lose your perspective of where tax savings and financial planning fit into the overall process.

The *Guide* takes an approach that is more accessible and useful than other estate planning books:

- Part I of the *Guide* will help you and the experts who work with you understand and use the essential estate planning documents (the basic documents you will have when your planning process is completed): financial statement, powers of attorney, will, living will, and trusts. Having a picture of the final objective in mind from the beginning will make later discussions and ideas far clearer. It will also facilitate your taking notes to discuss with your lawyer through each phase of the planning process.

- Part II covers the three basic wealth transfer taxes—the gift tax, the estate tax, and the generation-skipping transfer tax. A general understanding of each of these taxes will facilitate the entire planning process. You will be far better equipped to deal with your experts and accomplish your objectives.

- Part III looks at the various people your estate plan will affect and offers planning perspectives for different kinds of families. The American family can no longer be defined as mom, dad, 2.3 kids, and a station wagon. Many people needing estate planning are single. Whether they are single because they have never married, have been widowed, or have chosen alternative lifestyles, the simplistic approach of leaving everything to one's spouse is of no help. If you're single, you won't have to wade through countless chapters that assume you have a spouse to plan for. When minor children, particularly special children, are involved, there are numerous planning considerations. For the disabled adult these decisions are even more critical. Divorce is no longer uncommon and creates many estate planning concerns.

- Part IV analyzes tax, business, and investment implications of the various types of assets included in your estate and forms of ownership of these assets. Real estate, closely held businesses, life insurance—each has its own estate planning issues, which are covered in the *Guide*.

Throughout this book you will find practical planning suggestions, cautions warning you against common tax and planning traps, and notes and examples explaining how various planning options may affect you. All of these are highlighted for maximum accessibility.

Sample forms, agreements, and other useful aids follow many chapters, expanding on the discussions. Treat these forms as workbook pages. Make notes of your questions, personal preferences, and concerns in the margins. If you review these before meeting with your attorney and other estate planning professionals, you will be far better prepared to direct everyone to the issues important to you. Your meetings can be more productive, shorter, and less costly. For insurance agents, accountants, attorneys, and financial planners, each of these forms illustrates at least one approach to a particular planning problem and will assist you in planning for your clients.

Illustrative estate planning scenarios explain the effects of some of the planning opportunities discussed in the text and applied in the sample forms. These calculations have been prepared using state-of-the-art software developed by BNA Software, a division of the Bureau of National Affairs, Inc., and Commerce Clearing House. Finally, a few sample tax returns, prepared by the accounting firm Goldstein, Golub & Kessler, show some of the many tax filing requirements that you and your family will inevitably face.

No book can possibly cover every aspect of estate planning. The subject is too broad and too complex. Pension issues, state taxes, income taxes, investment strategies, and financial planning—all important topics—have barely been addressed. The only proper way to approach estate planning is to use all the experts who usually comprise an estate planning team: accountant, attorney, insurance agent, pension expert, financial planner, and so on. This book will help you focus on your needs and offer the best methods for addressing those needs. Having this knowledge will enable you to make better use of your estate planning team, keeping your costs and time involvement to a reasonable minimum. Most importantly, it will help you achieve the objectives of protecting your family and eventually giving the maximum amount of your wealth to those people you want it to benefit.

Part One

FIVE KEY PLANNING DOCUMENTS

1 FINANCIAL STATEMENT

The first step is to take stock of what you have. It's tough to plan until you know what you have to plan with, and for. Most estate or financial planning guides include a whole series of tables and charts to help you organize the information you need. If you use them, that's great. The problem is, these tables and charts are often intimidating, and they don't get used. Since most readers have seen business financial statements, the "For Your Notebook" section following this chapter contains a simplified financial reporting statement to help you pull together the vital information. You can choose any approach that works for you, however, as long as the task gets accomplished.

TIP: Use a format tailored for your needs. For example, most financial statement forms have separate columns for bonds, cash, stocks, and mutual funds. But you may have a combined account statement from one brokerage firm where most of your marketable assets are held. Group your assets as they're presented in that statement, or simply list the totals and attach a recent brokerage report to the financial statement.

WHAT DATA IS NEEDED AND WHY

What types of information are needed for proper estate planning? They are as follows:

1. *List of liquid assets.* This will include stocks, bonds, money market accounts, mutual funds, and other assets that can provide ready cash. The estate tax is generally due within nine months of death. Therefore, it's important to ascertain whether you have sufficient cash to meet expenses and taxes. Liquidity is an important factor in assessing insurance needs (see Chapter 19).

2. *Forms that show title.* Who owns the assets and in what form? The best estate plans can be defeated by holding assets in the wrong name. If you and your father own an asset as tenants in common, there will be different tax implications than if you own it as joint tenants (see Chapter 20). Title can affect whether the asset will pass through your estate or simply vest in a designated person on

your death. You and your spouse are each entitled to a $600,000 lifetime exemption from the estate and gift tax. If most family assets are held in one spouse's name, or jointly, this valuable exclusion can be largely wasted.

3. *Calculations showing tax basis.* Tax basis is the cost of the asset, plus improvements, less depreciation. Special rules apply if you received the property as an inheritance or gift, or through other transactions (apart from a purchase). This can be important in ascertaining which assets you should give away, sell, or keep in your estate. On your death, the tax basis of an asset is increased (stepped up) to equal its value for federal estate tax purposes. If you have an asset with a very low tax basis relative to the current value of that asset, retaining the asset in your estate in order to obtain the basis step-up can be important.

4. *Economic predictions.* An asset that is likely to appreciate substantially is often a better candidate for a gift than an asset whose value might decline.

A FINANCIAL STATEMENT HAS ADDITIONAL USES

You may have assumed that the only purpose of collecting financial data is to be able to plan your estate. This is incorrect, however. An example will illustrate another use:

EXAMPLE: Your spouse died a few years ago, and you live alone in an apartment. Your children have moved to different cities but visit often. You've taken the precaution of preparing all the basic estate planning documents: a will, a living will to advise doctors of what emergency medical care you do, and do not, want, and a power of attorney authorizing your daughter to handle your financial matters in case you're disabled. You suffer a long-term illness and are hospitalized for a few months. Your daughter flies into town eager to help, with power of attorney in hand. One problem—where does she begin? She has no information stating who your lawyer, accountant, and other professionals are. She knows about the will and living will, but where are they? She would like to handle your finances, but which banks do you deal with? What accounts do you have? Your tax return is due, but she can't locate the records or the name of your accountant. When you recuperate, you face interest and late charges and a lot more financial problems than you expected.

The solution is to have a financial statement that reports the vital information. Your financial report should include the names, addresses, and telephone numbers of all your estate planning professionals. For bank and brokerage accounts, include account names, numbers, and descriptions. Also indicate the name, address, and telephone number of the specific representative you deal with. A broker or banker who has known you for years is far more likely to help than a broker or banker at the main office who has never met you.

If you prepare a thorough financial report but don't revise it periodically, it won't be of great use in an emergency. There's a bonus for revising regularly: It's a lot easier to find the data you need. Also carefully consider where you should keep a copy of your financial report. Your safe-deposit box is an obvious place, but who else has access to the box? While it's probably a good idea to keep a current copy in your safe-deposit box, your attorney should have a copy with your will (this is probably kept in a fireproof vault—but ask to be sure), and your other planners will need working copies as well.

Finally, a current detailed financial statement is an essential tool to pursue proper financial planning to keep your estate growing.

CONCLUSION

A detailed financial report is one of the five key estate planning documents. Your extra efforts now in preparing it thoroughly and keeping it current will reap an immeasurable savings in time and energy for many years to come.

For Your Notebook:

SAMPLE PERSONAL FINANCIAL REPORT, INCLUDING ASSETS

ASSETS	Husband	Wife	Joint Property	Community Property	Total
Cash:					
1. XYZ Bank, Inc.					
2. ABC Money Market					
3. ABC, Inc. Brokerage Account					
4. Big Company Bonds					
5. AAA Inc.					
Insurance Policies:					
6. Universal Life					
7. Term					
Real Estate:					
8. Home					
9. Shopping Center Partners					
Retirement Assets:					
10. Keogh					
TOTAL ASSETS					
LIABILITIES					
11. Personal Credit Line					
12. Home Mortgage					
TOTAL LIABILITIES					
NET WORTH					

1. Account No. 223322. Representative—Ms. Jones, V.P., 123 Main St., Any City, NJ 12345. (000) 000-0000.

2. Account No. 999999. Representative—Mr. Jones, 222 Big St., Some City, FL 99999.

3. Account No. 00000. Broker—Mr. Smith. 0000 State St., New York, NY 99901. (212) 000-0000.

4. Purchased 1/1/85. Purchase price $45,101.

5. Purchased 56,000 shares of common stock on 2/31/67. Purchase price $323,000.

6. Policy No. 3333. Agent—Ted Jones, ABC Insurance, Inc., 555 Main St., Los Angeles, CA. (000) 000-0000. [List basic policy data here.]

7. Policy No. 000001. Agent—Rita Samson, Big Insurance, Inc., 0010 High St., Some City, KY. (000) 000-0000. [List basic policy data here.]

8. 666 Top St., Highland, SD. Purchased 3/3/57. Purchase price $56,000, improvements $234,000. Tax Lot: _____. Tax Block: _____.

9. 2.5 Units, 12% interest, in Connecticut real estate limited partnership. [Detail tax basis, general partner's name and address, tax identification number.]

10. Broker—Bill Jones, Bank Brokerage, 787 Low St., Big City, NY. (000) 000-0000. [Securities held could be listed or a copy of the brokerage statement attached.]

11. Account No. 99999-990-3. Big City Bank, 123 Main St., San Francisco, CA. (415) 000-0000.

12. Account No. 09090-33-3. Ed's Loan Company, Inc., 444 Slippery St., Big City, NY. (000) 000-0000. [Details concerning interest rate, escrow arrangements, and so on, could be listed.]

Figure 1.1. Sample personal financial report.

2 POWER OF ATTORNEY

A power of attorney is the most important, the simplest, and the least expensive estate planning document. It is a contract in which you grant another person, often your spouse, the power to act on your behalf in the event that you are unavailable for any reason. The power of attorney gives financial (or other) authority during disability. The person to whom you grant this authority is called your attorney-in-fact, or agent.

WHY YOU NEED ONE

The following examples show why it is important to have a prepared, *signed* power of attorney.

EXAMPLE: A widower had his attorney prepare a power of attorney, but he never signed it. He suffered an unexpected and severe heart attack and was hospitalized for an extended duration. Complications of the attack disabled him so that he no longer had the capacity to sign a power of attorney. His nearest family (a nephew and his wife) could not access his savings, and they didn't have sufficient funds of their own to meet the expenses of maintaining his home and paying medical bills. The family was forced to commence expensive proceedings to have the court appoint a guardian to access their uncle's funds in order to pay for his care and other expenses.

A power of attorney also can authorize your agent to make gifts and take other actions to minimize your estate tax.

EXAMPLE: Father began a regular gift program in which he and his wife each year join in making gifts of stock to their four children, their children's spouses, and their 10 grandchildren. The gifts are $20,000 each, the maximum amount that can be given away annually without any gift tax being due (see Chapter 7), for a total of $360,000. In December, Father falls ill and is unable to sign the necessary documents to make a transfer, so the couple makes no gifts in that year. The couple could incur an unnecessary additional estate tax cost of as much as $216,000. If the generation-skipping transfer tax is also considered, the tax cost could increase substantially. If an appropriate power of attorney had been prepared, Father's agent may have been able to handle the paperwork necessary to make the gifts and eliminate this unnecessary estate tax burden.

Be aware that a living trust is not a substitute for a power of attorney (see Chapter 4). A living trust is more expensive to prepare and difficult to implement, and even if you already have a living trust, you should still prepare and sign powers of attorney. Your living trust will only cover the assets that you legally transferred to it, while a power of attorney, if broadly written, can give your agent access to all of your assets in the jurisdiction where the power of attorney is valid. (On the other hand, since even a durable power of attorney immediately terminates on your death, it can never be considered a substitute for a will or trust arrangement.)

TYPES OF POWERS OF ATTORNEY

Durable and Springing Powers of Attorney

There are a number of different types of power of attorney. A durable power of attorney remains effective even though you are disabled. Special provisions generally must be included in your power of attorney for this to occur. This type can provide one of the most important benefits of a power of attorney. A springing power of attorney only "springs" into being when you become disabled. This prevents your agent from having any authority until you are actually disabled and need assistance. A power of attorney can be both durable and springing (see the sample power of attorney following this chapter). The argument against the springing power of attorney is that you should not grant any power of attorney unless you trust the person named. If you do trust your attorney-in-fact, why risk restricting the power of attorney until you become disabled? Questions could arise then about your disability and about whether the power of attorney has become effective.

NOTE: The rules differ from state to state. Consult with an attorney in your state to learn the specific rules that apply to you. For example, some states restrict the people you may name as an attorney-in-fact to close relatives. In some states it may be advisable to file (record) the power of attorney in the appropriate governmental office. Also, some state laws prescribe that a particular preprinted form of power of attorney be used. In these cases, one approach to consider is to sign both the standard, preprinted form and a power of attorney prepared by your attorney (because it can offer additional provisions and flexibility).

Power of Attorney for Business Matters

You should give careful consideration to the type and nature of the power of attorney used for your business affairs. For example, you may wish to grant a limited power of attorney to a close colleague to authorize him or her to perform certain functions relating to your business during a period when you are ill or otherwise unavailable. A business power of attorney may even provide for compensation. This should be considered an important planning component for every closely held business.

Power of Attorney for Investment Matters

Although there is no reason your banks and brokerage firms should not accept the power of attorney your lawyer prepares, they may first require their legal departments to review it. The resulting delays could defeat all benefits the power of attorney was intended to win. The solution is simple and only takes a few phone calls. Contact every bank and brokerage firm you deal with and request a copy of its standard form of power of attorney. Complete and execute the form and return it to them to maintain on file. Similar steps should be taken by your spouse if you're married. Although this may sound tedious, it really takes a minimum of time and, in an emergency, could prove to be invaluable. If you maintain substantial assets in mutual funds, caution is in order. Some of the larger mutual funds will not accept orders by a power of attorney.

Power of Attorney for Personal Matters

You should execute a separate power of attorney for personal financial matters. As indicated above, this could grant your spouse or children or others the right to handle all of your personal financial matters, saving time, money, and aggravation.

TERMS TO INCLUDE IN YOUR POWER OF ATTORNEY

Name one or more alternate agents in the event that the primary agent (your colleague or spouse) is unable or unwilling to take the necessary actions. If you own property in any state other than the one in which you live, it may be necessary to have a power of attorney written in compliance with the laws of that state. A springing power of attorney may be desirable—if your state laws permit a springing durable power of attorney (contains both features described above).

Although most powers of attorney are prepared on forms, a power of attorney is really a contract. Therefore, subject to a few possible limitations under the laws of your state, you can include almost any provision you deem appropriate. For example, your agent should sign the power of attorney, indicating his or her agreement to act in the manner described in the form and to indemnify you for any losses resulting from unauthorized actions. You may also wish to place restrictions on the scope of the attorney-in-fact's actions. For example, you may permit only the payment of certain emergency expenses; you may permit or not permit the sale of assets, the making of gifts, and so on.

IRS FORM 2848

If you are audited by the IRS one of the first things your attorney or accountant will request is that you sign a copy of Form 2848, Power of Attorney and Declaration of Representative. This form must be on file before any IRS agent will communicate with your accountant. Although the form is quite simple, there are a number of points and practical suggestions that can save time and reduce problems. It's always best to sign a number of extra copies of Form 2848 and have your accountant keep them in your file. As your case snakes its way through the IRS, the original power of attorney your accountant filed may get lost. It's also best to have more than one person in your accountant's office named in the form. If the IRS calls the day your accountant is on vacation, the IRS agent may refuse to speak with anyone else.

Read the form before you sign. You do not need to authorize your accountant to represent you for any years and taxes apart from what the particular audit is about. This is one way you can control what your accountant is doing without having to seek your approval. There are boxes to check to tell the IRS where to send communication concerning the audit. Don't allow your accountant to indicate that the correspondence should go only to him. You and your accountant should both receive copies, so you, too, will know what is going on. Extreme caution should be exercised with respect to the payment of any refund. Rarely should you check the box authorizing your accountant to receive any refund check.

CONCLUSION

Powers of attorney are an essential estate planning tool. Because of the simplicity, ease of preparation, and nominal cost, you and your adult family members all should have powers of attorney.

For Your Notebook:

SAMPLE DURABLE AND
SPRINGING POWER OF ATTORNEY
(WITH COMMENTS)

**FOR DISCUSSION WITH YOUR LAWYER ONLY
—DO NOT USE AS A POWER OF ATTORNEY**

KNOW ALL MEN BY THESE PRESENTS, that I GRANTOR NAME (the "Grantor"), residing at GRANTOR ADDRESS, in the State of STATENAME (the "State"), to provide for management of my person and financial affairs in a more orderly fashion, hereby declare as follows:

I.   APPOINTMENT OF ATTORNEY-IN-FACT

I hereby make, constitute, and appoint ("Grant") my spouse, SPOUSENAME, residing at GRANTOR ADDRESS, STATENAME, as my true and lawful Attorney-in-Fact, and Agent for me and in my name, place, and stead and for my benefit, or any alternate appointed in accordance with the provisions of this agreement (the "Attorney-in-Fact" or "Agent").

II.   POWERS OF ATTORNEY-IN-FACT

I grant to my Attorney-in-Fact all the powers and rights necessary to effect my wishes, including the power to:

A. Request, ask, demand, sue for, recover, sell, collect, forgive, receive, and hold money, debts, dues, commercial paper, checks, drafts, accounts, deposits, legacies, bequests, devises, notes, interests, stocks, bonds, certificates of deposit, annuities, pension and retirement benefits, insurance proceeds, any and all documents of title, choses in action, personal and real property, intangible and tangible property and property rights, and demands whatsoever, liquidated or unliquidated, as now are, or may become, owned by, or due, owing, payable, or belonging to me, or in which I have or may hereafter acquire interest; to have, use, and take all lawful means and equitable and legal remedies, procedures, and writs in my name for the collection and recovery thereof, and to adjust, sell, compromise, and agree for the same; and to make, execute and deliver for me, on my behalf and in my name, all endorsements, acceptances, releases, receipts, or other sufficient discharges for the same.

B. Prepare, sign, and file joint or separate income tax returns or declarations or estimated tax for any year or years; to prepare, sign, and file gift tax returns with respect to gifts made by me, or by my Attorney-in-Fact on my behalf, for any year or years; to consent to any gift and to utilize any gift-splitting provision or other tax election; and to prepare, sign, and file any claim for refund of any tax. This power is in addition to and not in limitation of the specific tax powers granted below.

C. Conduct, engage in and transact any lawful matter of any nature, on my behalf, and in my name. To maintain, improve, invest, manage, insure, lease, or encumber, and in any manner deal with any real, personal, tangible, or intangible property, or any interest in them, that I now own or may acquire, in my name and for my benefit, upon such terms and conditions as my agent shall deem proper.

D. Exercise or perform any act, power, duty, right, or obligation that I now have, or may acquire, including the legal right, power, or capacity to exercise or perform, in connection with, arising from, or relating to any person or property, real or personal, tangible or intangible, or matter whatsoever, including, without limiting the foregoing, the right to enter into a contract of sale and to sell any real, personal, tangible, or intangible property on my behalf, including but not limited to the property/properties located at: GRANTOR ADDRESS, STATENAME.

NOTE: It's preferable to list addresses of any real property that your agent may have to sell.

E. Make, receive, sign, endorse, acknowledge, deliver, and possess insurance policies, documents of title, bonds, debentures, checks, drafts, stocks, proxies, and warrants, relating to accounts or deposits in, or certificates of deposit, other debts and obligations, and such other instruments in writing of whatever kind and nature as may be necessary or proper in the exercise of the rights and powers herein granted.

F. Sell any and all shares of stocks, bonds, or other securities now or later belonging to me that may be issued by any association, trust, or corporation, whether private or public, and to make, execute, and deliver any assignment, or assignments, of any such shares of stocks, bonds, or other securities.

G. Conduct or participate in any business of any nature for me and in my name; execute partnership agreements and amendments thereto; incorporate, reorganize, merge, consolidate, recapitalize, sell, liquidate, or dissolve any business; elect or employ officers, directors, and agents; carry out the provisions of any agreement for the sale of any business interest or the stock therein; and exercise voting rights with respect to stock; either in person or by proxy, and exercise stock options.

H. Have access at any time or times to any safe-deposit box rented by me, and to remove all or any part of the contents thereof, and to surrender or relinquish said safe-deposit box. Any institution in which any such safe-deposit box may be located shall not incur any liability to me or my estate as a result of permitting my Attorney-in-Fact or Agent to exercise the powers herein granted.

I. Make outright gifts of cash or property to adults or, under the applicable Gifts to Minors Act in custodial form, to persons under the age of Twenty-One (21) years, in amounts not to exceed Ten Thousand Dollars ($10,000.00) to each donee in any calendar year. Permissible donees hereunder shall include my spouse, any children or stepchildren of mine and their descendants, or any descendant of a brother or sister of mine or of any person to whom I shall have been married, as well as any person who shall be married to any of the foregoing, and [name any other relatives or friends you wish].

NOTE: If you want your attorney-in-fact to be able to make gifts, this power should be specifically stated. This can be a very important estate planning tool.

J. Convey or assign any cash or other property of which I shall be possessed to the trustee or trustees of any trust that I may have created during my lifetime, provided that such trust is subject to my power of revocation, which power shall be exercisable hereunder by my agent.

K. Purchase United States Government Bonds known as "Flower Bonds," which may be used in payment of death taxes from my estate.

L. Appoint a substitute or alternate attorney-in-fact to have all powers and authority of the Attorney-in-Fact, except as provided below.

NOTE: Carefully review the broad authority given in this section. You may wish to narrow this. Exercise discretion in doing so, however, because it is impossible to know what situations your agent will face.

III. ADDITIONAL POWERS

In addition to and not by way of limitation upon any other powers conferred upon my Attorney-in-Fact and Agent herein, I grant to said Attorney-in-Fact full power and authority to do, take, and perform each and every act and thing whatsoever requisite, proper, or necessary to be done, in the exercise of any of the rights and powers herein granted, or available under law to an attorney-in-fact, as fully to all intents and purposes as I might or could do if I were personally present, with full power of substitution or revocation, hereby ratifying and confirming all that said Attorney-in-Fact shall lawfully do or cause to be done by virtue of this power of attorney and the rights and powers herein granted.

IV. POWERS RELATING TO TAX MATTERS

In addition to and not by way of limitation upon any other powers conferred upon my Attorney-in-Fact and Agent herein, I grant to said Attorney-in-Fact full power and authority to do, take, and perform each and every act and thing whatsoever requisite, proper, or necessary to be done, in connection with executing and filing any and all tax returns, receiving and cashing any refund checks with respect to any tax filing, and dealing with the Internal Revenue Service and any state and local tax authority concerning any gift, estate, inheritance, income, or other tax, and any audit or investigation of same. This power shall include, by way of example, and not limitation, the power to do all acts that could be authorized by my having properly executed a Form 2848, "Power of Attorney and Declaration of Representative," granting the broadest powers provided therein to my Attorney-in-Fact.

V. APPROVAL

I hereby approve and confirm all acts done by my Attorney-in-Fact on my behalf. I hereby ratify and confirm all acts whatsoever my said Attorney-in-Fact or Agent shall do or cause to be done, by virtue of this power of attorney.

VI. CONSTRUCTION

This instrument is to be construed and interpreted as a durable general power of attorney. The enumeration of specific items, rights, acts, or powers herein is not intended to, nor does it limit or restrict, and is not to be construed or interpreted as limiting or restricting, the general powers herein granted to said Attorney-in-Fact. This instrument is executed and delivered in the State, and the laws of the State shall govern all questions as to the validity of this power and the construction of its provisions. Should any provision or power in this document not be enforceable, such enforceability shall not affect the enforceability of the rest of this document.

VII. THIRD-PARTY RELIANCE

Third parties may rely upon the representations of my Attorney-in-Fact as to all matters relating to any power granted to my Attorney-in-Fact as my Agent, and no person who may act in reliance upon the representations of my Agent or the authority granted to my Agent shall incur any liability to me or my estate as a result of permitting my agent to exercise any power. Any third party may rely on a duly executed counterpart of this instrument, or a copy thereof, as fully and completely as if such third party had received the original of this instrument.

VIII. DISABILITY SHALL NOT AFFECT GRANT

This power of attorney shall not be affected by my disability as principal, and I do hereby so provide, it being my intention that all powers conferred upon my Attorney-in-Fact herein, or any substitute designated by me, shall remain at all times in full force and effect, notwithstanding my incapacity, disability, or death, or any uncertainty with regard thereto.

NOTE: The laws concerning a power of attorney's continuation after your disability differ by state. Consult a local attorney and reference any specific state statute providing for a durable power of attorney.

IX.   ALTERNATE ATTORNEY-IN-FACT

If SPOUSENAME is unwilling or unable to act as my agent, I appoint my ALTERNATE RELATIONSHIP, ALTERNATE NAME, who resides at ALTERNATE ADDRESS, as my Attorney-in-Fact and Agent (the "Alternate Attorney-in-Fact").

NOTE: Name as many alternate attorneys-in-fact as you can comfortably entrust with the responsibility and power. This provides greater assurance of a qualified agent in the event of an emergency in the future.

X.   INDEMNIFICATION OF THE ALTERNATE ATTORNEY-IN-FACT

The Grantor hereby agrees to indemnify and hold harmless the Alternate Attorney-in-Fact for any actions taken, or not taken, by the Alternate Attorney-in-Fact, where the Alternate Attorney-in-Fact acted in good faith and was not guilty of fraud, gross negligence, or willful misconduct.

XI.   EFFECTIVE DATE

A. The Grant to my Attorney-in-Fact shall take effect on the date hereof.

NOTE: If the primary attorney-in-fact is not your spouse or someone you trust fully, then make the authority of that person effective only on your disability. This is known as a springing power since it springs into effect upon your disability.

B. The Grant to my Alternate Attorney-in-Fact shall take effect only in the event of my subsequent disability or incapacity. This shall be the date upon which I am considered to be disabled by virtue of being unable to manage my affairs and property effectively for reasons such as mental illness, mental deficiency, physical illness or disability, advanced age, chronic use of drugs, chronic intoxication, confinement, kidnapping, detention by a foreign power, or disappearance, or for any other reason allowable by statute or law. In addition to any other method acceptable to any third party relying upon the effectiveness of the Grant to my Alternate Attorney-in-Fact, or any method allowed by law, it shall be deemed conclusive proof that the Grant to my Alternate Attorney-in-Fact is effective upon there being a sworn statement, executed by my Attorney-in-Fact, spouse, natural children, or any Two (2) doctors properly licensed to practice in the State.

NOTE: Consult with a local attorney to learn whether your state provides for a springing power of attorney, which only becomes effective on your disability. Specifically reference the particular statute in the form.

XII. TERMINATION OF GRANT

1. The Grant of the Power of Attorney to my spouse shall terminate at the earlier of the date of her substantial disability, the termination of our marriage through divorce, the execution of a separation agreement, or the delivery of a writing to such Attorney-in-Fact executed by me, prior to my being disabled, terminating such Grant.

NOTE: Delete this paragraph if you're not married.

---

2. The Grant of the Power of Attorney to my Alternate Attorney-in-Fact shall terminate at the earlier of the date of his or her substantial disability, or the delivery of a writing to such Alternate Attorney-in-Fact executed by me, prior to my being disabled, terminating such Grant.

3. Any Attorney-in-Fact or Agent may resign by providing written notice to me (or my guardian or committee) with copy to the next named Attorney-in-Fact or a court of competent jurisdiction.

IN WITNESS WHEREOF, I have hereunto set my hand and seal this DAY of MONTH, 1991, acknowledging that I have read and understood the powers and rights herein granted and that I voluntarily choose to make the Grant.

Grantor/Principal

_____

GRANTOR NAME

Attorney-in-Fact

_____

SPOUSENAME

Alternate Attorney-in-Fact

_____

ALTERNATE NAME

NOTE: Most power-of-attorney forms do not contain a place for your agent to sign. This signature can make it easier for your agent to use the power of attorney, because anyone accepting it can verify his or her signature on the form.

[NOTARY FORMS AND WITNESS LINES OMITTED]

3 WILL

It's your money, and you can do what you want with it. If you want to get on an airplane, go to Las Vegas, and gamble away your entire $3 million estate, that's your prerogative. If there are no people dependent on you for support, maintenance, and basic living expenses, then your gambling spree is your estate plan. Every attorney, accountant, insurance agent, and financial planner would be aghast. It would be far more reasonable to craft an estate plan that minimizes estate taxes and provides funds, whether in trust or direct, for your minor heirs.

But, it's worth repeating: It's your money and you're free to do what you want. By all means, review the options available with your estate planning team of experts. But the final decision is yours.

To this end, the most common, and certainly one of the most important, document is your will. It is *the* basic document for disposing of your estate. A valid will can ensure that your assets will be distributed to the people you choose (children, spouse, friends, and so on) and in the manner you choose (outright transfer, in trust, to a guardian). It is the vehicle by which you can appoint the guardian to care for your minor children, special children, elderly parents, or other dependents in the event of your death; the executor to handle the winding up of your personal financial matters and the distribution of your estate; and the trustees to handle the financial aspects of any trust set up under your will. Each of these important decisions is discussed below. The sample will in the "For Your Notebook" section following this chapter contains detailed practical illustrations of each. The notes interspersed in the sample will highlight some of the alternative approaches you might want to discuss with your tax adviser.

WHO GETS THE PROPERTY AND HOW

One of the most basic uses of a will is to state who should receive your assets and in what manner. For most people, it is fairly obvious that their largess will go to their immediate family, and perhaps a few select friends or others with whom they have a significant tie. (Later chapters will discuss different ways to structure assets given to your spouse and children and give the tax implications of each. For example, if you're married, the fact that you can give an unlimited amount of assets to your surviving spouse without incurring any estate tax cost is a strong encouragement for such transfers.)

If you have a charitable intent, you may already know which charities you want to benefit. However, if the amounts are significant, it's worth verifying that the charity is recognized by the IRS as tax-exempt and that it has a good record for applying most of its monies for charitable causes, and not for administration expense (see Chapter 14).

How to Distribute Your Property

The best way to distribute your property to the designated recipients will depend on factors such as the following:

- *The amount of money and other assets involved.* The larger the amount, the more likely that a trust arrangement with professional management will be appropriate (see Chapter 4).
- *The nature of the property.* CDs and similar investments may not be that difficult to reinvest. A partially vacant shopping center, a manufacturing company, or other business venture will need special arrangements. If buy-out agreements don't suffice, a trust arrangement may be appropriate (see Chapters 16 and 17).
- *The age and ability of the recipient.* The younger and less able the recipient, the more important that some mechanism of formal control be used. If the amounts are not large enough to warrant a trust, a Uniform Gifts to Minors Act account may suffice (see Chapter 11).

Making Your Intended Distributions Happen

When your lawyer drafts your will, be careful to consider what will happen to your distributions under different scenarios. What if your estate declines substantially because hazardous waste is found on your business plant, or the stock market crashes? Assets may not end up where you want. The safest approach is to draft provisions so that maximum and minimum amounts and percentages of your estate are used for each bequest. Suppose, for example, that your estate is worth $2 million, and so you decide to leave $10,000 to a close friend, a proportion you consider to be appropriate. If you're unexpectedly faced with a calamity, however, the result could be that your friend gets $10,000 and your children not much more. A cautionary approach would be to have your lawyer use language like the following: "I leave $10,000 to my good friend Joe Smith, who resides at 123 Main Street, Anytown, USA, not to exceed 1 percent of my adjusted gross estate." This phrase will protect you in the event of a change.

The same dilemma could occur in a case where most of your property passes outside your $2 million probate estate, even though it is included in your taxable estate. For example, if you own a $1.8 million house jointly with your wife, the house won't go through probate. Instead, your wife will receive title on your death, which would only leave $200,000 in your estate. The $10,000 legacy to your friend becomes much more significant now and may be money you would have preferred to give your children. The solution is quite simple. Carefully and thoroughly update your personal financial statement, looking up actual deeds and other documents to verify how title is held. You might be surprised to find how little are the assets that will pass through your estate.

GUARDIANS

If you have minor children, the single most important decision to make in preparing a will, and almost always the most difficult and agonizing, is whom to appoint as a guardian. You may have a living spouse, but what if you both die in a car crash? What if you die and your spouse is permanently disabled? The safest approach is always to name guardians. Your choice should be someone who is compassionate and has, or could have, a warm relationship with the potential charges.

The following five points can make the selection of a guardian somewhat easier:

1. There are few restrictions on how many conditions you can set for a guardian. For example, your younger sister may be quite mature, but she is single and you prefer that the guardian for your children be married. You can name your sister as an alternate and specify that her appointment as guardian be contingent upon her being married and at least 25 years of age.

2. Name as many alternates as you can. That way, you will have backups for those who don't meet the criteria. The sample will following this chapter illustrates a way of appointing multiple alternatives.

3. You may feel more secure if you name one person to be in charge of the money you leave to your dependents and another to watch and care for them. This approach can provide some checks and balances, since at least two different people will have a fiduciary responsibility for your dependents.

4. Your choice of guardian is not carved in stone. You can always change your will, either by having a new will prepared or simply executing an amendment (codicil).

CAUTION: For a codicil to your will to be valid, it must be executed with all of the same formalities as your will.

---

5. Finally, the decision about who should be a guardian is of a more personal than legal nature. Try your best to make preliminary

decisions before you meet with your lawyer—it's a lot more economical to make preliminary choices without your lawyer's clock running.

EXECUTOR AND TRUSTEE

The role of an executor and trustee, unlike that of a guardian, is primarily financial in nature. That role is to martial assets, invest, make distributions and payments, and provide record keeping. However, the functions have enough in common that the same attributes of compassion needed by a guardian are also valuable in an executor or trustee. This is the reason many people go to great lengths to choose individual executors and trustees rather than to rely on banks or other impersonal, corporate appointees.

On the other hand, there are times when the stability, skill, and longevity of a corporate trustee might be necessary: (1) No suitable relative or friend may be found. (2) The trust might be for such a long duration that having an individual trustee would not be feasible. (3) The nature of the assets may be such that no individual you know would be capable of managing them, and a sale would not be the best economic option.

As with a guardian, make preliminary choices of the executor and trustees before meeting with your lawyer. If you find yourself agonizing over who to choose, consider that you can name two or more executors or trustees as coexecutors, or cotrustees. This can provide some checks and balances. However, two people who disagree can be problematic. Remember that if you don't feel comfortable with your choices, you can change them any time before your death or disability.

CONTENTS AND MECHANICS

Say it the way you mean it. Most wills are simply cold statements of fact: "I appoint John Doe as my Executor." But they don't have to be and, in fact, should not be. If you have two brothers, John Doe and Sam Doe, will Sam feel insulted that you chose John instead of him? He might if the typical clause above is used. Consider the following alternative: "I appoint my dear brother John Doe as my Executor. I name my dear brother Sam Doe as my alternate Executor in the event that John Doe is either unwilling or unable to serve as Executor. Although he is the younger sibling, the choice of John as Executor has been made out of consideration for the substantial commitments by brother Sam Doe has made to many worthwhile charitable organizations. I would feel wrong taking his time away from these for administering my estate."

It's a bit longer, but you've turned a potential insult of the older of your two surviving brothers into a compliment. Any time you make a choice that is potentially unpopular, or could be interpreted as insulting or even unfair, try to couch it in more agreeable terms. Your will is your final word, and it's always best to leave on a good note.

Letter of Last Instructions

Drafting a letter of last instructions, or the "two-tissue-box letter" as it has been called, should be part of the preparation of every will. Some things simply don't belong in the will proper: a personal statement, last words to loved ones, the disposition of personal effects and jewelry (this may change frequently, so that it is not worth the cost and trouble to keep changing your will), funeral instructions, and the like. A copy of this letter can be kept in your safe-deposit box, another copy given to your lawyer for safekeeping with your will, and possibly a third copy given to your intended executor.

NOTE: Some states won't permit such a letter to be legally binding.

Formalities of Execution

A will is a formal document and must be executed precisely as required by your state's laws. Although a sample will is presented in the following pages, technical issues are not addressed in this chapter. To protect your interests and to meet your personal goals, it is incumbent upon you to retain counsel at least to prepare the final version of the necessary documents.

CONCLUSION

Your will is one of your most important estate planning documents. It is vitally important first to evaluate carefully all of your alternatives for taking care of your loved ones and your affairs after you're gone, and then to seek a competent estate attorney to draft your will and any of the other necessary documents.

For Your Notebook:

SAMPLE WILL WITH Q-TIP TRUST
AND CREDIT SHELTER TRUST
(WITH COMMENTS)

**FOR DISCUSSION WITH YOUR LAWYER
ONLY—DO NOT USE AS A WILL**

LAST WILL AND TESTAMENT

I, YOUR NAME, residing at YOUR ADDRESS, in the City of YOUR CITY, State of STATENAME, do make, publish, and declare this to be my Last Will and Testament, hereby revoking any and all prior wills, codicils, and testamentary dispositions by me at any time heretofore made.

I.   PAYMENT OF EXPENSES AND DEBTS

I direct that any expenses of my last illness and funeral, as well as any of my debts, be paid as soon after my death as would be advantageous to the administration of my estate. These debts shall not include: (i) obligations secured by mortgages on real estate or cooperative apartments, which debts I direct my Executor to pay at his discretion; or (ii) debts owing insurance companies secured by insurance policies, which debts I intend should first be satisfied out of the proceeds of the policies securing them. This section shall not serve to revive any of my debts barred by the statute of limitations.

II.   DEATH TAXES

I direct that all estate, inheritance, succession, transfer, and other death taxes imposed upon or in relation to any property included in my estate, whether such property passes under or outside the provisions of this Will, and whether such taxes be imposed by domestic or foreign jurisdiction, be charged against and paid from my residuary estate (as defined below) without apportionment. Should my residuary estate not be sufficient to meet such taxes, I direct that the excess next be paid from the Credit Shelter Trust. The following taxes are excluded from this provision: taxes on the qualified terminable interest property included in my gross estate through the application of Code Section 2044, and taxes on any generation-skipping transfer that shall be charged against the property generating such tax as provided in Code Section 2603(b).

NOTE: Careful consideration must be given to how taxes will be paid. Many wills simply state that taxes will be paid from your residuary estate (what's left after all other transfers). This may not be appropriate if you make several transfers before the residuary clause goes into effect, or if significant property is transferred outside your will (for example, property held in joint title with someone other than your spouse). Have your estate planner make projections of how the tax costs will be allocated under different assumptions. You don't want to risk drastically reducing an important bequest. State taxes are important to consider.

III.   SPECIFIC BEQUESTS OF TANGIBLE PERSONAL PROPERTY

I give and bequeath my DESCRIBE TANGIBLE PROPERTY to NAME OF RECIPIENT. If he/she does not survive me, then all property appointed under this section shall be disposed of as provided under General Bequest of Tangible Personal Property.

NOTE: Use this provision to give a painting, ring, or other personal item to a specific person. Consider the tax allocation for such property.

IV.   GENERAL BEQUEST OF TANGIBLE PERSONAL PROPERTY

A. I give and bequeath all of my tangible personal property, not disposed of pursuant to prior provisions of this Will, wherever located, to my spouse, SPOUSE NAME. If my spouse does not survive me, I give and bequeath this personal property to my children, and the issue of any deceased child of mine, in such proportions or shares, and upon such terms and conditions as the Executor, in the exercise of absolute discretion, may direct in a written instrument delivered to each appointee with respect to the specific article or articles so appointed. Without intending any legal obligation, I have requested the Executor to dispose of this personal property as I have specified in a separate memorandum. The receipt by the appointee, if adult or if a minor of his or her parent, guardian, or the person with whom he or she resides, shall be a full and sufficient discharge to the Executor from all liabilities with respect to the specific articles so appointed. I direct that all articles not effectively appointed under this or other provisions of my Will shall be sold by my Executor, and I give and bequeath the net proceeds thereof to and among my children and the issue of any deceased child of mine in such proportions and amounts as shall equalize, so far as may be practical, the value of the articles previously appointed to or for the benefit of each of my children and the issue of any deceased child of mine, per stirpes.

B. All costs, if any, of shipping, packing, and insuring any of my personal property transferred under any section of this Will shall be paid by my estate. In addition, any insurance policy covering personal property shall, to the extent advantageous to the administration of my estate, be transferred with the property insured.

V.   REAL PROPERTY GENERALLY

I give, devise, and bequeath to my spouse, if my spouse shall survive me: (i) all real property, including any interests in real property, wherever situated; and (ii) all stock in any cooperative apartment corporation, together with the appurtenant proprietary lease covering that apartment, that I own at the time of my death and that my spouse and I shall be occupying any portion of as a place of residence, whether permanent, temporary, or seasonal.

VI.   UNIFIED CREDIT SHELTER SPRINKLE TRUST FOR SPOUSE AND CHILDREN

NOTE: You are entitled to a lifetime credit that exempts $600,000 of property transfers. If you're married, you can give all of your assets free of tax to your surviving spouse. This approach, however, wastes your lifetime exclusion and may result in a larger tax on your spouse's estate when he or she dies, since he or she will own all of the assets. This section is intended to use up as much of your lifetime exemption as possible to minimize the total tax when both your estate and your spouse's estate are considered (see Chapter 9).

A. If my spouse survives me, I give to my Trustees, in trust, the largest amount that will not result in any federal estate tax payable after giving effect to the unified credit to which I am entitled, as well as any other credits applicable to my estate. In determining the credits applicable, the state death tax credit shall only be considered to the extent that it will not increase the state death tax liability. The amount so calculated shall be reduced by the following: (i) the value of property transferred under previous sections of this Will; (ii) property passing outside of this Will that is included in my gross estate and does not qualify for the marital deduction (or for which no marital deduction is claimed); and (iii) administration expenses and principal payments on debts that are not allowed as deductions for my federal estate tax. For the purpose of establishing the amount disposed of by this section, the values finally fixed in the federal estate tax proceeding relating to my estate shall be used. In making the determinations required under this section, it is my intent that this Unified Credit Shelter Sprinkle Trust be funded so as to make the maximum use of my unified credit, even if the result is a reduction in the amount to be included in a Q-TIP Trust, if one is provided below. Disclaimers shall not be considered in making the calculations under this section.

NOTE: There are several approaches to arriving at the desired amount of assets to place in this credit shelter (bypass) trust. The attorney drafting your will can advise you on the best approach for you. The provision for state death taxes should depend on the type of death tax your state has.

B. My Trustees shall hold, manage, and invest the amounts held in this trust. My Trustees shall collect and receive any income and, to the extent and at such times as the Trustees in their absolute discretion shall determine, shall pay it to or for the benefit of one or more members of a class consisting of my spouse, my children, CHILDREN'S NAMES AND ADDRESSES, and other descendants living from time to time, and my mother, MOTHER'S NAME, who resides at MOTHER'S ADDRESS (collectively, the "Recipients"). However, in no event may the trustees provide any amounts to my mother when such amounts would jeopardize the income or assets that the Trustees deem necessary for the support and welfare of my spouse or children. Any net income not so paid over or applied for the benefit of the Recipients shall be accumulated and added to the principal of the trust, at least annually, and thereafter shall be held, administered, and disposed of as a part of the trust.

NOTE: This provision calls for a sprinkling of income to provide for an elderly parent who may be in need, but the same method could be used to provide for any relative. Carefully review the effects this may have on medicaid and similar planning for the elderly recipient.

C. My Trustees are also authorized to pay to, or apply for the benefit of, one or more members of a class consisting of the Recipients such parts of the principal of the trust as my Trustees in their absolute discretion shall deem necessary or advisable for the health, support, and maintenance of the Recipients in each of their respective, accustomed manners of living. These payments and applications may be made irrespective of the fact that such payments may exhaust the principal of the trust being held for the benefit of any persons. The determinations of my Trustees as to the amount of principal payments or applications under this section shall be final and conclusive on all persons with any interest in this trust. Upon the making of any payments or applications under this section my Trustees shall be fully released and discharged from any further liability or accountability.

VII. RESIDUARY INCLUDING Q-TIP TRUST FOR SPOUSE

All the rest, residue, and remainder of my property, wherever situated, and all property that I shall be entitled to dispose of at my death after deducting all my debts, funeral expenses and any expenses of the administration of my estate (my "residuary estate") shall be disposed of as follows:

A. Provision for the payment of any death or similar taxes, if required under this Will, shall be made.

B. Q-TIP Trust: If my spouse, SPOUSE'S NAME, survives me, then all the rest, residue, and remainder of my property and estate (my residuary estate), whether real, personal, tangible, or intangible, or of any kind and wheresoever situated, of which I shall die seized or possessed, or of which I shall be entitled to dispose at the time of my death, I give, devise, and bequeath to the Trustees hereinafter named, in trust, to hold, manage, and invest such property. My Trustees shall collect the income from this trust, and are instructed to pay over the net income to my spouse, or to apply such income for his or her benefit in convenient installments but at least quarterannually, during his or her lifetime. This section is intended as a qualified terminable interest property (Q-TIP) trust under Code Section 2056(b)(7) and shall be interpreted to so qualify. I direct my Executor to give consideration to minimizing the federal estate tax due on my death, but to also consider the federal estate tax likely to be payable by my spouse's estate. Any decisions by my Executor as to whether to elect under Code Section 2056(b)(7) to qualify this trust, or any part of this trust, for the federal estate tax marital deduction shall be made in the Executor's absolute discretion and shall be final and conclusive.

NOTE: The Q-TIP approach provides your surviving spouse with access to all of the income and needed principal from the amount placed in trust. Because it qualifies for the unlimited marital deduction, there will be no federal estate tax due on the assets placed in this trust. Further, you decide what happens to the assets after your spouse's death. This can be very important in the event of a divorce or of the remarriage of your surviving spouse. Disclaimers of the Q-TIP property by your spouse may also be addressed in your will.

C. Upon the death of my spouse if my spouse survives me, the principal and any undistributed income not then added to principal of the Q-TIP Trust (or if my spouse does not survive me, upon my death, my residuary estate) shall be disposed of as follows:

1. If any child of mine has previously died, the share set aside for such child shall be set aside for his or her then living descendants if any, and I give, devise, and bequeath the same to such descendants, in equal shares per stirpes. These transfers shall be either in trust, or free from trust in accordance with the principles set forth in the following sections.

2. If any child of mine then shall have reached the age of Thirty-Five (35), the share set aside for such child shall be transferred, conveyed, and paid over, and I give, devise, and bequeath the same to such child.

3. If any child of mine then shall not have reached the age of Thirty-Five (35), the share set aside for such child shall be held in trust by, and I give, devise, and bequeath the same to, the Trustee hereinafter named, for the following uses and purposes (the "Distribution by Age"):

a. To manage and invest the assets of each trust, to collect the income from the trust, and if the child is under the age of Twenty-Five (25) at the time his or her share is set aside, to apply the net income, and as much of the principal as is determined by the Trustee in his or her sole discretion for such child's care, support, maintenance, education, or general welfare until he or she reaches the age of Twenty-Five (25), to such extent and at such time and in such manner as the Trustees, in their absolute discretion, shall determine, without court order and without regard to the duty of any person to support such child. Any net income not so applied shall be added to the principal of the trust and thereafter shall be held, administered, and disposed of as a part thereof.

NOTE: This section creates a separate trust for each child. The purpose is to guarantee each child the benefits of equal inheritances (or whatever amounts you intend), and to permit the distribution of the trust in three installments as the child grows up. When the assets are not large enough to warrant this treatment, or if you prefer to have all of the assets combined in the event that one child has special needs or an emergency, then the use of a single trust for all children would be appropriate.

---

b. When such child reaches the age of Twenty-Five (25), the Trustee shall transfer, convey, and pay over to such child One-Third (1/3) of the principal of the trust, as it shall then be constituted. When such child reaches the age of Thirty (30), the Trustee shall transfer, convey, and pay over to such child One-Half (1/2) of the principal balance of the trust, as it shall then be constituted. When such child reaches the age of Thirty-Five (35), the Trustee shall transfer, convey, and pay over to such child the entire remaining balance of the trust, as it shall then be constituted. Upon the death of such child before reaching the age of Thirty-Five (35), the Trustee shall transfer the principal of the trust to such persons other than the child, his or her estate, his or her creditors, or the creditors of his or her estate, to such extent, in such amounts or proportions, and in such lawful interests or estates, whether absolute or in trust, as such child may by his or her Last Will and Testament appoint by a specific reference to this power.

c. If the power of appointment is for any reason not validly exercised in whole or in part by such child, the principal of the trust, to the extent not validly appointed by such child, shall, upon his or her death, be transferred to such child's then living descendants, in equal shares per stirpes, or if no such descendant is then living, the principal of the trust shall, upon his or her death, be transferred to such child's then living spouse. If there is no living spouse, then, upon his or her death, the principal of the trust shall be divided into a sufficient number of equal shares so that there shall be set aside one such share for each child of mine then living, or for the issue of any deceased child of mine, per stirpes, such shares to be disposed of as provided for in this section. Any beneficiary of such amounts under the age of Thirty-Five (35) shall have such amounts held in trust as provided above, unless the application of the section concerning the Rule of Perpetuities would require otherwise.

4. Notwithstanding anything contained in this section to the contrary, if at any time during the life of any child or any one or more of his or her issue, any financial emergency arises as a result of accident, illness, or other unusual circumstances, the Trustees are authorized, in their discretion, to pay to such child or to any one or more of his or her issue, or to apply for his or her or their benefit, from the capital of the trust estate, the amount or amounts as the Trustees may deem advisable in the circumstances.

5. My children shall include: CHILDREN'S NAMES, and any later-born children.

VIII. BEQUESTS AND DEVISES TO PERSONS UNDER AGE THIRTY-FIVE GENERALLY

A. If any child of mine, or issue of a deceased child, or any other individual under the age of Thirty-Five (35) years, becomes entitled to any property from my estate upon my death, or any property from any trust created hereunder upon the termination thereof, the share set aside for such person shall be held in trust, and I give, devise, and bequeath the same to the Trustees, in trust, as provided for the following uses and purposes: to manage, invest, and reinvest the same, to collect the income thereof, and to distribute such principal and interest in accordance with the Distribution by Age provided for in the section above.

B. If any tangible personal property shall at any time be held as part of such individual's trust, the Trustees shall have no duty to convert the same into productive property, and the expenses of the safekeeping thereof, including insurance, shall be a proper charge against the assets of the trust.

C. If my Executor or the Trustees, in the exercise of their absolute discretion, shall determine at any time not to transfer in trust or not to continue to hold in trust any part or all of such property, they shall have full power and authority to transfer and pay over such property, or any part thereof, without bond, to such individual, if an adult under the law of the state of his or her domicile at the time of such payment, or to his or her parent, or to the guardian of his or her person or property, or to a custodian for such individual under any Uniform Gifts to Minors Act or Uniform Transfers to Minors Act, pursuant to which a custodian is acting or may be appointed, or to the person with whom such individual resides.

D. The receipt by such individual, if an adult, or by the individual's parent, guardian, or custodian, or by any other person to whom any principal or income is transferred and paid over pursuant to any of the above provisions, shall be a full discharge to my Executor or the Trustees from all liability with respect to such transfer.

IX.   APPOINTMENT OF TESTAMENTARY GUARDIAN

I appoint my spouse to be guardian of the person and property of each of my minor children. In the event that my spouse dies during the minority of any of my children without having appointed a successor guardian, or if he or she predeceases me, I appoint MR. FIRST GUARDIAN and MRS. FIRST GUARDIAN, husband and wife, who reside at FIRST GUARDIANS' ADDRESS, as guardian. If they are unable or unwilling to serve as guardian, I appoint MR. SECOND GUARDIAN and MRS. SECOND GUARDIAN, husband and wife, who reside at SECOND GUARDIANS' ADDRESS, as guardian. If they are unable or unwilling to serve as guardian, I appoint MR. THIRD GUARDIAN and MRS. THIRD GUARDIAN, husband and wife, who reside at THIRD GUARDIANS' AD-DRESS, as guardian. Should none of the couples set forth above be able or willing to serve as guardian, then the first-named person in this section who is able and willing to serve shall serve as guardian.

NOTE: Name as many alternate guardians as you can to ensure proper care for any minor or special children or for a disabled relative in your care. The approach used is to have the first couple serve if you prefer to have your children live in a family environment.

X.   APPOINTMENT OF FIDUCIARIES

A. I appoint my spouse as Executor of this, my Last Will and Testament. If my spouse is unable or unwilling to serve as Executor, I appoint MR. FIRST FIDUCIARY, who resides at FIRST FIDUCIARY'S ADDRESS, as Executor. If he or she is unable or unwilling to serve as Executor, I appoint MR. SECOND FIDUCIARY and MRS. SECOND FIDUCIARY, husband and wife, who reside at SECOND FIDUCIARIES' ADDRESS, jointly as Executor. If they are unable or unwilling to serve as Executor, I appoint MRS. THIRD FIDUCIARY, who resides at THIRD FIDUCIARY'S ADDRESS, as Executor.

NOTE: Unlike the case with a guardian, there is no need to have a family unit. You still should name as many alternates as you can. People can serve either alone or together as fiduciary (executor or guardian). There are a number of instances where it is preferable, or even necessary, to have two people serve together as co-trustees. However, it's usually best to have only one executor. Consult your attorney.

B. I appoint the following persons as Trustees:

I appoint my spouse and MR. FIRST FIDUCIARY as Co-Trustees of every trust established under the residuary clause of this, my Last Will and Testament. If either is unable or unwilling to serve as Trustee of such trust, I appoint the persons named in the section appointing fiduciaries as Trustee of such Trust.

NOTE: You could appoint different people to be the trustees for different trusts if you were concerned that someone wouldn't work well as both trustee and beneficiary.

C. The following provisions apply to the above-named fiduciaries:

1. If any person is the sole Executor or Trustee acting under this Will, or under any trust created under this Will, I authorize such person to designate, in his or her reasonable discretion, any bank or trust company as Co-Trustee to act jointly with him or her. Any such designation of a Co-Trustee may be revoked by the Executor or Trustee at any time before such Co-Trustee qualifies. The last of the persons set forth herein to act as Executor or Trustee is empowered at any time, while acting as a Executor or Trustee hereunder, to designate any individual, bank, or trust company as a successor Executor or Trustee, and any successor Executor or Trustee, while acting as an Executor or Trustee hereunder, shall have the same authority to designate a successor Executor or Trustee. Any designation of a successor Executor or Trustee, pursuant to the authority granted in this section, may be revoked by the Executor or Trustee making such designation at any time before such successor Executor or Trustee qualifies.

2. Any designation of a successor Executor or Trustee, or any revocation of such designation, pursuant to the authority granted in this section, shall be in a written instrument, duly executed and acknowledged by the Executor or Trustee exercising such authority and filed in the court in which this Will is admitted to probate.

D. During the time that any Trustee acting under any trust created under this Will is also a beneficiary of that trust, the Trustee shall be disqualified from acting as a Trustee and shall not be deemed to be a Trustee for the purpose of making any discretionary allocations of receipts or expenses between principal and income in her or his own favor.

E. Any individual Executor or Trustee may resign at any time by filing an acknowledged instrument in the court in which this Will is admitted to probate. The resignation shall take effect upon the filing, whether or not a successor Executor or Trustee has been appointed.

F. No Executor or Trustee, or successor to either, designated in accordance with the provisions of this section, shall be required to furnish any bond or other security including any bond that may be required for the payment of commissions to any individual Executor or Trustee for the performance of his or her duties under this Will or under any trust formed under this Will in any jurisdiction. If any bond is required by law, statute, or rule of court, no sureties shall be required on such bond.

XI. EXECUTOR AND TRUSTEES, MISCELLANEOUS PROVISIONS

A. Neither my Executor nor my Trustees shall be responsible for the use made by any person of any payment of income or principal made to that person. They are not obliged to see to the proper use or application by such person of any distributions made to, or for the benefit of, such person.

B. At any time prior to the completion of the funding of any trust, my Executor may exercise any of the powers granted to my Trustees relating to the distribution of the income and principal of such trust and treat the monies so paid or applied as a partial funding of such trust.

C. In the exercise of any discretionary powers over the payment or application of income or principal under this Will or any trust created under this Will, the judgment of my Executor or my Trustees, as the case may be, as to the amount of any payment or distribution, and as to the advisability thereof, shall be final and conclusive upon all persons beneficially interested in my estate or in any trust. Upon making any payment or distribution of income or principal as provided by this, my Will, my Executor and Trustees shall be fully discharged of liability with respect to such payment or distribution and from further liability or accountability.

D. In determining the amounts of income and principal, if any, that shall be paid or disbursed pursuant to any discretionary powers given herein, my Executor and Trustees shall not be required to take into consideration any assets or other sources of income of the person for whose benefit such powers might be exercised.

E. In determining the value of the principal of any trust fund created by this Will at any time or times, the decision of my Executor or my Trustees shall be deemed correct.

XII. RULE AGAINST PERPETUITIES—TRUST TERMINATION

Notwithstanding any provision of this Will to the contrary, all trusts created under this Will shall terminate upon the expiration of Twenty-One (21) years after the death of the last surviving of all of my descendants living at the date of my death. If any trust created under this Will has not terminated earlier, the Trustees shall transfer at that time the trust funds in their possession to the persons entitled to receive the trust income, in the same shares in which the income is then being paid, or made payable, to them.

XIII. SIMULTANEOUS DEATH

A. If my spouse shall die simultaneously with me or in such circumstances as to render it difficult to determine who died first, then I direct that my spouse shall be deemed to have survived me and that the provisions of this Will shall be construed upon the assumption that he or she so survived.

B. If any beneficiary under this Will, other than my spouse, shall die simultaneously with another beneficiary under this Will or in such circumstances as to render it difficult to determine who predeceased the other, and if the rights of one of them depend upon his or her having survived the other, then I direct that the beneficiary whose rights depend upon such survivorship shall be deemed to have predeceased the other beneficiary and that the provisions of this Will shall be construed upon the assumption.

C. If any beneficiary under this Will, other than my spouse, shall die within Thirty (30) days after my death, such beneficiary shall be deemed to have predeceased me and the provisions of this Will shall be construed accordingly.

XIV. SPENDTHRIFT PROVISION

Except as otherwise may be provided in this Will, no transfer disposition, charge, or encumbrance on the income or principal of any trust by any beneficiary under this Will by way of anticipation shall be valid or in any way binding upon my Trustees. The right of any beneficiary to any payment of income or principal is subject to any charge or deduction that my Executor or Trustees make against it under the authority granted to them by any statute or law or by any provision of this Will. No beneficiary shall have the right to transfer, dispose of, assign, or encumber such income or principal until the assets shall be paid to that beneficiary by my Trustees. No income or principal shall be liable to any claim by any creditor of any such beneficiary.

XV. COMPENSATION OF EXECUTOR AND TRUSTEES

Except for my spouse, any Executor or Trustees shall be entitled to receive as compensation for services rendered under this Will or under any trust created under this Will the commissions that he or she would be entitled to receive in each such capacity under the laws of the state in effect at the time such commissions are payable. My Executor and Trustees are authorized to make payments to themselves on account of any part of such commissions, without court order. No interest shall be paid on such payments.

XVI. POWERS OF EXECUTOR AND TRUSTEES

In the administration of any property, whether real, personal, tangible, or intangible, included in my estate, or of any trust created under this Will, whether owned by me at the time of my death or subsequently acquired by my Executor or my Trustees, including any accumulated income, my Executor or my Trustees shall, except as may be otherwise provided in this Will, have the following powers to be exercised in their absolute discretion:

A. To sell or otherwise dispose of any assets at such times, in such manner (for cash or on credit), and upon such terms and conditions as they shall deem advisable.

B. To abandon any property, real or personal, that they deem worthless or not of sufficient value to warrant keeping; to abstain from the payment of taxes, utility charges, assessments, and maintenance of any such property; to permit any such property to be lost by tax sale or other proceedings; and to convey any property for a nominal or no consideration if they believe the continued ownership thereof inadvisable.

C. To complete, extend, modify, or renew any loans, notes, bonds, mortgages, contracts, or any other obligations that I may owe or own, to which I may be a party, or which may be liens or charges against any of my property or against my estate, whether or not I am liable, in such manner as they may believe advisable; to sell or release any claims or demands of my estate or of any trust estate against others or of others against my estate or any trust estate as they may believe advisable, including the acceptance of deeds of real or personal property in satisfaction of bonds and mortgages, and to make any payments in connection therewith that they may believe advisable.

D. To purchase or exchange real estate (whether or not it qualifies under Code Section 1031) or other property at such times, in such manner, and upon such terms as they deem advisable; to invest in such bonds, preferred or common stocks, mortgages, interests in any kind of investment trust or common trust fund, or other evidences of rights, interests, or obligations, secured or unsecured, or in such other property, real or personal, as they shall deem advisable, whether or not any investment shall produce income or be of a wasting nature, and without regard to any statute, decision, or other law concerning the investment of trust funds or the amount that shall be invested in any one security or in any one kind of investment, and whether or not any investment shall be included within the class of investments prescribed for the investment of trust funds by the laws of the state in which I shall be domiciled at the time of my death, from time to time in effect.

E. To retain for such periods of time as they shall deem advisable any investments or other property of which I shall die seized or possessed or to which I shall be in any manner entitled at the time of my death.

F. To hold any property or assets uninvested for such reasonable periods of time as they believe advisable, without personal liability for any loss of income or other opportunity or holding costs.

G. To buy, own, manage, maintain, improve, lease (for any term whether or not it extends beyond the terms of the trusts created under this Will, or the term fixed by any statute or other applicable law), mortgage, exchange, partition, or otherwise transfer or encumber any real or personal property or any interest therein, or any interest in any venture, corporation, or partnership owning an interest in real property, and perform any and all acts incident to these powers or necessary to carry out these powers; to accept and invest, or not invest, any proceeds of an insurance or condemnation payment; to make alterations in any buildings now or hereafter located on any such property or to demolish the same; to construct new buildings; to do all this without authorizations by any court and in such manner and upon such terms and conditions as they shall deem advisable; and to enter into contracts or grant options with respect to any of the above for any term, whether or not it extends beyond the term fixed by any statute or other applicable law.

H. To prepare and file tax, franchise, or similar returns and to exercise at such times and in such manner as they may deem advisable any rights of election or other rights that may be available to them under the provisions of tax laws of the United States or any state or local jurisdiction or foreign country, including but not limited to the power to make such decisions as they reasonably believe advisable in all of the circumstances (regardless of whether the decision is the most advantageous for my estate as a whole). These decisions may concern the date to value my estate; the claiming of expenses or deductions for estate tax or income tax purposes; the filing of joint income, gift, or other tax returns with my spouse, if there is any; the payment of any taxes or collection of any refunds relative to such returns; and, in connection with the foregoing, to make or not to make such adjustments or transfers between principal and income as they, in their absolute discretion, may deem equitable in the circumstances.

I. To foreclose mortgages and bid on property under foreclosure, or to take title to property by conveyance in lieu of foreclosure, either with or without payment of consideration; to continue investments after maturity, either with or without renewal or extension, on such terms as they shall deem advisable; to consent to the modification, renewal, or extension of any note, agreement, or guaranty, whether or not it is secure, and release obligors or refrain from instituting suits or actions against such obligors for deficiencies, with or without consideration and on such terms as they shall deem advisable; to use any part of the property held under this Will as they shall deem advisable for the protection of any investment in real or personal property or in any mortgage.

J. To borrow from themselves (but only on arm's-length terms and upon execution of a written note) or from any other party, whether for the purposes of raising funds to pay taxes or otherwise, and to give or not give security therefor, all upon such terms and for such periods as they shall deem advisable.

K. To make loans, either secured or unsecured, in such amounts, upon such terms, at such rates of interest, and to such persons (including the beneficiary of any trust created herein), firms, or corporations as they may determine.

L. To exercise or dispose of any options, privileges, or rights; to become a party to, or deposit securities or other property under, or accept securities issued under, any voting trust agreement; to grant options for the sale of property for any term, whether or not it extends beyond the terms of the trust created under this Will, or for the term fixed by any statute, decision, or other law.

M. To vote upon any proposition or election at any meeting of stock or security holders, and to grant proxies, discretionary or otherwise, to vote at any meeting or any adjournments thereof.

N. To assent to participate in any reorganization, readjustment, recapitalization, consolidation, merger, dissolution, sale, or purchase of assets, lease, mortgage, contract, or other action or proceedings by any corporation or other party; to deposit securities or other property, or become a party to any agreement or plan for any such action or proceeding or for the protection of creditors or holders of securities; to subscribe to new securities issued pursuant to any such action or proceeding; to delegate discretionary powers to any reorganization, protective, or similar committee; to exchange any property for any other property in connection with any of the above; to pay any assessments or other expenses in connection with any of the above.

O. To carry on any business owned by me (in whole or part, directly or indirectly) or in which I may be engaged at the time of my death for such period of time as they may deem advisable, or to sell or liquidate such business.

P. To pay, adjust, compromise, settle, or refer to arbitration any claim in favor of or against my estate or the trusts created by this Will, and to institute, prosecute, withdraw, or defend such legal proceedings as they shall deem advisable.

Q. To employ and pay the compensation of such accountants, custodians, experts, counsel (legal or investment), and other agents as they shall deem advisable and to delegate other agents as they shall deem advisable; to reasonably delegate discretionary powers to, and to rely upon information or advice furnished by, such accountants, custodians, experts, counsel, or other agents, while, however, remaining fully responsible for supervising and controlling same. If a bank or trust company shall be acting as Executor or Trustee hereunder, no payments shall be made to said bank or trust company for custodian or investment counsel services.

R. Notwithstanding anything to the contrary in this Will, in no event shall any part of the principal or income of any trust be used for the care, health, support, or maintenance of any person during any time that he or she may be a patient or a resident in a facility operated by or with the funds of any state or other governmental agency. It is my intention that so long as public funds are available and said person is a patient or a resident in a facility assisted with public funds, no part of the principal of any trust shall be made available for his or her health, support, or maintenance, or for reimbursement to the institution or the government providing for such health, support, or maintenance.

S. To pay any expenses, costs, fees, taxes, penalties, or other charges and to charge the same against the principal or income, or partly against the principal and partly against the income, of the whole or any part of my estate or of all or any of the trusts, parts, funds, or shares created by this Will, except as otherwise expressly provided with respect to estate, transfer, succession, or other inheritance taxes.

T. To set up reserves for taxes, assessments, insurance, repairs, depreciation, obsolescence, and general maintenance on all buildings, leaseholds, easements, or other real property interests, or other property held by them out of rents, profits, or other income received on such buildings or other property.

U. To hold property in their names as Executor or Trustees, or, to the extent permitted by law and in such form as will pass by delivery, in their names without designation of any fiduciary capacity, or in the name of a nominee, so long as reasonable precautions have been taken to protect the interests of my estate, or any trust in such property; to entrust custody of any securities, cash, or other property held by them hereunder to one or more of their number.

V. By instrument or instruments signed by all persons acting as my Executor and Trustees, qualified and acting as such at any time, to delegate, in whole or in part, to any person or persons (including any of my Executors or Trustees) the authority and power to (i) sign checks, drafts, or orders for the payment or withdrawal of funds from any bank account in which funds of my estate or any trust created under this Will shall be deposited; (ii) endorse for sale, transfer, or delivery, or sell, transfer, or deliver, or purchase or otherwise acquire, any and all stocks, stock warrants, stock rights, bonds, or other securities whatsoever; and (iii) gain access to any safe-deposit box or boxes in which assets of my estate or any trust created hereunder may be located or which may be in the names of my Executor or Trustees and remove part or all of the contents of any such safe-deposit box and release and surrender them.

W. To form, reorganize, liquidate, or dissolve such corporations, partnerships, associations, joint ventures, or other arrangements as they shall deem advisable in connection with the administration or distribution of my estate or any trust, part, fund, or share thereof, and to transfer to such corporations such property as they shall deem advisable.

X. To pay any legacy or make any division, distribution, or partition of property in kind or otherwise and to allot any property, including an undivided interest therein, to any trust, fund, or share, whether or not the same kind of property is allotted to other trusts, funds, or shares, except as otherwise hereinafter expressly provided with respect to the use of property that would not qualify for the marital deduction.

Y. To select any method that they believe advisable for payment of the taxes levied on my estate by any taxing authority and arrange for or enter into any agreements with the appropriate taxing authority for such purpose, and, without limiting the foregoing, to elect to extend the time for payment of taxes levied on my estate by any taxing authority for such periods as are permitted by the Internal Revenue Code or the laws of any jurisdiction, including the election pursuant to Internal Revenue Code Section 6166; to pay part or all of the federal estate taxes levied on my estate, in two or more equal installments, notwithstanding that the effect of any method selected, or election made, may be to defer the final settlement of my estate or subject it to interest charges or penalties. My Executor in his or her sole discretion, may refrain from making any payment out of the principal or income of my estate, or any trust created hereunder, until such time as he or she shall have paid in full, or made full provision for, the payment of all of the debts of my estate and all taxes levied thereon by any taxing authority.

Z. To make such payments on account of the Executor's or Trustees' commissions and attorneys' fees in advance of the settlement of their accounts, as they may determine to be just and reasonable, without the necessity of any petition or approval of any court or the consent of any persons interested in my estate.

AA. Any individual Executor or Trustee acting hereunder is authorized at any time and from time to time by revocable power of attorney to delegate to any one or more of his Co-Executors or Co-Trustees any duty or power conferred upon him or her hereunder and regardless of whether any such delegation relates to a discretionary or ministerial power. Any such power of attorney and any revocation of any such power of attorney shall be in writing and delivered to the Co-Executor or Co-Trustee to whom the duty or power has been delegated.

AB. Generally, to exercise all such rights and powers, and to do all such acts, and to enter into all such agreements as persons owning similar property in their own rights might lawfully exercise, do, or enter into.

AC. To execute and deliver any and all instruments in writing that my Executor or my Trustees may deem advisable in order to carry out any of the foregoing powers. No party to any such instrument in writing signed by my Executor or my Trustees shall be obligated to inquire into its validity.

AD. With regard to an incapacitated beneficiary:

1. If any beneficiary of my estate shall, in the opinion of my Executor or Trustees, become incapacitated (whether by reason of illness or other cause), my Executor or Trustees in their absolute discretion, in lieu of paying all or part of the net income or principal or of any legacy to such beneficiary as is otherwise authorized or directed by this Will, may dispose of the income or principal by making payment to a legally appointed guardian, committee, or conservator of such beneficiary; or may dispose of the income or principal by making payment to such beneficiary's attorney-in-fact under a durable power of attorney, or to any person with whom such beneficiary resides or who has charge of his or her care; and the income or principal will be applied directly for the benefit of such beneficiary.

2. To make any payment or application described in this section without bond or other security and without prior judicial approval, and the receipt of the amount of such payment or application shall completely release and discharge my Executor or Trustees from all further liability or accountability therefor.

AE. Notwithstanding anything to the contrary contained in this Will, if my Trustees of any trust created hereunder (or, if any such trust shall not have been funded, the Executor of this Will) shall determine that the aggregate value or the character or nature of the assets of such trust (or the estate assets available to fund such trust) makes it inadvisable, inconvenient, or uneconomical to continue the administration of (or to fund) such trust, then the Trustees or Executor, in the exercise of absolute discretion, may transfer and pay over the trust estate (or the estate assets available to fund such trust), equally or unequally, to one or more persons then eligible to receive the net income from such trust. If the Executor of this Will shall determine not to fund such trust and the Trustees of such trust should not be the same, the Executor of this Will shall obtain the consent of the Trustees of such trust before distributing the estate assets otherwise available for funding such trust.

Except as otherwise provided in this Will, in any case in which my Executor or my Trustees are required or permitted to divide my estate or any part thereof into trusts, funds, or shares, they shall not be required physically to divide any of the investments or other property held hereunder but may assign undivided interests therein to the various trusts, funds, and shares, provided that no such undivided holding shall be deemed to defer or postpone the vesting or distribution in accordance with the terms of this Will of any property so held in trust.

The foregoing powers, authority, and discretion granted to my Executor and Trustees are in addition to and not in limitation of the powers, authority, and discretion vested in them by operation of law. These powers may be exercised by them as often and from time to time as they may deem necessary or advisable, without application to or approval by any court, and shall remain exercisable after the termination of any trust until actual or final distribution.

NOTE: The general approach in most wills is to give the executors and trustees the broadest possible authority. The advantage of this is that whatever situation arises, the executor and trustees will have sufficient authority to deal with it. However, this is not required. If you believe that some of the powers are excessive, discuss the changes you would like with your lawyer.

XVII.   SERVICE OF PROCESS, SETTLEMENTS

It shall not be necessary to serve with process any minor or incompetent in any judicial proceeding in connection with this Will (including, without limitation, proceedings involving the administration of my estate) in which any competent adult party to such proceedings has the same interest as such minor or incompetent. Any nonjudicial settlement of the accounts of my Executor and Trustees executed by all of the persons required to be served by said section, after taking into consideration the foregoing provisions of this section, shall be final and conclusive on all persons interested, or who may become interested, in my estate (including, without limitation, all minors, unborns, or incompetents).

XVIII.   PERSONS DEALING WITH EXECUTOR OR TRUSTEES

No person dealing with my Executor or my Trustees shall be bound to see to the application or disposition of cash or other property transferred to my Executor or my Trustees, or to inquire into the authority for or propriety of any action by my Executor or Trustees.

XIX.   NO INTEREST ON LEGACIES

It is my wish that all legacies under this Will shall be satisfied by my Executor as soon as may be practicable after my death, but I direct that no legacy shall bear interest if unpaid at the time specified by law.

XX.   DEFINITIONS, CONSTRUCTION

A. All references in this Will to the Internal Revenue Code are to the Internal Revenue Code of 1986, as amended, and shall be deemed to refer to corresponding provisions of any subsequent federal tax law.

B. Captions, titles, and section numbers (and letter designations) are inserted for convenience only and should not be read to broaden or limit the scope of any provision.

C. As used in this Will:

1. The term "death taxes" shall mean all estate, inheritance, transfer, succession, and other death taxes or duties of any nature, including any interest or penalties thereon.

2. The terms "unified credit," "gross estate," "marital deduction," and "interests in property that pass or have passed" shall have the same meaning and effect as under the provisions of the Internal Revenue Code.

3. The words "Executor," "Executors," "Co-Executor," "fiduciary," "Trustee," and "Trustees" shall mean and include the persons originally designated herein and any

person appointed as a Co-Trustee or as a successor in accordance with the provisions of this Will, and shall be construed as masculine, feminine, or neuter, or in the singular or plural, as the sense requires.

    4. The term "State" means STATE NAME.

D. For purposes of this Will, masculine terms shall be read as the feminine or neuter equivalent, singular terms as the plural equivalent, and vice versa, all as the sense may require.

    IN WITNESS WHEREOF, I, the said YOUR NAME, sign, seal, publish, and declare this as my Last Will and Testament, in the presence of the persons witnessing it at my request, this MONTH DAY, YEAR.

                                        _____ (L.S.)

    Signed, sealed, published, and declared by YOUR NAME, the Testator above named, as and for his or her Last Will and Testament, in our presence, and we, at his request, and in his or her presence and in the presence of each other, have hereunto signed our names as attesting witnesses and added opposite thereto our respective places of residence, all on the day and year last above written.

Address:

_____

Witness Name

_____

Witness Signature

Address:

_____

Witness Name

_____

Witness Signature

Address:

_____

Witness Name

_____

Witness Signature

STATE OF STATENAME   )

              :   ss.:

COUNTY OF COUNTYNAME)

    Each of the undersigned, individually and severally, being duly sworn, deposes and says:

    The within Will, consisting of ____ pages, each page of which was initialed by Testator except for the ____th page, which was signed by Testator, was subscribed in our presence and sight by YOUR NAME, the within named Testator, in the MONTH DAY, YEAR, at ADDRESS WHERE WILL SIGNED.

Said Testator declared the instrument so subscribed to be his or her Last Will and Testament.

Each of the undersigned thereupon signed as a witness at the end of said Will, at the request of said YOUR NAME Testator, and in his or her presence and sight and in the presence and sight of each other.

Said Testator was, at the time of so executing said Will, over the age of eighteen years and, in the respective opinions of the undersigned, of sound mind, memory, and understanding and not under any restraint or in any respect incompetent to make a Will.

The Testator, in the respective opinions of the undersigned, could read, write, and converse in the English language and was suffering from no defect of sight, hearing, or speech, or from any other physical or mental impairment that would affect his or her capacity to make a valid Will. The Will was executed as a single original instrument and was not executed in counterparts.

Each of the undersigned was acquainted with said Testator at such time and makes this affidavit at his or her request.

The within Will was shown to the undersigned at the time this affidavit was made, and was examined by each of them as to the signature of said Testator and of the undersigned.

The foregoing instrument was executed by the Testator, YOUR NAME, and witnessed by each of the undersigned affiants under the supervision of LAWYER'S NAME, an attorney-at-law.

_____

_____

_____

[NOTARY FORMS OMITTED]

CAUTION: The format for signing a will, the number of witnesses, and so forth, varies by state. Since it's critical that a will be executed in conformity with applicable law, be sure to consult an attorney.

For Your Notebook:

RELIGIOUS IMPLICATIONS OF A WILL, JEWISH LAW (*HALACHA*) AND INHERITANCE

By Rabbi Aryeh Weil[1] and Martin Shenkman

Although many parents prefer to leave their estates to their children in equal shares, biblical law prescribes certain specific distributions of assets following death. For example, under biblical law, a widow is entitled to support and maintenance for life, or until remarriage. A widow could also elect to forego, at any time, this support and instead claim a lump sum settlement provided for in her marriage contract (*ketubah*). Sons are generally the exclusive heirs, with the first-born son being entitled to a double portion. Single daughters are to receive support and maintenance while they remain single and a dowry upon marriage.[2] Here is the problem: What you can do when your will provides for the distribution you believe best for your family, but you would also like to show allegiance to the requirements of traditional Jewish law. There is a practical approach to achieving both objectives with little difficulty.

The solution is generally found through a combination of two documents: (1) a will reflecting your intended distributions of your estate, drafted in accordance with current civil law; and (2) a document creating a means of circumventing the biblical inheritance requirements without technically violating them, drafted in accordance with Jewish law. The ease of compliance should serve as an encouragement to those concerned about complying with the religious precepts.

To understand the suggested approach, some of the basic principles and issues should be noted. Jewish law makes an important distinction between an *inter vivos* (lifetime) gift and a testamentary (effective on death) bequest. Generally, a person can give any property while alive, and in any manner. This is because the biblical laws of inheritance only apply to assets owned at the time of death. The obvious solution, then, would be to make an *inter vivos* gift to the heir, such as a daughter, who would receive a less-than-equal share under Jewish law. But there is a little more to it than that.

If you gave a deed to your daughter for property that was only to be transferred upon your death, this would not be effective under Jewish law. At the instant of your death, the Jewish laws of inheritance (*yerusha*) would apply, and the assets would have to be distributed accordingly. Alternatively, if you attempted to make a gift that was to become effective at a later date, a number of additional problems

[1] Rabbi Aryeh Weil is the rabbi of Congregation Bnai Yeshurun in Teaneck, New Jersey. He is also vice president of the Rabbinical Council of America and is an adjunct on the faculty of Rockland Community College of the State University of New York. The authors acknowledge the assistance of Rabbi Willig and Israel Polak in the preparation of the *shtar chov*.
[2] Numbers XXVII, 5–11.

would be raised. One is that the transfer of most property requires a formal act (*kinyan*). A *kinyan* cannot be effective for property that is not owned at the time of the gift transaction. Also, for a transfer to be effective under Jewish law, a *kinyan* generally must be completed at the time of the transfer, obviously not possible for a future gift.

The solution here is the creation of a debt in favor of the persons you wish to have inherit property in excess of what they would be entitled to under Jewish law. This technique creates a technical compliance with biblical law through a separate contractual document (a *shtar*), which creates a fictional debt (a *chov*). There is no prohibition in Jewish law concerning the creation of such a debt. The debt is stated to mature one minute prior to your death. The heirs are given the option of paying this substantial debt or, as an alternative, agreeing to the distribution provided for under your secular will. The intent is for them to comply with this alternative in order to preserve a greater inheritance for themselves.

EXAMPLE: Father leaves an estate worth $3 million. His will provides that First Son, Second Son, and Daughter each receive $1 million. Biblical law would require the following distribution: First Son, $2 million; Second Son, $1 million; and Daughter, support and a dowry. Father executes a conditional *shtar chov* creating a debt of $2 million in favor of Daughter. First Son can agree to the equal one-third allocations provided for in Father's will, or he can attempt to secure his $2 million inheritance provided under Jewish law and then make a payment of $2 million to Daughter. The choice will be obvious; each child will receive an equal $1 million inheritance as their father intended, and Father's estate technically will have been distributed in accordance with the precepts of Jewish law. The fictitious debt will lapse by its own terms.

All authorities are not in full agreement concerning the effectiveness of this approach under Jewish law. From a civil perspective, the creation of this fictional debt could conceivably raise a number of issues. Although the contractual form of debt (*shtar chov*) does not have to contain a fixed maturity date or stated interest rate (two factors used to identify a debt for tax and civil purposes), there is no guarantee that the debt will not be regarded as a true indebtedness for all purposes.

If the debt is, in fact, a valid indebtedness, could the payee enforce the payment of the amount due and hold your estate liable? What if one of the heirs wished to create problems for the other family members by using the documents as part of a will challenge? If the debt is recognized under civil law, will the imputed interest rates provided under the Internal Revenue Code apply to create income and expense for family members? Would the eventual relief of the debt without payment (which is obviously not intended) create relief of indebtedness income? Does the creation of the debt itself trigger a gift tax? It is hoped, although no assurance can be given, that should such a situation ever arise, the civil legal and tax authorities would recognize the intent and purpose of the transaction and not permit such unwarranted and harsh results to occur.

Two steps can be taken to minimize this risk: First, some of the language used in the contractual arrangements creating the debt should be the appropriate Hebrew terms, so as to distinguish the document from what may be considered a contractual debt (*shtar chov*) under civil law. Second, there does not seem to be any delivery requirements to make the *shtar chov* valid under religious law. As a result, only a single executed copy of the *shtar chov* should be prepared. This copy should be held in safekeeping by your rabbi. This alone should serve as a substantial safeguard to avoid unintended problems.

As a final step in addressing the compliance with the biblical laws of inheritance, it is suggested that an additional paragraph be added to your secular will. This additional provision has two purposes. The first is to provide for some amount of money that should be distributed in accordance with Jewish law. This will serve to remind your heirs of the rules and customs involved and thus will encourage them to take similar steps to make their estate plans conform to Jewish law. The second objective of the additional provision is to provide language that will make the distributions called for under your secular will come closer to compliance with the biblical requirements of inheritance. As discussed above, everyone is free to complete *inter vivos* gifts. Thus, all transfers under the will could be stated to have been effected by gift transfers, effective one minute prior to your death, and in accordance with the completion of a proper *kinyan* as required under Jewish law. This language should provide some basis for a rabbinic court (*Bet Din*) to sanction the distributions under your secular will on the basis of your conformity with local custom and certain minority rabbinic opinions concerning inheritance.

For Your Notebook:

PROPOSED LANGUAGE TO ADD TO SECULAR WILL IN CONFORMITY WITH JEWISH LAW

It is my intent that transfers of property made under this Section shall be in conformity with Jewish law (*Halacha*). Therefore, for the sole purpose of meeting this objective, I provide as follows:

1. I hereby devise and bequeath the sum of One Thousand Dollars ($1,000.00) to my heirs, as defined in accordance with *Halacha,* to be divided among them in strict accordance with *Halacha.*

2. Each and every distribution or other transfer of any property under this Will, except for the bequest set forth in Subsection 1., above, shall be deemed to be made by way of matanah, effective the instant prior to my death, as required by Halacha. Each such transfer shall be deemed to have been completed through a proper *kinyan,* as appropriate for each type of property, and as defined by *Halacha.*

For Your Notebook:

CONDITIONAL *SHTAR CHOV*

WHEREAS, the undersigned testator ("Testator")

I, the Testator, hereby accept upon myself this *Chov* to [NAME OF PERSON TO RE-CEIVE DISTRIBUTION UNDER YOUR SECULAR WILL, WHO IS NOT AN HEIR UNDER BIBLICAL LAW], the sum of [AN AMOUNT IN EXCESS OF THE BEQUESTS TO SUCH PERSON] Dollars, effective immediately, but not payable until one minute before my death, on the condition that I do not retract this obligation at any time prior to my death. All the property that is mine at that time, both real and personal, shall serve as security for the payment of the said obligation.

I hereby stipulate that my heirs, as defined by biblical law (Torah) as interpreted in accordance with Orthodox Jewish law (*Halacha*) (the "Heirs") shall be given the option of paying the above obligation, or, in lieu thereof, of carrying out the terms as specified in my Last Will and Testament, executed on DATE OF YOUR WILL, and, in addition, carrying out all transfers of property upon my death that are considered "nontestamentary transfers" in accordance with the laws of the State of [NAME OF YOUR STATE]. Should my Heirs choose and comply with this option, then this Conditional *Shtar Chov* shall become void.

The above condition(s) is (are) made in accordance with the laws of the Torah, as derived from Numbers XXVII, 5–11.

Any dispute arising out of this document, or the transactions contemplated hereunder, shall be brought before, and settled in a court of Jewish law, a *Bet Din*.

Signed this MONTH DAY, YEAR, at ADDRESS WHERE EXECUTED.

_____
YOUR NAME (SIGNATURE)

For Your Notebook:

RELIGIOUS IMPLICATIONS OF A WILL, ISLAMIC LAW AND INHERITANCE

By James B. Boskey[1]

The law of inheritance is the largest, and probably the most important, "legal" subject in Koran, the holy book of Islam, and has been one of the most analyzed legal subjects in Islamic law. Mohammed, the prophet of Islam, was an important social reformer, and one of the major elements of his social reforms can be seen best through the changes he made in the way in which inheritances were to pass under Islamic law.

While there are several schools of Islam, each of which varies to some extent in its interpretation of the Koranic injunctions with regard to inheritance, there are many general principles that are common to them. Among the most important is the limitation on freedom of testation. A Muslim may only pass one-third of his or her estate by will, the remainder passing in accordance with the law of intestate succession, and there are various limitations even on that limited freedom of testation.

The intestate-succession scheme that is set out in the Koran is a very complex one that cannot be fully described in the short compass available here. The clearest exposition in English of that scheme is Noel J. Coulson's *A History of Islamic Law*,[2] although even that volume deals largely with the law of the Sunni schools.

The basic approach to succession taken by the Koran was to provide inheritance to the descendants and patrilineal ascendants of the decedent. One of the most radical reforms for the time was the requirement that daughters were to be provided with two-thirds of the inheritance taken by sons, and that, in absence of sons, daughters take two-thirds of the estate. Other important aspects were the right of patrilineal kin to take in preference to matrilineal kin in almost all situations, the limited rights granted to widows (such rights being in large part restricted to life interests in certain portions of the decedent's property), and the provision for the establishment of *Waqfs* (charitable trusts).

Most modern Islamic states still implement, in large part, the traditional Koranic law of inheritance, although the right of individuals to pick and choose amongst the doctrines of the various schools of Islamic law maintains some flexibility. The general inheritance scheme is one that many Muslims, even in the United States, may wish to adopt by will even though it is not imposed on them. In drafting a will taking account of this perspective, care must be taken to identify the school of Islamic law whose principles will govern the inheritance scheme.

---

[1] James B. Boskey is a professor of law at Seton Hall Law School, Newark, New Jersey. He studied Islamic law as part of an L.L.M. program at the London School of Economics and Political Science.

[2] Edinburgh University Press, 1964.

4 TRUST

A trust is one of the most important estate planning tools, and one of the most versatile. Trusts can be prepared to address many different circumstances, as illustrated throughout this book.

CAUTION: Trusts can have varying income, estate, and gift tax consequences. While many of the estate and gift tax implications are addressed in later chapters, a full review is well beyond the scope of this book. Therefore, it is vitally important that before you set up any trust arrangement, you review all of these tax implications with your tax adviser and attorney.

WHAT IS A TRUST?

A trust is a legal relationship in which property is transferred to one or more trustees. The trustees (whether individuals, banks, trust companies, or others) are owners of the property transferred to them as trustees. Ownership normally means that property can be used as the owner sees fit and for his or her benefit. However, ownership means something different with a trust. Although they are owners, the trustees may not use the property for their benefit (unless they happen to be beneficiaries). Instead, the trustees are fiduciaries and guardians of the trust property and have the responsibility to see to it that the property is used only as provided in the trust agreement, or as required by law. The trustees merely own legal title to the property; the equitable title is owned by the beneficiaries, who can benefit from the trust property.

The person who sets up the trust is called the settlor, donor, or grantor. The trust agreement itself is a contract, which can be extremely flexible and can include any provision you want, as long as it doesn't conflict with state law.

TYPES OF TRUSTS

By Structure

A trust can be revocable or irrevocable. The first type can be changed after you set it up; the second generally cannot. While it sounds advantageous to have the flexibility to change a trust, there can be a substantial cost in doing so. The assets in a properly structured irrevocable trust can generally avoid being included in your estate for tax purposes, but the assets in a revocable trust do have to be included. Revocable trusts, therefore, are suitable for uses other than saving estate tax. They can be used to protect you and your family in the event of disability, to minimize probate costs, and to provide for professional management of assets.

A trust can be funded or unfunded. A funded trust is one with assets, and an unfunded trust is one to which assets have not yet been transferred. For example, you could establish a trust now with nominal assets for the benefit of your children. On your death, your will could "pour over" assets into the trust. Another approach would be to establish the same trust under your will, allowing you to avoid the costs of a second legal document, tax filings, and the like.

Thus, a trust also can be established by you during your life (*inter vivos*), or after your death through your will (testamentary). You may wish to set up an *inter vivos* trust to hold insurance in order to keep it out of your estate, or to provide protection in the event of disability. Testamentary trusts can be set up for your surviving spouse, under your will, or for minor children so that the management of assets to be given to them after your death is provided for.

By Use

Trusts can be categorized by their uses, as indicated below. Many of these uses are addressed in later chapters, while this chapter will be reserved for general considerations—except in the case of the living trust, which is not described elsewhere in the book.

- When a couple divorces, a trust can be set up to provide for their children (Chapter 13).
- A living trust (see below) can be used to accomplish many of the same objectives as a power of attorney and even some of the objectives as a living will and health care proxy (Chapter 5).
- Trusts can be set up to benefit grandchildren (Chapter 8).
- If you're married, a qualified terminable interest property (Q-TIP) trust is a basic estate planning technique that enables you to give your spouse the income from your assets and limited access to the assets themselves, but ensures that on your spouse's death the assets will be distributed to the beneficiaries you designate (Chapter 9).
- If your spouse is not a United States citizen, a special trust called a qualified domestic trust (Q-DOT) may be used to qualify for the marital deduction on your death (Chapter 10).

- There are also several different types of trusts appropriate for minor children including 2503(c) and 2503(b) trusts (Chapter 11).
- When a special child is involved, a trust is an essential tool to provide for your child in the event of your disability or death (Chapter 12).
- If you plan a major charitable gift but wish to retain some use of the property for a period of time, you may use either a charitable lead trust or a charitable remainder trust. The format of both of these trusts is largely dictated by the IRS (Chapter 14).
- One of the most common uses of trusts is to own life insurance and keep it from being taxed in your estate or, if you're married, in your spouse's estate (Chapter 19).

TYPICAL TRUST PROVISIONS

Many trusts are used for a specialized purpose and will require special provisions. These are discussed in the individual chapters referred to above. However, there are a number of provisions common to most trusts, perhaps the most important of which is to name the trustee.

Trustee Selection

The trustee (or trustees) is the person who will be responsible for administering whatever assets you put in trust, and most likely he or she will do so when you are no longer available, as a result of your disability or death. Because the assets may be the primary, or even the sole, source of income for the people dearest to you, the greatest care should be used in selecting a trustee. Unlike the case with a guardian or trustee under a will or revocable trust, where you can readily execute a codicil to change the designations, your ability to change a trustee under an irrevocable trust is limited. If you reserve the right to dismiss a trustee and appoint a new trustee, the assets of the trust will probably be included in your estate. You should carefully evaluate whether the person chosen has both the ability to handle the financial matters and the emotional sensitivity to care for the needs of your loved ones (or even yourself, depending on the type of trust used).

You can name more than one person to serve at the same time as trustee, providing a checks-and-balances system, if this will help ensure that your wishes will be met. An institution or individual as co-trustees is a commom approach. But consider whether having more than one person serve as a trustee will create conflict and unnecessary fees and administrative burdens. In some instances, such as when state law requires, or when a trustee is also a beneficiary, it may be necessary to have co-trustees.

Whatever choice you make, be sure that the trust contains detailed provisions for succession. A trust can last a long time. Name alternate co-trustees in the event that a previously named trustee can't, or won't, serve. As a final backstop, also name a trust company, bank, or trustee to be appointed by your lawyer's firm.

Grantor Rights

It is natural for those who set up a trust to want to reserve some powers for themselves. If you intend to remove the trust property from your estate and avoid being taxed on the trust's income, any power or right that you wish to retain must be carefully reviewed with your tax adviser. Retained powers can taint the trust as a grantor trust for income tax purposes, which will cause all trust income to be taxed to you. (This will occur when, on an actuarial basis using IRS-prescribed tables, you have more than a 5 percent reversionary interest in the trust.) Retained powers can also cause all of the assets in the trust to be taxed in your estate (see Chapter 6).

Revocability

The distinction between a revocable and irrevocable trust was discussed above. Once you and your advisers have decided on the approach to use, a provision should be included in the trust explicitly stating either that it's irrevocable or that you've reserved the power to revoke, and under what conditions.

Trustee Rights

Some consideration should be given to the powers that you grant the trustee over the trust property. Most trusts contain a listing of very broad powers that the trustee is given in addition to any powers that state law may provide. One of the most important provisions, for example, specifies how the trustee should divide the trust income, and whether he or she has the right to invade the assets of the trust to make payments. The reason broad rights are generally given is so that the trustee will have the ability to deal with any emergency that may occur in the future. These rights, however, can be limited to achieving certain objectives. You don't have to grant broad powers; you can restrict them in various ways if you and your attorney think it advisable.

TIP: Although you may be presented with a form of trust agreement by your attorney, a bank trust department, or your insurance company, there is no required form (with the exception of certain charitable trusts for which the IRS prescribes the form). You can, subject to any limitations imposed by state law, include any provisions in your trust that you want. Other than the additional legal costs of making changes, you should not feel constrained to use any form that doesn't accomplish your objectives. However, if you intend to use a bank or trust company as trustee, they are likely to have their own restrictions for small trusts in order to make it practical to administer them.

A REVOCABLE LIVING TRUST

A revocable living trust (sometimes called a "living trust" or "loving trust") is the most talked about estate planning technique of recent years—unfortunately, mostly for the wrong reasons. (Note that a living trust is not the same as a living will, which is described in the next chapter. A living will only specifies your wishes for health care if you should become disabled, while a living trust specifies disposition and management of assets.)

These trusts have been touted as the answer for all estate planning woes. Proponents argue that you can save probate costs, which can be exorbitant, and that you can avoid having your assets disclosed to the public. Reality, however, can be quite different. Probate is not necessarily the evil and excessively expensive process many people claim while establishing a living trust can become just that.

Drawbacks of a Living Trust

To properly set up a living trust, you must go through a number of time-consuming and potentially costly steps:

- You must retain a lawyer to prepare a trust document, which if done right, is not such a simple matter. And the trust document is only step one.
- You then must arrange to transfer assets to the trust. In the case of real estate, you will have to have a deed executed and, depending on where you live, complete various tax and other forms.
- If the property has a mortgage, you will have to review the mortgage for a due-on-sale clause and, most likely, notify your bank.
- The title insurance company should be asked whether a new policy in the name of the trust is required.
- Insurance policies on real estate and art will have to be changed to show the name of the trust.
- To transfer personal property you will need a bill of sale or other document.
- New bank accounts may have to be opened.
- A separate tax identification number will have to be obtained.
- Tax and other filings may be required.

- Once all of this is done, you have to be careful to conduct any business or investment activities for the trust under the trust name and to keep them separate from nontrust activities, which are conducted under your name—a hassle.

Even if all of the above should turn out to be cheaper than probate costs, it still might not make sense to do financially. This is because the costs of setting up your living trust will be incurred now, whereas the probate costs may not be incurred for 20 or more years. There is a time value to money. The money you spend today won't be available to earn interest as it would be if you did not set up the living trust.

Also consider that a living trust is not a substitute for a will. You must have a will in any case, because there is no assurance that every asset of yours will be in the trust. Even if your will simply states that all assets under the will are to be poured over into your living trust, this still should be done. So, instead of eliminating the cost of a will, you've increased your legal costs by having two documents when one may have sufficed. (This is not a reason to forego a living trust in favor of a will. As will be explained below, there are definite advantages and benefits that a living trust can offer. It's just best to examine these realistically.)

CAUTION: If a pour-over will arrangement is used, be certain that your lawyer has reviewed the laws applicable in your state to ensure that the provision will be effective. For example, the order in which the documents are executed may be important.

Finally, the great secrecy many people hope to obtain through a living trust may not be realized. If your will contains a pour-over provision, it will be probated, and the probate process may pull the trust into the public record. If there are any legal disputes among beneficiaries or others, or if the trust is contested, all of this will occur in court records, which are open to the public. So there may be little advantage to the supposed secrecy of a living trust. On the other hand, unless you're a well-known public figure, just because your will is probated doesn't mean the tabloids will be holding the presses to print new headlines.

Benefits of a Living Trust

With all of the above caveats, is there any reason left to use a revocable living trust? Absolutely. It remains a vitally important and useful estate planning technique. A review of the real benefits it can provide will help you better understand how it should be used and what provisions it can contain:

- One use of a revocable trust is to have your disability insurance policies made payable to it. Alternate trustees can be named to take over in the event of your disability. They should have less problems using assets for your benefit than someone acting under a power of attorney, since the assets in your living trust are already in the trust's name.

- A living trust is also likely to have more detailed provisions for accountability and court review than a power of attorney. Thus, when the assets and needs are sufficient, a living trust can be a much better option than a power of attorney.

- For the elderly or others not able or wishing to handle all of their financial matters, a living trust can be an excellent way to have a co-trustee assume primary responsibility for the management of assets. The trust document can include detailed criteria for this management.

- Since the trust is revocable, you can change and fine-tune the provisions before you're disabled in order to prepare for the best management of the trust in such an event, or to prepare for your heirs' taking over after your death.

- A living trust is an excellent vehicle for a single person who can't rely on immediate family to handle financial matters in the event of disability.

- A comparison should also be made to another option for providing for financial management of a disabled or incompetent person— having a court appoint a guardian, conservator, or committee. The definitions and functions differ under each state's laws. The key point still is that the matters the proponents of living trusts saw as problems of wills are also problems with the use of a guardianship or similar approaches. A court will have to become involved; numerous filings and petitions will have to be made; hearings will have to be attended, and so forth. It's an expensive and time-consuming process, which a living trust can help avoid.

Drafting Considerations

The broad use to which a living trust can be put requires the drafting of a comprehensive document. When a living trust is prepared to serve you during illness or disability, many of the provisions normally used in a power of attorney should be incorporated. When a living trust is to serve as the primary estate document transferring your assets to your heirs, then many of the provisions included in your will (trusts for minors, trusts for your spouse, appointment of a fiduciary and alternates, and so forth) should be incorporated. Finally, since the living trust is a trust, many of the provisions discussed in each of the chapters concerning trusts should be addressed. For example, if your life insurance policies will be held in your living trust (not generally recommended), the provisions in the insurance trust in Chapter 19 should be included.

CONCLUSION

A trust is one of the most important tools to use in your estate planning. Because of the broad discretion that you have in drafting a trust and the many uses to which a trust can be put, you should have expert guidance in setting one up.

5 LIVING WILL

Medical technology and treatments are complex and are rapidly changing. Many medical procedures can be extremely costly. Some treatments can be very painful and have undesirable side effects. Your financial and estate planning can be jeopardized when your last months or years are spent in agony or without the minimal quality of life you desire, and when large health care bills deplete your estate.

The recommended approaches include the preparation of either a living will or a health care proxy (durable power of attorney with medical directives), or both. The decisions are difficult and will require consideration of a host of potential problems. State laws are rapidly changing, so it's essential to consult a lawyer about what can and cannot be done. The problems arise, in part, when there is conflict between the state's interests in preserving life and your personal desires and rights regarding what should, and shouldn't, be done with you.

CAUTION: Concern for Dying, located in New York City, can provide a form that should be valid in your state. Although they make every effort to keep such forms current, it is still best to consult with the lawyer handling your estate planning. Another reason for doing so is that these documents are a critical component of your estate plan, and your lawyer should be aware of your goals and objectives.

THE DOCUMENTS

When it comes time to make difficult decisions, what if you don't have the mental capacity to do so? The result may be that doctors, courts, or others, in spite of trying to ascertain and fulfill your wishes, may take steps that are the opposite of what you would have wanted. One step that you can take now to forestall these consequences is to prepare and execute a living will and a medical directive power of attorney, or health care proxy. These documents can help clarify your decisions about what quality of life you want to maintain and can appoint a specific person to make any necessary decisions in order to carry out your desires in the event that you are unable to do so.

Why two documents? The first, the living will, can be used to set forth your objectives and feelings regarding the type of care you generally want, or don't want. It is the place where you can describe the type of lifestyle you want to have—the quality of life that you consider a minimum necessity. One of the most important roles of the living will is that it may be the only written evidence of what your wishes are. Thus, as clearly and precisely as possible, your living will should state your feelings and desires about quality of life, religious convictions, and whether you want to refuse or not refuse medical treatment.

You should specifically state whether you would want artificial nutrition and hydration. If you don't want artificial feeding, even if discontinuing it could hasten death, you should state this. But what about pain medication and other treatments or procedures to reduce pain? Should they be administered even if they hasten death? Are there any mechanical means of prolonging life that should be used? The difficulty in addressing these questions is that it is impossible to know which treatments will be necessary or available. Another document can provide some assistance with this dilemma.

The second document (many forms combine the two), a health care proxy or power of attorney with medical directives, is also essential, because it provides a mechanism for decisions to be made when and where the need arises. It's impossible to foresee every possible illness you might have, or every possible treatment your doctors might prescribe. By appointing a person to act in your behalf, decisions can be made based on your condition at the time, the available medical procedures and advice, and your wishes. Decide whom to appoint very carefully. Many loved ones, however sensitive to your feelings, simply may not be able to make the very difficult decisions that would accord with your desires. Also, consult your lawyer to learn any requirements that your state may impose on health care agents.

RELIGIOUS CONSIDERATIONS

Religious doctrines may specifically address what can be done medically to sustain, or not sustain, life. However indifferent you may presently feel about the effects of the tenets of your faith on these decisions, it can be a terrible mistake not to discuss these issues with your clergy. Your family's religious convictions should be considered, too. It may be possible to carry out your wishes by making only modifications and still be within the prescribed limits of your faith.

If, after consulting your clergy and holding discussions with your family, you decide to take a position contrary to the tenets of your faith, your living will should say so. The sample form in the "For Your Notebook" section following this chapter contains such a clause. However, if you decide that you want to adhere to the tenets of your faith, it is just as important to state this. When doing so, you should be very precise in your description of the religious doctrines to which you adhere.

Further, it is strongly recommended that you provide the name and address of a clergy member to be consulted for interpretation of your religious beliefs, and, as a backup, the name of a religious organization or institution.

EXPRESS YOUR DESIRE TO HAVE EVERY LIFE-SAVING MEASURE PERFORMED

With so much press and attention given to the right to die, euthanasia, declination of medical procedures, and related issues, one very important fact has been obscured. Whether for religious or personal reasons, you may want every life-saving procedure available to be performed. You may want to have cardiac resuscitation; mechanical respiration, nutrition, and hydration; and other extraordinary measures. Make your wishes known. Even though such measures may be expected to be taken in the absence of contrary instructions, given the current legal climate concerning living wills, it may be just as important to state your desire for full treatment as the reverse.

WALLET CARD

No matter how much care you take to prepare and sign a living will and health care proxy, in an emergency situation they may do little good. Properly prepared documents are far too bulky to carry in your wallet or purse. If you're wheeled into an emergency room or intensive-care unit and are unable to communicate your feelings, the only means your attending physicians may have to learn your general wishes and know that you've signed the appropriate documents is if you have some evidence of them with you. Carry a wallet-sized card giving a basic statement of your desires, and telling that you've signed a living will and heath care proxy and who should be contacted to obtain them. In some states certain items can be noted on your driver's license.

CAUTION: Don't arbitrarily sign a preprinted wallet card prepared by any organization without carefully reviewing what it says, since it may not reflect your desires. Further, if the name of the sponsoring organization is on the card, it may in itself convey a certain position that is not consistent with your desires.

CONCLUSION

When you want to specify that extraordinary life-saving measures should *not* be performed, the approach used is to execute a living will stating your intent. An accompanying power of attorney should be signed granting to certain named persons the right to make any decisions and perform any acts necessary to carry out your wishes as set forth in the living will. Discuss your feelings with your lawyer, doctor, clergy, and family. The very process of discussing these matters is, perhaps, as important as actually signing the documents. Not only will the talking help you crystallize your feelings, it will also inform in a more direct, personal, and fuller way than can be done in a document, the very people who might be involved in making decisions for you.

For Your Notebook:

SAMPLE LIVING WILL
(WITH COMMENTS)

**FOR DISCUSSION WITH YOUR LAWYER ONLY
—DO NOT USE AS A LIVING WILL**

DIRECTION TO WITHHOLD MAINTENANCE AND MEDICAL TREATMENT

I, YOUR NAME, residing at YOUR ADDRESS, being an adult and of sound mind, and being competent and otherwise capable of making the decisions set forth in this Living Will, make this declaration as a directive to be followed if for any reason I become incapacitated and incompetent, and, thus, unable to participate in decisions regarding my medical care, this statement shall stand as an expression of my wishes and directions.

WHEREFORE, I wish to direct the actions of my family, friends, clergy, physicians, nurses, and all those concerned with my care, as provided in this declaration.

WHEREFORE, I recognize that death is as much a reality as birth, growth, maturity, and old age. It is the one certainty of life.

NOW THEREFORE, I declare my wishes to be as follows:

I.   NO HEROIC MEDICAL EFFORTS

If I (i) have an incurable or irreversible, severe mental or severe physical condition; (ii) am in a state of permanent unconsciousness or profound dementia; (iii) am severely injured; and in any of these cases there is no reasonable expectation of my recovering from such severe, permanent condition and regaining any meaningful quality of life, then in any such event it is my desire and intent that heroic life-sustaining procedures and extraordinary maintenance of medical treatment be withheld and withdrawn. It is not my desire to prolong my life through mechanical means when my body is no longer able to perform vital bodily functions on its own, and when there is little likelihood that I will ever regain any meaningful quality of life. The severity and permanence of illness, injury, or disability are of such a nature or degree, or the condition is accompanied by such pain, that the average person might contemplate the decisions addressed herein (regardless of whether such person would make the decisions I have made).

In any such event, I direct all physicians and medical facilities in whose care I may be, and my family and all those concerned with my care, to refrain from and cease extraordinary or heroic life-sustaining procedures and artificial maintenance and/or medical treatment. The procedures and treatment to be withheld and withdrawn include, without limitation: surgery, antibiotics, cardiac and pulmonary resuscitation, and ventilation or other respiratory support.

II.   NUTRITION AND HYDRATION

Specifically excluded from this request is artificially administered nutrition and hydration (feeding and fluids), which I request to be given when appropriate.

NOTE: Artificial feeding and hydration can be quite controversial, the issue being whether they are viewed as medical treatment or as ordinary care. Some people view these measures as invasive medical treatment. In some states, if you don't specifically declare that you don't want artificial nutrition and hydration, such care cannot be refused. In some states, your proxy need not know your wishes specifically about medical treatments other than nutrition and hydration—for example, a ventilator or dialyses. They can make judgments based on your condition. As with any medical treatment, nutrition and hydration have side effects, such as causing infection or aspiration. Also, people may lapse into a coma more quickly and thus be spared the pain of dying if they are *not* given nutritional supplements. To put a demented person on artificial feeding often requires physical restraints, which is not the quality of life that many people want. Finally, religious tenets can view either the provision or denial of nutrition and hydration as particularly problematic, and thus forbidden.

III. MEDICATION AND TREATMENTS TO ALLEVIATE PAIN AND SUFFERING

In any such event where procedures and treatment are to be withheld or withdrawn, I desire that all treatment and measures for my comfort, and to alleviate my pain, be continued, even if such measures shorten my life.

IV. CAREFUL CONSIDERATION HAS BEEN MADE

These decisions and requests are made after careful consideration and reflection. These decisions are made to avoid the indignity, pain, and difficulties, both for myself and my family, of prolonged, hopeless deterioration and dependence when I am in a condition described above.

NOTE: To make very detailed specifications of procedures to apply or not apply has drawbacks. Medical technology changes rapidly, providing new options, and medical situations don't always develop in a way you can foresee. A patient dying from leukemia took every precaution, but he caught a cold. His spleen began to expand causing excruciating pain. Finally, he had to have his spleen removed to eliminate the pain, which was still part of managing his dying. Fortunately, he was competent to make this decision. If he had had a living will that had a blanket prohibition against surgery, and he had not been competent to make his own decisions, a very difficult dilemma would have resulted. Therefore, the best approach may be the use of a health care proxy in which you communicate your desires with the health care agent and your doctor. In some states a durable power of attorney is used.

V. RELIGIOUS CONVICTIONS

I do not want the effectiveness of this directive to be conditional upon its conforming to any religious doctrines or beliefs to which I may be believed to subscribe.

NOTE: You are never obligated to adhere to any particular religious doctrine, but you should at least discuss your living will with your clergy. It may be too late to change your directives when you begin to feel differently about your religious affiliations or beliefs.

VI. NO TIME LIMIT

I have considered the possibility of limiting the effectiveness of this instrument to a fixed period of time from the date hereof and have decided that it shall remain in full force and effect for as long as I may live unless a written notice of revocation is delivered to each holder of this Living Will, as set forth in Exhibit A.

NOTE: This approach raises several problems. State law may prohibit an indefinite duration. Your medical directives can only be updated to reflect changes in medical innovation if you revise your forms. See comments in the power-of-attorney termination provision below.

VII. ATTORNEY-IN-FACT; AGENT

I recognize that a time may come when I cannot participate in my medical care decisions (even if there are favorable prospects for my eventual recovery) and also that it is not possible for me to anticipate the very wide variety of medical decisions that may need to be made in the future and give written directions. Accordingly, I have executed this Living Will and a separate Durable Power of Attorney with Medical Decision Powers of even date (attached hereto as Exhibit B), appointing my NAME OF HEALTH CARE AGENT, residing at AGENT'S ADDRESS, as my true and lawful Attorney-in-Fact and Health Care Agent. If HEALTH CARE AGENT NAME is unwilling or unable to act as my agent, I appoint FIRST ALTERNATE AGENT, who resides at FIRST ALTERNATE'S ADDRESS, as my Agent. If FIRST ALTERNATE AGENT is unwilling or unable to act as my Agent, I appoint SECOND ALTERNATE AGENT, who resides at SECOND ALTERNATE'S ADDRESS, as my Agent.

If all of the above Agents and Attorneys-in-Fact have predeceased me or are unable or unwilling for any reason to serve as my Medical-Decision Attorney-in-Fact, but one is required by law solely in order to direct the withholding or withdrawal of life-sustaining treatment in accordance with my objectives as stated herein, I authorize my attending physician to appoint such an attorney in writing, upon consultation with one or more of my relatives, friends, or other persons or agencies reasonably believed to be interested in my well-being.

VIII. MORALLY BINDING

These directions are the exercise of my right to refuse treatment. Therefore, I expect my family, physicians, and all those concerned with my care to regard themselves as legally (whether or not the law at the time of the execution or implementation of this Living Will requires such) and morally bound to act in accordance with these directions, and in so doing to be free from any liability and responsibility for having followed my directions.

IX. CONSTRUCTION

Should legislation or regulations be enacted after the execution of this Living Will, then this Living Will shall, to the extent necessary to make it valid and enforceable, be interpreted so as to comply with such future legislation or regulations. The titles and captions contained in this article are for convenience only and should not be read to affect the meaning of any provision. Should any provision in this Living Will be declared invalid or unenforceable, the remaining provision shall not be affected so long as they can be applied in a manner to carry out my wishes as set forth herein.

IN WITNESS WHEREOF, I have executed this declaration MONTH DAY, YEAR.

YOUR NAME

DECLARATION OF WITNESSES TO LIVING WILL

I, _____, _____ and _____, each hereby declare and attest that: (i) the foregoing instrument was personally signed, sealed, and delivered by YOUR NAME, in my presence, and thereupon I, at his or her request and in his or her presence and in the presence of the other witnesses, have hereunto subscribed my name as a witness; (ii) I did not sign the above signature of YOUR NAME for or at his or her direction; (iii) I am acquainted with YOUR NAME and believe him or her to be of sound mind and under no constraint or undue influence; (iv) I am not related to YOUR NAME by blood or marriage; (v) I am not entitled to any portion of the estate of YOUR NAME under any Will of YOUR NAME or Codicil now existing, nor am I so entitled by operation of law; (vi) I do not have any present or inchoate claim against any portion of his or her medical care; (vii) I am not a physician or an employee of any attending physician, hospital, or health care facility in which he or she is a patient; and (viii) I am over Eighteen (18) years of age.

Address:

_____

Witness Name

_____

_____

Witness Signature

_____

Address:

_____

Witness Name

_____

_____

Witness Signature

_____

Address:

_____

Witness Name

_____

_____

Witness Signature

_____

STATE OF STATE NAME   )

                                              :

COUNTY OF NAME OF COUNTY)

BE IT REMEMBERED, that on this MONTH DAY, YEAR, before me, the subscriber, an attorney/notary of the State of STATE NAME, personally appeared YOUR NAME, who, I am satisfied, is the principal mentioned in, and who executed the within "Living Will: Direction to Withhold Maintenance and Medical Treatment" and acknowledged that he or she signed, sealed, and delivered the same as his or her act and deed, for the use and purposes therein expressed.

_____

Name of Notary

EXHIBIT A

IDENTIFICATION OF PERSONS GIVEN COPIES OF LIVING WILL

A copy of this Living Will and Durable Power of Attorney with Medical Decision Powers has been provided to:

(1) My spouse: SPOUSE'S NAME
                      YOUR ADDRESS

(2) My Lawyer: LAWYER'S NAME
                      LAWYER'S ADDRESS

(3) My Physician: DOCTOR'S NAME
                      DOCTOR'S ADDRESS

(5) My Health Care Agent: AGENT'S NAME
                                  AGENT'S ADDRESS

(4) Concern For Dying: The Living Will Registry
                            Concern For Dying
                            250 West 57th Street
                            New York, New York 10107
                            (212) 246-6962

NOTE: If you're alone and don't have close family or friends who would know your wishes and where your living will would be, consider sending a copy to The Living Will Registry. This is a place where you can be sure a copy will be found. You will be given a plastic wallet card indicating that your living will has been filed with The Registry, so that in an emergency a hospital or other health care provider can obtain a copy. Concern For Dying can assist you by providing legal forms, which are updated regularly for all 50 states.

EXHIBIT B

DURABLE POWER OF ATTORNEY WITH MEDICAL DECISION POWERS

I, YOUR NAME, residing at YOUR ADDRESS, to provide for management of my person and financial affairs in a more orderly fashion, and in connection with the execution of a Living Will: Direction to Withhold Maintenance and Medical Treatment, hereby declare as follows:

I.   APPOINTMENT OF ATTORNEY-IN-FACT AND HEALTH CARE AGENT

I hereby make, constitute, and appoint ("Grant") NAME OF HEALTH CARE AGENT, residing at AGENT'S ADDRESS, as my true and lawful Attorney-in-Fact and Health Care Agent for me and in my name, place, and stead and for my benefit, or any alternate appointed in accordance with the provisions of this agreement (the "Agent").

II.   POWERS OF AGENT

I grant to my Agent all the powers and rights necessary to effect my wishes, solely for the purposes and objectives specifically set forth in the Living Will: Directive To Withhold Maintenance and Medical Treatment (my "Wishes"), to which this Durable Power of Attorney with Medical Decision Powers is attached, including the power to:

A. Request, ask, demand, sue for, recover, sell, collect, forgive, receive, and hold money, debts, dues, commercial paper, checks, drafts, accounts, deposits, legacies, bequests, devises, notes, interests, stocks, bonds, certificates of deposit, annuities, pension and retirement benefits, insurance proceeds, any and all documents of title, choses in action, personal and real property, intangible and tangible property and property rights, and demands whatsoever, liquidated or unliquidated, as now are, or may become, owned by, or due, owing, payable, or belonging to me, or in which I have or may hereafter acquire interest, to have, use, and take all lawful means and equitable and legal remedies, procedures, and writs in my name for the collection and recovery thereof, and to adjust, sell, compromise, and agree for the same, and to make, execute, and deliver for me, on my behalf and in my name, all endorsements, acceptances, releases, receipts, or other sufficient discharges for them.

NOTE: This section is intended to provide your Agent with the financial where-withal to implement your health care decisions, which could be critical to ensure that your desires are carried out. The effect this may have on the validity of this durable power of attorney with medical decision powers must be carefully reviewed with your attorney, because some states do not permit you to grant an agent authority over medical and financial matters in the same document.

B. Conduct, engage in, and transact any lawful business of any nature on my behalf and in my name. To maintain, improve, invest, manage, insure, lease, or encumber, and in any manner deal with any real, personal, tangible, or intangible property, or any interest in them, that I now own or may acquire, in my name and for my benefit, upon such terms and conditions as my agent shall deem proper and necessary to provide the funds necessary to carry out my Wishes.

C. Exercise or perform any act, power, duty, right, or obligation that I now have, or may acquire, including the legal right, power, or capacity to exercise or perform, in connection with, arising from, or relating to any person or property, real or personal, tangible or intangible, or matter whatsoever, including, without limiting the foregoing, the right to enter into a contract of sale and to sell any real, personal, tangible, or intangible property on my behalf, upon such terms and conditions as my agent shall deem proper and necessary to provide the funds necessary to carry out my Wishes.

D. Make, receive, sign, endorse, acknowledge, deliver, and possess insurance policies, documents of title, bonds, debentures, checks, drafts, stocks, proxies, warrants, relating to accounts or deposits in, or certificates of deposit, other debts and obligations, and such other instruments in writing of whatever kind and nature as may be necessary or proper in the exercise of the rights and powers herein granted for the purpose of providing funds necessary to carry out my Wishes.

E. Sell any and all shares of stocks, bonds, or other securities now or later belonging to me that may be issued by any association, trust, or corporation, whether private or public, and to make, execute, and deliver any assignment, or assignments, of any such shares of stocks, bonds, or other securities for the purpose of providing funds necessary to carry out my Wishes.

F. Conduct or participate in any business of any nature for me and in my name; execute partnership agreements and amendments thereto; sell, liquidate, or dissolve any business; carry out the provisions of any agreement for the sale of any business interest or the stock therein; and exercise voting rights with respect to stock, either in person or by proxy; and exercise stock options for the purpose of providing funds necessary to carry out my Wishes.

G. Have access at any time or times to any safe-deposit box rented by me, and to remove all or any part of the contents thereof, and to surrender or relinquish said safe-deposit box for the purpose of providing funds necessary to carry out my Wishes. Any institution in which any such safe-deposit box may be located shall not incur any liability to me or my estate as a result of permitting my Attorney-in-Fact or Agent to exercise the powers herein granted.

H. Convey or assign any cash or other property of which I shall be possessed to the trustee or trustees of any trust that I may have created during my lifetime, for the purpose of providing funds necessary to carry out my Wishes.

In addition to, and not by way of limitation, upon any other powers conferred upon my Attorney-in-Fact and Agent herein, I grant to said Attorney-in-Fact full power and authority to do, take, and perform each and every act and thing whatsoever requisite, proper, or necessary to be done, in the exercise of any of the rights and powers herein granted, for the purposes and objectives specifically set forth in the Living Will: Directive To Withhold Maintenance and Medical Treatment to which this Durable Power of Attorney with Medical Decision Powers is attached; I grant any power available under law to an attorney-in-fact acting in the capacity and for the purposes herein indicated, as fully to all intents and purposes as I might or could do if were personally present.

III. APPROVAL

I hereby ratify and confirm all that said Attorney-in-Fact shall lawfully do or cause to be done by virtue of this Durable Power of Attorney with Medical Decision Powers and the rights and powers herein granted.

IV. GRANT OF MEDICAL DECISION POWERS

I specifically designate my Agent to make medical treatment decisions for me in the event that I am comatose or otherwise unable to make such decisions for myself including any decisions with respect to life-sustaining measures, artificial feeding, artificial hydration, and other matters as more specifically set forth in the Living Will: Direction to Withhold Maintenance and Medical Treatment, to which this Durable Power of Attorney with Medical Decision Powers is attached.

V. INDEMNIFICATION OF THE ALTERNATE ATTORNEY-IN-FACT

The Grantor hereby agrees to indemnify and hold harmless the Agent for any actions taken, or not taken, by the Alternate Agent, when the Alternate Agent acted in good faith and was not guilty of fraud, gross negligence, or willful misconduct.

VI. CONSTRUCTION

This instrument is to be construed and interpreted as a durable general power of attorney. The enumeration of specific items, rights, acts, or powers herein is not intended to nor does it limit or restrict, and is not to be construed or interpreted as limiting or restricting, the general powers herein granted to said Agent. This instrument is executed and delivered in the State of STATE NAME, and the laws of the State of STATE NAME shall govern all questions as to the validity of this power and the construction of its provisions. Should any provision or power in this document not be enforceable, such enforceability shall not affect the enforceability of the rest of this document. In this regard, I specifically state that I have granted my Agent certain authority and power over my financial matters to ensure the carrying out of my Wishes. Should this grant be prohibited by any law presently existing or hereinafter enacted, it is my specific desire that such grant be interpreted in the broadest manner permitted by such law, and that in the event such grant is prohibited, that every other provision of this Durable Power of Attorney with Medical Decision Powers remains fully valid and enforceable.

VII. THIRD-PARTY RELIANCE

Third parties, including but not limited to medical professionals, hospitals, banking institutions, brokerage firms, and the like, may rely upon the representations of my Agent as to all matters relating to any power granted to my Agent as my Agent, Attorney-in-Fact, and Health Care Agent, and no person who may act in reliance upon the representations of my Agent or the authority granted to my Agent shall incur any liability to me or my estate as a result of permitting my Agent to exercise any power. Any third party may rely on a duly executed counterpart of this instrument, but not a copy thereof unless such copy is certified by my Agent as being a true copy of the original hereof, as fully and completely as if such third party had received the original of this instrument.

VIII. DISABILITY SHALL NOT AFFECT GRANT

REFERENCE TO APPLICABLE STATE LAW authorizes me to provide that this power of attorney shall not be affected by my disability as principal, and I do hereby so provide, it being my intention that all powers conferred upon my Agent herein or any substitute designated by me shall remain at all times in full force and effect, notwithstanding my incapacity, disability, or any uncertainty with regard thereto.

IX.   ALTERNATE AGENT

A. If HEALTH CARE AGENT NAME is unwilling or unable to act as my agent, I appoint FIRST ALTERNATE AGENT, who resides at FIRST ALTERNATE'S ADDRESS, as my Agent. If FIRST ALTERNATE AGENT is unwilling or unable to act as my Agent, I appoint SECOND ALTERNATE AGENT, who resides at SECOND ALTERNATE'S ADDRESS, as my Agent and Agent.

NOTE: Some state laws may restrict the number of alternates you can name or whether agents can act jointly. The safest approach is to revise your living will and this durable power of attorney on a regular basis to ensure conformity with applicable laws and having a capable and willing agent.

B. Any Agent or Agent may resign by providing written notice to me (or my guardian or committee) with copy to the next named Agent or a court of competent jurisdiction.

X.   EFFECTIVE DATE; TERMINATION

The Grant shall take effect on the date this Durable Power of Attorney with Medical Decision Powers is executed. The Grant shall terminate at the earlier of my executing a document terminating the Grant or Three (3) years from the date this agreement is executed.

NOTE: Consider a termination date so that you will be forced to reconsider your decisions to be sure they still reflect your feelings and are at least somewhat current with medical technology. A short period, such as one year, is certainly preferable, as long as you don't forget to revise it. State law may also limit the duration of this power of attorney.

IN WITNESS WHEREOF, I have hereunto set my hand and seal this MONTH DAY, YEAR.

YOUR NAME

[WITNESS AND NOTARY FORMS OMITTED]

NOTE: Special restrictions and requirements may apply regarding who can be a witness (health care providers are often excluded) and how many witnesses are required. A brief statement of the witness's knowledge of and relationship to you is also appropriate.

For Your Notebook:

RELIGIOUS IMPLICATIONS OF A LIVING WILL, JEWISH LAW (*HALACHA*) CONSIDERATIONS

By Rabbi Aryeh Weil[1] and Martin Shenkman

Jewish law has profound implications for the contents of any living will or health care proxy. This brief discussion can at best raise enough points to encourage those concerned to pursue the issues with competent rabbinic authority.

Jewish law has a strong predilection toward saving life (*pikuach nefesh*), and this is reflected in much of the literature addressing living wills and right-to-die issues. The sanctity of life is of paramount importance. The fact that the laws of the Jewish Sabbath are suspended when health and life are at risk is but one example. Biblical law creates an affirmative duty (*mitzvah*) to sustain and preserve life and to seek sustenance and care. The almost insurmountable hurdles that would face a Jewish court before someone could be convicted of a capital crime are evidence of the lengths to which one must go to preserve life. Thus, steps to hasten the demise of any sick person are generally forbidden, and euthanasia is forbidden. However, when death is certain and the patient is in substantial pain or discomfort, it may be permissible *not* to postpone death by *not* taking steps to preserve life through artificial means. The determination of the certainty of death, the discomfort of the patient, and the means that can be foregone are complicated questions both from a medical perspective and from that of Jewish law. Therefore, for the situation when you might be in a position of incompetence, or otherwise be constrained from communicating your desire that your treatment accord with Jewish law, a living will and health care proxy are the solution, although the application of these documents is nearly the opposite of their usual secular purpose (because of the emphasis on preserving life).

The timing of decisions is vitally important. Once a patient is connected to mechanical life-support systems, it is far more difficult from a religious perspective to remove these devices than it would have been to avoid connecting them in the first place.

Jewish law does not demand that every possible life-saving measure be taken in every circumstance, but the identification of which steps can be taken and which can be avoided should be resolved between you and your rabbi while you are able to do so.

Two other issues of Jewish law have relevance to the living will—the determination of death, and the permissible treatment of the body after death.

[1] Rabbi Aryeh Weil is the rabbi of Congregation Bnai Yeshurun in Teaneck, New Jersey. He is also vice president of the Rabbinical Council of America and is an adjunct on the faculty of Rockland Community College of the State University of New York.

NOTE: The variation in Jewish legal interpretations is significant. Therefore, you should discuss your concerns with your rabbi and list a specific rabbi and organization in your living will as the source to contact the regarding the application of Jewish law to you and your condition.

A common secular definition of death is based on the irreversible cessation of all brain function. Historically, the definition of death under Jewish law was based on a cessation of cardiac and respiratory activity. However, the advance of medical technology has raised questions concerning this definition. As a result, there is some debate within the Jewish community as to what definition of Jewish law should apply. To comply with Jewish law, your living will and health care proxy should state that the Jewish definition of death should be used and that your health care decisions should be made accordingly. You should consult with your rabbi to identify and include a more specific definition. Alternatively, you can rely on the approach suggested above of naming your rabbi and a specific religious organization to resolve questions of a religious nature.

Postmortem procedures, such as autopsies and dissections, are generally prohibited by Jewish law. Certain interpretations may permit organ donations under specific conditions; however, considerable controversy remains. As a result, anyone wishing to comply with religious law should carefully consider executing a living will and health care proxy, and carrying a wallet card that states clearly his or her personal desire that no postmortem procedures be carried out without the prior consultation of competent rabbinic authority concerning the acceptability of the suggested procedures, under the circumstances and in light of Jewish law.

NOTE: For additional information, contact Agudath Israel of America, 84 William Street, New York, New York 10038, Telephone (212) 797-9000, or Rabinical Council of America, 275 Seventh Avenue, New York, New York 10001.

For Your Notebook:

RELIGIOUS IMPLICATIONS OF A LIVING WILL, PERSPECTIVES FOR CATHOLICS

By Monsignor Harold P. Darcy[1]

Catholic Christians, like all members of the human race, must some day confront death. They believe, of course, that in death life is transformed through the Death and Resurrection of Jesus Christ into Eternal Life. As a matter of fact, Catholics look upon the act of dying as the most perfect human act they will ever perform. Consequently, it is not necessary for them to use every means available to prolong life; their eternal destiny is in God.

Those who have entered into the process of dying should be provided with whatever assistance they desire to alleviate pain and to prepare themselves emotionally and spiritually for death, but they do not have to undergo medical treatments that would not render them reasonable benefit. They do not have to use extraordinary means to prolong life. They should be able to give informed consent, which implies that they know the risks involved in either accepting or refusing treatment. In observing the Fifth Commandment, a person has the duty to care for his or her own body, but this does not signify that all remedies must be used in all circumstances. Unfortunately, decisions in these matters are very complex, and, as medical science advances, the desirability of certain procedures may change.

Human beings who are terminally ill have the primary right to decide what medical treatment they will accept, provided this does not mean actively assisted suicide or euthanasia. Not only should they be informed about the diagnosis, but they also should be told about the prognosis, the treatment suggested, and other available options, together with the benefits and risks, respectively.

Obviously, when a person is not able to make judgments in an emergency with respect to medical treatment, others must make them for him or her. Usually, members of the family will do this, but they must make the judgment call in accord with the dying person's personal wishes, if they are known, particularly regarding the use of artificial or extraordinary means to prolong life. Each person should decide beforehand what kind of life-prolonging means he or she would want. Good planning for health care decisions will ensure that the dying person will receive the full dignity that should characterize the process of dying.

---

[1] Monsignor Harold P. Darcy is chairman of the Medical Moral Committee of the Archdiocese of Newark, New Jersey; he is also chaplain and professor at Seton Hall University School of Law.

Delegating health care directives to others is one way to deal with the event of incapacity to make such decisions for oneself. These directives are commonly known as a living will or a durable power of attorney. A living will is a curious notion itself. In our common-law tradition, a will becomes effective only after death; it has no power until death has taken place. A living will, however, has effect only while the person lives. These documents should be reviewed periodically, because a person's wishes might change or because the document might become outdated and might give rise to doubts as to whether it still expresses the person's wishes.

The notions of the living will and the durable power of attorney are still evolving. However, it appears likely that acceptable living-will instruments, bearing different nomenclature, will be accepted throughout the United States. Any such instrument must conform to local law. The Catholic Church does not discourage living wills, but it does urge much caution and great care in developing these legal documents.

In our time, the withholding or the withdrawal of medical treatment from a severely ill or dying person is discussed at great length. This is especially true today in the areas of nutrition and hydration—the withholding or withdrawing of artificially provided food and water from unconscious, seriously ill, or dying patients. Some form of medical technology is involved here, for example, naso-gastric tube, intravenous tube, and so forth. These cases are most crucial when dealing with the patient who is permanently unconscious but not dying.

The typical case would be that the patient has been involved in an accident or has suffered another type of brain damage, but his or her brain is not progressively deteriorating nor is the patient dying from some other illness or disease. With normal care, the patient will live for many years. One acceptable Catholic opinion would allow for the termination of food and water in such cases; another would not. Those who hold the former opinion (approval of termination) stress that the primary responsibility is to fulfill the spiritual purpose of life, which involves a certain degree of cognitive-affective function. But, they argue, if the cognitive-affective function is no longer possible, then it is not necessary to prolong life. So, the inability to swallow is a pathology from which the person will die, and it is not necessary to prevent this by the use of medical technology.

The position that advocates that food and water must be provided holds that the spiritual purpose of life still can be enhanced by the unconscious patient, if that person has intended that all of his or her suffering be offered to God in union with the suffering of Christ. Besides, there have been instances in which a person has been diagnosed as permanently unconscious and subsequently has regained consciousness. According to this opinion, food and water are not primarily forms of therapeutic medical treatment; rather, they are the basic means of sustaining life, without which the patient would die.

Artificially assisted nutrition and hydration are not usually burdensome; they are ordinary medical technology—readily available, not excessively expensive, and provided easily. The withdrawal of nutrition and hydration induces a new cause of death, starvation, and dehydration.

A Papal Encyclical on Christian Ethics or Moral Theology is expected in the near future. It may treat some of the foregoing matters.

Part Two

THE THREE-HEADED TAX BEAST: ESTATE, GIFT, AND GENERATION-SKIPPING TRANSFER TAXES

6 ESTATE TAX

The estate tax is a transfer charge assessed on property owned by you at the time of your death. This simple explanation, however, belies the range and complexity of the actual tax. There are a number of exclusions and deductions. Also, the definition of property owned at the time of death includes items that many people find surprising. With federal estate tax rates as high as 55 percent (60 percent when certain phase-outs are in effect), and state taxes adding to this, planning to minimize the burden is essential if you want to pass on the maximum amount of assets to your heirs. This chapter provides a brief overview of the estate tax, and the next two chapters outline the two related transfer taxes—the gift tax and the generation-skipping transfer tax. The remainder of this book helps you learn how to minimize the tremendous burden these taxes impose.

BASIC ESTATE AND GIFT TAX CONCEPTS

Unified Rules

The tax paid on property you transfer to someone *before* you die is called a gift tax. The tax you pay on property transferred *after your death* (by your will or as a result of joint ownership) is called an estate tax. However, the gift and estate taxes are called "unified" because the same tax rates, deductions, and rules generally apply to both. Thus, the gift and estate taxes are in many respects a single tax that is assessed progressively throughout your lifetime, with the last installment due nine months after your death (on your estate tax return). This can be compared to an income tax in which you pay estimated taxes but only file one return for your entire lifetime.

All property transfers are added together; the unified gift or estate tax is calculated; then the tax already paid is subtracted (so you don't pay tax twice on the same property transfer). The purpose of this approach is to push your property transfers (whether subject to the gift or estate tax) into the highest marginal estate tax bracket. Therefore, even if you don't pay tax twice on the same property transfer, you can pay additional tax on a prior transfer as you're pushed into higher tax brackets.

There are a number of deductions permitted in calculating the estate tax and gift tax. For estate tax purposes, you can deduct funeral and administrative expenses and liabilities. For gift tax purposes, you can deduct the annual $10,000 per donee exclusion (see next chapter). You can deduct property transfers to qualifying charities in calculating both taxes (see Chapter 14). The most important adjustment in calculating the unified gift and estate tax is a once-in-a-lifetime unified credit.

Unified Credit

You are entitled to reduce the amount of property transfers you make, whether as gifts during your lifetime or by will or other methods after your death, by a single $600,000 credit. This credit effectively eliminates the first $192,800 of estate tax you would otherwise have to pay. When you have a large estate that is taxed at the highest marginal gift and estate tax rates (in the 55 percent effective tax bracket), the savings can be hundreds of thousands of dollars. As a result of the unified credit, there will be no federal estate tax due if your assets are less than $600,000 (actually, you can have substantially more assets and still avoid any tax because of the other deductions available). State tax laws may differ, however, so merely having $600,000 or less in assets will not ensure you an estate free of any transfer taxes.

The unified credit is one of the most important tax planning tools, but it also can be one of the least properly used. For example, when you are making gifts, it is always best to use the annual $10,000 per donee exclusions to the maximum extent possible. This is because any gift that comes under the annual exclusion will not use up any of your unified credit—that is, when you make a gift in excess of $10,000 to any person during the same year, part of your unified credit is taken up. It is usually advisable to save your unified credit for the future. But one of the most common mistakes is the failure to use this credit. Many taxpayers are inclined to leave everything to their surviving spouse on their death because there is no tax on property transferred under the marital deduction. The problem is that this common approach can result in bunching assets in the estate of the last spouse to die, subjecting the second estate to an unnecessarily large estate tax (see Chapter 9).

IDENTIFYING YOUR GROSS ESTATE

The first step in calculating the estate tax is to identify all property and property interests that are included in what is called your gross estate. Once these are identified, they must be valued. The sum of all properties you own, after a reduction for certain expenses and other allowable adjustments, will be the base on which your estate tax is calculated. The Form 706, Estate Tax Return, that appears in the "For Your Notebook" section following this chapter provides an illustration of all these steps.

In addition, the comprehensive estate planning example in the "For Your Notebook" section following Chapter 16 illustrates in worksheet format the process of determining your gross estate and the base on which the estate tax will be calculated.

What's Included

Generally, your gross estate includes all property, whether real estate (land and buildings), personal property (furniture, jewelry, and so forth), or intangible property (copyrights, licenses, and the like), required to be included in your estate under the estate tax rules.

Assets included in your gross estate consist of any interests you had in property at the time of your death that are included in your probate estate. For example, a bonus you were entitled to at the time of your death is included in your gross estate. If you own insurance on the life of another person, perhaps under a cross-purchase buy-out agreement, the value of this policy is included in your gross estate (see Chapter 16). Business and partnership interests are included. The fact that your surviving spouse may have an interest under state law concepts of dower or courtesy (spouse's claim to your assets) does not affect the inclusion of these assets in your gross estate for tax purposes.

Property to be included in your estate is very broadly defined. Even property that you gave away during your life may have to be included in your gross estate. For example, if you transferred property but retained the right to the income, or even the right to designate who would obtain the income, these assets can be brought back into your gross estate. If you transferred property to another party but specified that they could only use and enjoy that property after your death, the entire value of this property is included in your estate. If you transferred property but reserved the right to change who would be able to enjoy that property, the property is included in your estate. Insurance proceeds receivable by the executor of your estate, or by any other beneficiary if you retained incidents of ownership in the policy, will be taxed in your estate (see Chapter 19). If you had a general power of appointment over property (you could designate who would get the property), the value of that property is included in your gross estate.

Valuation of the Assets

The fair value of the assets at the date of your death is the amount to be included in your gross estate. The value to be used is called the "fair market value." This is the price at which the property would change hands between a willing buyer and a willing seller, neither being under any compulsion to buy or to sell, and both having reasonable knowledge of the relevant facts. When a stock traded on a public exchange is included in your estate, the value is easily found in any major newspaper. For assets like real estate and closely held business interests, valuation can be a substantial point of contention between your estate and the IRS. A special valuation rule is provided for farms, ranches, and certain property used in a closely held business (see Chapter 18).

Another special rule permits your executor to value your assets at a date six months after your death (called the "alternate valuation date"), rather than under the general rule using the date of your death. The rationale for this rule is quite simple: If you had died in September 1987, just before the October stock market crash, the value of your estate would have been based on historically high stock prices. Your estate tax would be due nine months later, following the market crash. Your executor would be in an unworkable bind. The estate tax easily could have exceeded the entire value of your estate. The alternate valuation date provides what can be an important degree of flexibility to address changing market conditions. If this alternate valuation date is elected, it applies to all property included in your gross estate that hasn't been disposed of prior to the alternate valuation date.

Deductions from Your Gross Estate

Your estate is allowed deductions for funeral expenses, estate administrative expenses, claims against your estate, debts relating to any property included in your gross estate, charitable bequests (Chapter 14), and qualifying bequests to your surviving spouse (Chapters 9 and 10). If expenses could qualify for deduction on either your estate tax return or income tax return, you must select one place to claim the deduction (a double benefit is not permitted). Losses, such as a casualty loss, are also deductible.

When all of these items are deducted from your gross estate, the result is your taxable estate. An intervening step of determining an adjusted gross estate can be calculated by reducing your gross estate by certain expenses, debts, and losses.

CALCULATING THE ESTATE TAX

The federal estate tax is figured as follows: A tentative tax is calculated on the sum of your taxable estate, as determined above, increased by your adjusted taxable gifts made after 1976. These are gifts made in most years before your death on which you incurred a gift tax. The idea is that since a single tax structure is used for estate and gift tax purposes, all taxable transfers should be added and subjected to the same graduated tax rate schedule. Gifts included in this tentative tax calculation are included based on their fair market value when the gifts were made. This tentative tax amount is then reduced by the gift taxes that were paid on your gifts made after 1976. There are a number of credits that may also be applied to reduce your estate tax. These include a credit for prior transfers, a credit for death taxes paid to your state, and so forth.

CONCLUSION

The estate tax is a complex and broad transfer tax that can substantially diminish the assets you had hoped to pass on to your heirs. However, with an understanding of the general rules discussed in this chapter, and with attention to the planning strategies offered here and in all of the following chapters, you can go a long way toward ensuring that your family and other designated heirs will be your primary beneficiaries, and not Uncle Sam.

For Your Notebook:

INSURANCE ILLUSTRATION OF REPLACING ASSETS EQUAL TO UNIFIED CREDIT

FACTS AND COMMENTS

If you're married, it doesn't make sense to waste the credit by leaving all of your assets to your spouse. This approach will just bunch assets in the surviving spouse's estate and cause them to be taxed at a higher rate. To use the maximum credit, each spouse should have $600,000 of assets to transfer through his or her estate (tax estate, not probate estate) at death.

But what if you're a doctor, accountant, lawyer, or other professional, and you want to shelter assets from business creditors and potential malpractice claimants? Does it pay for you to keep $600,000 of assets in order to use your $600,000 unified credit when this entails a risk of subjecting the assets to the claim of creditors and to lawsuits? There is a relatively simple solution:

EXAMPLE: Assume that instead of keeping your $600,000 of assets, you transfer all of the assets to your spouse. On your spouse's death, this will create an additional estate tax cost of approximately $330,000 [55% rate × $600,000] (which could have been avoided had you kept the assets and bequeathed them to a credit shelter or bypass trust—see the sample will in Chapter 3). You can replace this amount ($330,000) with a life insurance policy owned by an irrevocable life insurance trust, so that the proceeds won't be included in either your estate or your spouse's estate (see Chapter 13). If you're 40 and your spouse is 37, the cost of this insurance will be $943 per year for 12 years. The present value of these payments (the worth in today's dollars), assuming a 10 percent interest rate, is only $6,425 [($943 premium × 12 years) × 6.8137 present value factor of an annuity]. Legal fees could be under $1,000, and the accounting costs for a simple trust return may not add much more to the cost of having your individual and business returns prepared. Thus, for about $7,500 and change, you can protect your assets and cover the additional cost of losing your unified credit. The illustrations and assumptions follow.

```
$330,000 JOINT COMPLIFE PLAN - INSURANCE PAYABLE ON SECOND DEATH          PAGE 1 OF 2
FOR  JOHN DOE                AGE  40  MALE.          BASIC AMOUNT .................    $99,000
     JANE DOE                AGE  37  FEMALE.        ADDITIONAL PROTECTION ........   $231,000##

INITIAL ANNUAL PREMIUM        $942.88                                      QUIK PAY PLUS
----------- DIVIDENDS PURCHASE ADDITIONS FOR 11 YEARS AND THEN REDUCE PREMIUMS WITH ANY EXCESS TO ADDITIONS -----------
                    1             2            3                 4              5
      END         TOTAL        ANNUAL                      ------- CASH VALUES --------
      OF          INSUR-        CASH        TOTAL
      YEAR        ANCE*        OUTLAY*     PAYMENTS*          TOTAL*          GUAR.
      ------------------------------------------------------------------------------------

       1          330000         943         943               72              0
       2          330000         943        1886              858             680
       3          330000         943        2829             1719            1388
       4          330000         943        3772             2664            2127
       5          330000         943        4714             3699            2896
       6          330000         943        5657             4833            3698
       7          330000         943        6600             6075            4532
       8          330000         943        7543             7436            5401
       9          330000         943        8486             8925            6304
      10          330000         943        9429            10553            7244

      11          330000         943       10372            12429            8221
      12          330000         943       11315            13632            9236
      13          330000           0       11315            14783           10291
      14          330000           0       11315            16039           11384
      15          330000           0       11315            17451           12517
      16          330000           0       11315            18978           13690
      17          330000           0       11315            20631           14905
      18          330000           0       11315            22418           16161
      19          330000           0       11315            24348           17461
      20          330000           0       11315            26431           18804

      46          330000           0       11315           185817           64547
      63          730865           0       11315           730865           99000
      ------------------------------------------------------------------------------------

ASSUMES THAT BOTH INSUREDS REMAIN ALIVE.

##THE PREMIUM FOR THE ADDITIONAL PROTECTION PORTION OF THE TOTAL INSURANCE IS NOT GUARANTEED.  INCREASED PREMIUM
  MAY BE REQUIRED TO MAINTAIN COVERAGE.
*ILLUSTRATED DIVIDENDS (1991 SCALE) REFLECT CLAIM, EXPENSE AND INVESTMENT EXPERIENCE AND ARE NOT ESTIMATES OR
  GUARANTEES OF FUTURE RESULTS.  THEY MAY BE LARGER OR SMALLER THAN ILLUSTRATED.  THIS ILLUSTRATION DOES NOT REFLECT
  THAT MONEY IS PAID AND RECEIVED AT DIFFERENT TIMES.  9.34% VARIABLE RATE LOAN PROVISION.
LUMP SUMS AND UNSCHEDULED INCREASES IN ADDITIONAL PREMIUMS ARE SUBJECT TO NEW UNDERWRITING AND SERVICE FEES.
NN SELECT/SELECT   1 NJ       02/20/91
ILLUSTRATION NO. 022091-100644
```

Figure 6.1. Insurance illustration of replacing assets equal to unified credit.

Product Description

The Joint Life Protection policy is also referred to as Joint CompLife. The policy provides a death benefit at the death of the second of two insureds. The policy consists of Basic Amount and can have Additional Protection. The Additional Protection consists of one-year term insurance and paid-up additions. The premium for the Additional Protection portion of the total insurance is not guaranteed. Changes in the dividend scale may require an increased premium to maintain coverage. The premium on the policy is payable until the insured with the younger adjusted age reaches adjusted age 100.

QUIK PAY PLUS

This ledger illustrates Premium Payment Option 3 which can be found in the contract. The Quik Pay Plus payment period is based on the illustrated dividend scale. If dividends are lower than illustrated, additional payments may be required.

Initial Premiums	Annual	Monthly
Basic Amount (includes Policy Fee)	$942.88	$82.29

Underwriting Amount

The Underwriting Amount for each insured is $165,000

Policy Change Note

Policy changes (e.g., dropping Additional Premiums and changing dividend options) require written notice to the Company using a policy change form. Policy changes, including Lump Sums after issue and unscheduled increases in Additional Premiums, are subject to new underwriting and service fees.

Adjusted Ages and Life Expectancies

The adjusted age is the insured's actual age plus an adjustment that considers the insured's issue classification.
First insured's age adjustment 0 years.
Second Insured's age adjustment 0 years.
The joint life expectancy of the two insured's is 46 years.

ILLUSTRATION NO. 022091-100644

Figure 6.1. *Continued.*

For Your Notebook:

SAMPLE ESTATE TAX RETURN, FORM 706

FACTS AND COMMENTS

The estate plan illustrated in the attached return for Mr. John Q. Taxpayer relies on two basic techniques to achieve a zero estate tax cost: (1) the unified credit to shelter up to $600,000 (actually $587,500 in the example), which is not transferred outright to the surviving spouse to avoid having it included in her estate on her death; and (2) the marital deduction, which eliminates tax on the remainder of the estate.

The decedent's will provided that an amount equal to the unified credit would pass to his children outright (not in a credit shelter trust), ensuring that both spouses' estates will make substantial use of the unified credit.

The calculation of the unified credit amount is illustrated under the heading, "Share per Will Article VI." As with all calculations and reporting on an estate tax return, the provisions of the decedent's will must be closely analyzed. The calculation shows that the maximum unified credit of $600,000 was reduced by $12,500 of administrative expenses, which was reported on the estate's income tax return. Therefore, the estate tax deduction for these expenses was waived. Since the estate will not pay any estate tax, there is no benefit to claiming the deduction of the estate tax return. However, the estate will owe income tax on income earned by the estate. For example, the deduction is claimed on the estate's income tax return. This has the affect of reducing the remaining assets which can be protected from the estate tax by the unified credit.

The marital deduction is claimed on Schedule M. Items 9 and 10 are calculated in accordance with the formula clauses contained in the decedent's will. The effect of these formulas is to reduce the estate tax to zero through the unlimited marital deduction.

Finally, there is an index of exhibits that were attached to this estate tax return. The actual exhibits have not been included, but this index illustrates the kinds of material you will often file.

Form 706

Form 706
(Rev. July 1990)
Department of the Treasury
Internal Revenue Service

United States Estate (and Generation-Skipping Transfer) Tax Return
Estate of a citizen or resident of the United States (see separate instructions). To be filed for decedents dying after December 31, 1989, and before January 1, 1993.
For Paperwork Reduction Act Notice, see page 1 of the instructions.

OMB No. 1545-0015
Expires 6-30-93

Part 1.—Decedent and Executor

1a Decedent's first name and middle initial (and maiden name, if any) **John Q.**	**1b** Decedent's last name **Taxpayer**
	2 Decedent's social security no. **123 : 45 : 6789**
3a Domicile at time of death (county and state) **New York, New York**	**3b** Year domicile established **1973** **4** Date of birth **9/10/28** **5** Date of death **April 1, 1988**
6a Name of executor (see instructions) **John Executor**	**6b** Executor's address (number and street including apartment number or rural route; city, town, or post office; state; and ZIP code) **123 Park Avenue** **New York, NY 10001**
6c Executor's social security number (see instructions) **987 : 65 : 4321**	
7a Name and location of court where will was probated or estate administered **Surrogates Court, New York County**	**7b** Case number **1111/22**
8 If decedent died testate, check here ▶ [X] and attach a certified copy of the will.	**9** If Form 4768 is attached, check here ▶ [X]
10 If Schedule R-1 is attached, check here ▶ ☐	

Part 2.—Tax Computation

1	Total gross estate (from Part 5, Recapitulation, page 3, item 10)	**1** 5,714,658
2	Total allowable deductions (from Part 5, Recapitulation, page 3, item 20)	**2** 5,114,658
3	Taxable estate (subtract line 2 from line 1)	**3** 600,000
4	Adjusted taxable gifts (total taxable gifts (within the meaning of section 2503) made by the decedent after December 31, 1976, other than gifts that are includible in decedent's gross estate (section 2001(b))	**4** -0-
5	Add lines 3 and 4	**5** 600,000
6	Tentative tax on the amount on line 5 from Table A in the instructions	**6** 192,800
7a	If line 5 exceeds $10,000,000, enter the lesser of line 5 or $21,040,000. If line 5 is $10,000,000 or less, skip lines 7a and 7b and enter zero on line 7c	**7a**
b	Subtract $10,000,000 from line 7a	**7b**
c	Enter 5% (.05) of line 7b	**7c** -0-
8	Total tentative tax (add lines 6 and 7c)	**8** 192,800
9	Total gift tax payable with respect to gifts made by the decedent after December 31, 1976. Include gift taxes paid by the decedent's spouse for such spouse's share of split gifts (section 2513) only if the decedent was the donor of these gifts and they are includible in the decedent's gross estate (see instructions).	**9** -0-
10	Gross estate tax (subtract line 9 from line 8)	**10** 192,800
11	Unified credit against estate tax from Table B in the instructions.	**11** 192,800
12	Adjustment to unified credit. (This adjustment may not exceed $6,000. See instructions.)	**12**
13	Allowable unified credit (subtract line 12 from line 11)	**13** 192,800
14	Subtract line 13 from line 10 (but do not enter less than zero)	**14** -0-
15	Credit for state death taxes. Do not enter more than line 14. Compute credit by using amount on line 3 less $60,000. See Table C in the instructions and **attach credit evidence** (see instructions)	**15** -0-
16	Subtract line 15 from line 14	**16** -0-
17	Credit for Federal gift taxes on pre-1977 gifts (section 2012)(attach computation)	**17**
18	Credit for foreign death taxes (from Schedule(s) P). (Attach Form(s) 706CE)	**18**
19	Credit for tax on prior transfers (from Schedule Q)	**19**
20	Total (add lines 17, 18, and 19)	**20** -0-
21	Net estate tax (subtract line 20 from line 16)	**21** -0-
22	Generation-skipping transfer taxes (from Schedule R, Part 2, line 10)	**22** -0-
23	Section 4980A increased estate tax (from Schedule S, Part I, line 17) (see instructions)	**23** -0-
24	Total transfer taxes (add lines 21, 22, and 23) . Extension.	**24** -0-
25	Prior payments. Explain in an attached statement . Payment	**25** 28,000
26	United States Treasury bonds redeemed in payment of estate tax	**26**
27	Total (add lines 25 and 26)	**27** 28,000
28	Balance due (or overpayment) (subtract line 27 from line 24). Refund	**28** (28,000)

Under penalties of perjury, I declare that I have examined this return, including accompanying schedules and statements, and to the best of my knowledge and belief, it is true, correct, and complete. Declaration of preparer other than the executor is based on all information of which preparer has any knowledge.

Signature(s) of executor(s)   Date

Signature of preparer other than executor   Address (and ZIP code)   Date

Figure 6.2. Sample Estate Tax Return.

Form 706 (Rev. 7-90)

Estate of: John Q. Taxpayer

Part 3.—Elections by the Executor

Please check the "Yes" or "No" box for each question.

		Yes	No
1	Do you elect alternate valuation?		X
2	Do you elect special use valuation? . . . . If "Yes," you must complete and attach Schedule A-1		X
3	Do you elect to pay the taxes in installments as described in section 6166? . . . . If "Yes," you must attach the additional information described in the instructions.		X
4	Do you elect to postpone the part of the taxes attributable to a reversionary or remainder interest as described in section 6163? . . .		X

Part 4.—General Information (Note: *Please attach the necessary supplemental documents.* **You must attach the death certificate.**)

Authorization to receive confidential tax information under Regulations section 601.502(c)(3)(ii), to act as the estate's representative before the Internal Revenue Service, and to make written or oral presentations on behalf of the estate if return prepared by an attorney, accountant, or enrolled agent for the executor:

Name of representative (print or type) John J. Doe, Esq.	State NY	Address (number, street, and room or suite no., city, state, and ZIP code) Doe, Smith Jones; 891 5th Avenue; New York, NY 1017

I declare that I am the ☐ attorney ☐ accountant ☐ enrolled agent **(you must check the applicable box)** for the executor and prepared this return for the executor. I am not under suspension or disbarment from practice before the Internal Revenue Service and am qualified to practice in the state shown above.

Signature	CAF number	Date	Telephone number 212-555-1212

1   Death certificate number and issuing authority (attach a copy of the death certificate to this return).
New York City, Dept. of Health

2   Decedent's business or occupation. If retired, check here ▶ ☐ and state decedent's former business or occupation.
Executive

3   Marital status of the decedent at time of death:
    ☒ Married
    ☐ Widow or widower—Name, SSN and date of death of deceased spouse ▶ -
    -
    ☐ Single
    ☐ Legally separated
    ☐ Divorced—Date divorce decree became final ▶

4a Surviving spouse's name Mary Taxpayer	4b Social security number 001 : 23 : 4567	4c Amount received (see instructions) 4,576,533

5   Individuals (other than the surviving spouse), trusts, or other estates who receive benefits from the estate (do not include charitable beneficiaries shown in Schedule O) (see instructions). For Privacy Act Notice (applicable to individual beneficiaries only), see the Instructions for Form 1040.

Name of individual, trust, or estate receiving $5,000 or more	Identifying number	Relationship to decedent	Amount (see instructions)
John Q. Taxpayer, Jr.	555-55-5555	Son	146,875
James J. Taxpayer	865-22-4321	Son	146,875
Mary I. Taxpayer	007-22-3333	Step-Daughter	146,875
David Taxpayer	136-85-5555	Step-Son	146,875

All unascertainable beneficiaries and those who receive less than $5,000 . . . . ▶		
Total		587,500

(Continued on next page)

Figure 6.2. *Continued.*

Part 4.—General Information (continued)

	Please check the "Yes" or "No" box for each question.			Yes	No
6	Does the gross estate contain any section 2044 property (qualified terminable interest property (QTIP) from a prior gift or estate)(see instructions)?				X
7a	Have Federal gift tax returns ever been filed?			X	
	If "Yes," please attach copies of the returns, if available, and furnish the following information:				
7b	Period(s) covered	7c	Internal Revenue office(s) where filed		
	If you answer "Yes" to any of questions 8–16, you must attach additional information as described in the Instructions.				
8a	Was there any insurance on the decedent's life that is not included on the return as part of the gross estate?			X	
b	Did the decedent own any insurance on the life of another that is not included in the gross estate?				X
9	Did the decedent at the time of death own any property as a joint tenant with right of survivorship in which (1) one or more of the other joint tenants was someone other than the decedent's spouse, and (2) less than the full value of the property is included on the return as part of the gross estate? If "Yes," you must complete and attach Schedule E.				X
10	Did the decedent, at the time of death, own any interest in a partnership or unincorporated business or any stock in an inactive or closely held corporation?			X	
11a	Did the decedent make any transfer described in section 2035, 2036, 2037, or 2038 (see the instructions for Schedule G)? If "Yes," you must complete and attach Schedule G				X
b	If "Yes," was it a valuation freeze subject to section 2036(c)?				
12	Were there in existence at the time of the decedent's death:				
a	Any trusts created by the decedent during his or her lifetime?				X
b	Any trusts not created by the decedent under which the decedent possessed any power, beneficial interest, or trusteeship?				X
13	Did the decedent ever possess, exercise, or release any general power of appointment? If "Yes," you must complete and attach Schedule H.				X
14	Was the marital deduction computed under the transitional rule of Public Law 97-34, section 403(e)(3) (Economic Recovery Tax Act of 1981)?				X
	If "Yes," attach a separate computation of the marital deduction, enter the amount on item 18 of the Recapitulation, and note on item 18 "computation attached."				
15	Was the decedent, immediately before death, receiving an annuity described in the "General" paragraph of the instructions for Schedule I? If "Yes," you must complete and attach Schedule I.				X
16	Did the decedent have a total "excess retirement accumulation" (as defined in section 4980A(d)) in qualified employer plans and individual retirement plans? If "Yes," you must complete and attach Schedule S.			X	

Part 5.—Recapitulation

Item number	Gross estate	Alternate value	Value at date of death
1	Schedule A—Real Estate		1,519,755
2	Schedule B—Stocks and Bonds		681,436
3	Schedule C—Mortgages, Notes, and Cash		593,711
4	Schedule D—Insurance on the Decedent's Life (attach Form(s) 712)		1,539,306
5	Schedule E—Jointly Owned Property (attach Form(s) 712 for life insurance)		
6	Schedule F—Other Miscellaneous Property (attach Form(s) 712 for life insurance) . .		
7	Schedule G—Transfers During Decedent's Life (attach Form(s) 712 for life insurance) .		
8	Schedule H—Powers of Appointment		
9	Schedule I—Annuities		1,380,450
10	Total gross estate (add items 1 through 9). Enter here and on line 1 of the Tax Computation.		5,714,658

Item number	Deductions	Amount
11	Schedule J—Funeral Expenses and Expenses Incurred in Administering Property Subject to Claims	13,307
12	Schedule K—Debts of the Decedent	524,818
13	Schedule K—Mortgages and Liens	
14	Total of items 11 through 13	538,125
15	Allowable amount of deductions from item 14 (see the instructions for item 15 of the Recapitulation)	538,125
16	Schedule L—Net Losses During Administration	
17	Schedule L—Expenses Incurred in Administering Property Not Subject to Claims	
18	Schedule M—Bequests, etc., to Surviving Spouse	4,576,533
19	Schedule O—Charitable, Public, and Similar Gifts and Bequests	
20	Total allowable deductions (add items 15 through 19). Enter here and on line 2 of the Tax Computation	5,114,658

Figure 6.2. *Continued.*

Estate of: John Q. Taxpayer

SCHEDULE B—Stocks and Bonds

(For jointly owned property that must be disclosed on Schedule E, see the Instructions for Schedule E.)

Item number	Description including face amount of bonds or number of shares and par value where needed for identification. Give CUSIP number if available.	Unit value	Alternate valuation date	Alternate value	Value at date of death
1	45 Shares Common – Class A	7,135.00			321,075
	168 Shares Common – Class B	7,135.00			1,198,680
	Total from continuation schedule(s) (or additional sheet(s)) attached to this schedule . . .				
	TOTAL. (Also enter on Part 5, Recapitulation, page 3, at item 2.)				1,519,755

(If more space is needed, attach the continuation schedule from the end of this package or additional sheets of the same size.)
(The instructions to Schedule B are in the separate instructions.)

Schedule B—Page 10

Figure 6.2. *Continued.*

Estate of: John Q. Taxpayer

SCHEDULE D—Insurance on the Decedent's Life
You must attach a Form 712 for each policy.

Item number	Description	Alternate valuation date	Alternate value	Value at date of death
1	Life Insurance Company Policy No. See Attached Form 712			129,700
2	Life Insurance Company Policy No. See Attached Form 712			40,200
3	Life Insurance Company Policy No. See Attached Form 712			63,100
4	Life InsuranceCompany Policy No. See Attached Form 712			448,436
5	Life Insurance Company Policy No. See Attached Form 712 $72,601 The value of item 5 has been excluded from the gross estate because the decedent possessed no incidents of ownership in the policy at his death. Forms 712 are attached as Exhibit B.			
	Total from continuation schedule(s) (or additional sheet(s)) attached to this schedule . . .			
	TOTAL. (Also enter on Part 5, Recapitulation, page 3, at item 4.)			681,436

(If more space is needed, attach the continuation schedule from the end of this package or additional sheets of the same size.)

Schedule D—Page 12

Figure 6.2. *Continued.*

Estate of: John Q. Taxpayer

SCHEDULE E—Jointly Owned Property

(If you elect section 2032A valuation, you must complete Schedule E and Schedule A-1.)

PART 1.— Qualified Joint Interests—Interests Held by the Decedent and His or Her Spouse as the Only Joint Tenants (Section 2040(b)(2))

Item number	Description For securities, give CUSIP number, if available.	Alternate valuation date	Alternate value	Value at date of death
1	Condominium – Apt. 101-N Sunnyside, Florida Value based on appraisal Exhibit A			1,100,000
2	57,447.22 Shares Paine Webber Cash Fund Account			57,447
3	Cash - checking account First National Bank, N.A. A/C Palm Beach, Florida			29,974
	Total from continuation schedule(s) (or additional sheet(s)) attached to this schedule			
1a	Totals 1a			1,187,421
1b	Amounts included in gross estate (one-half of line 1a) 1b			593,711

PART 2.—All Other Joint Interests

2a State the name and address of each surviving co-tenant. If there are more than three surviving co-tenants, list the additional co-tenants on an attached sheet.

Name	Address (number and street, city, state, and ZIP code)
A.	
B.	
C.	

Item number	Enter letter for co-tenant	Description (including alternate valuation date if any) For securities, give CUSIP number, if available.	Percentage includible	Includible alternate value	Includible value at date of death
		Total from continuation schedule(s) (or additional sheet(s)) attached to this schedule			
2b		Total other joint interests 2b			

3   **Total includible joint interests** (add lines 1b and 2b). Also enter on Part 5, Recapitulation, page 3, at item 5   593,711

(If more space is needed, attach the continuation schedule from the end of this package or additional sheets of the same size.)

Schedule E—Page 14

Figure 6.2. *Continued.*

Estate of: John Q. Taxpayer

SCHEDULE F—Other Miscellaneous Property Not Reportable Under Any Other Schedule
(For jointly owned property that must be disclosed on Schedule E, see the Instructions for Schedule E.)
(If you elect section 2032A valuation, you must complete Schedule F and Schedule A-1.)

		Yes	No
1	Did the decedent at the time of death own any articles of artistic or collectible value in excess of $3,000 or any collections whose artistic or collectible value combined at date of death exceeded $10,000?		X
	If "Yes," full details must be submitted on this schedule.		
2	Has the decedent's estate, spouse, or any other person, received (or will receive) any bonus or award as a result of the decedent's employment or death?		X
	If "Yes," full details must be submitted on this schedule.		
3	Did the decedent at the time of death have, or have access to, a safe deposit box?		X
	If "Yes," state location, and if held in joint names of decedent and another, state name and relationship of joint depositor.		

If any of the contents of the safe deposit box are omitted from the schedules in this return, explain fully why omitted.

Item number	Description For securities, give CUSIP number, if available.	Alternate valuation date	Alternate value	Value at date of death
1	Partnership Interest – SS Associates			139,000
2	Partnership Interest – XYZ Partners, L.P.			1,387,627
3	M Holdings Corp. Liquidating Trust			2,679
4	Personal Effects			10,000
	Total from continuation schedule(s) (or additional sheet(s)) attached to this schedule . . .			
	TOTAL. (Also enter on Part 5, Recapitulation, page 3, at item 6.)			1,539,306

(If more space is needed, attach the continuation schedule from the end of this package or additional sheets of the same size.)

Schedule F—Page 16

Figure 6.2. *Continued.*

Estate of: John Q. Taxpayer

SCHEDULE I—Annuities

Note: *Generally, no exclusion is allowed for the estates of decedents dying after December 31, 1984 (see instructions).*

		Yes	No
A Are you excluding from the decedent's gross estate the value of a lump-sum distribution described in section 2039(f)(2)?			X

If "Yes," you must attach the information required by the instructions.

Item number	Description Show the entire value of the annuity before any exclusions.	Alternate valuation date	Includible alternate value	Includible value at date of death
1	Individual Retirement Account Account No. 123 XYZ Company – Custodian Payable to: Mary Taxpayer as beneficiary			929,763
2	ABC Profit Sharing Plan and Trust Payable to: Mary Taxpayer as beneficiary			450,687
3	ABC Employee Pension Trust – all benefits funded through life insurance as listed on schedule D			-0-
	Total from continuation schedule(s) (or additional sheet(s)) attached to this schedule			
	TOTAL. (Also enter on Part 5, Recapitulation, page 3, at item 9.)			1,380,450

(If more space is needed, attach the continuation schedule from the end of this package or additional sheets of the same size.)
(The instructions to Schedule I are in the separate instructions.)

Figure 6.2. *Continued.*

Estate of: John Q. Taxpayer

SCHEDULE J—Funeral Expenses and Expenses Incurred in Administering Property Subject to Claims

Note: *Do not list on this schedule expenses of administering property not subject to claims. For those expenses, see the Instructions for Schedule L.*

If executors' commissions, attorney fees, etc., are claimed and allowed as a deduction for estate tax purposes, they are not allowable as a deduction in computing the taxable income of the estate for Federal income tax purposes. They are allowable as an income tax deduction on Form 1041 if a waiver is filed to waive the deduction on Form 706 (see the Form 1041 instructions).

Item number	Description	Expense amount	Total Amount
1	A. **Funeral expenses:** Lovely Chapel Mount Cemetery Hill Monument Co.	8,197 2,973 2,137	
	Total funeral expenses		13,307
	B. **Administration expenses:**		
1	Executors' commissions—amount estimated/agreed upon/paid. (Strike out the words that do not apply.) . . . . waived		
2	Attorney fees—amount estimated/agreed upon/paid. (Strike out the words that do not apply.) . . . . . . Not taken on 706		
3	Accountant fees—amount estimated/agreed upon/paid. (Strike out the words that do not apply.)		
4	Miscellaneous expenses: Administrative expenses not taken on 706	Expense amount	
	Total miscellaneous expenses from continuation schedule(s) (or additional sheet(s)) attached to this schedule		
	Total miscellaneous expenses		
	TOTAL. (Also enter on Part 5, Recapitulation, page 3, at item 11.)		13,307

(If more space is needed, attach the continuation schedule from the end of this package or additional sheets of the same size.)

Schedule J—Page 20

Figure 6.2. *Continued.*

Estate of: John Q. Taxpayer

SCHEDULE K—Debts of the Decedent, and Mortgages and Liens

Item number	Debts of the Decedent—Creditor and nature of claim, and allowable death taxes	Amount unpaid to date	Amount in contest	Amount claimed as a deduction
1	Loan payable to AB Interest payable at 6.5%; demand loan Interest accrued to date of death	10,656		10,656 583
2	Loan payable to CD Interest payable at 6.5%; demand loan Interest accrued to date of death	421,590		421,590 1,877
3	Internal Revenue Service 1979 Tax Exam Tax Interest accrued to date of death			4,018 6,734
4	Loan payable to EF Floating interest rate; demand loan Interest accrued to date of death			76,251 3,109
	Total from continuation schedule(s) (or additional sheet(s)) attached to this schedule			–0–
	TOTAL. (Also enter on Part 5, Recapitulation, page 3, at item 12.)			524,818

Item number	Mortgages and Liens—Description	Amount
1		
	Total from continuation schedule(s) (or additional sheet(s)) attached to this schedule	
	TOTAL. (Also enter on Part 5, Recapitulation, page 3, at item 13.)	NONE

(If more space is needed, attach the continuation schedule from the end of this package or additional sheets of the same size.)
(The instructions to Schedule K are in the separate instructions.)

Schedule K —Page 22

Figure 6.2. *Continued.*

(Make copies of this schedule before completing it if you will need more than one schedule.)

Estate of: John Q. Taxpayer

CONTINUATION SCHEDULE

Continuation of Schedule _____K_____

(Enter letter of schedule you are continuing)

Item number	Description For securities, give CUSIP number, if available.	Unit value (Sch B or E only)	Alternate valuation date	Alternate value	Value at date of death or amount deductible
1	Internal Revenue Service Examination of 1980 tax return – amount undertermined as yet.				
	TOTAL. (Carry forward to main schedule.).				

See instructions on next page.   **Continuation Schedule—Page 35**

Figure 6.2. *Continued.*

Estate of: John Q. Taxpayer

SCHEDULE M—Bequests, etc., to Surviving Spouse

Terminable Interest (QTIP) Marital Deduction.—If you elect to claim a marital deduction for qualified terminable interest property (QTIP) under section 2056(b)(7), you MUST list on Part 2 of Schedule M all of the property for which you are making the election. Listing property on Part 2 constitutes the making of the QTIP election. No marital deduction will be allowed for any terminable interest property that is listed on Part 1 of Schedule M.

		Yes	N
1	Did any property pass to the surviving spouse as a result of a qualified disclaimer? . . . . If "Yes," attach a copy of the written disclaimer required by section 2518(b).		X —
2	Is the surviving spouse a U.S. citizen?	X	
3	**Qualified Domestic Trust.**—Do you elect under section 2056A(d) to treat any trusts reported on Schedule M as qualified domestic trusts? (see instructions)		X
4	**Election out of QTIP Treatment of Annuities.**—Do you elect under section 2056(b)(7)(C)(ii) to not treat as qualified terminable interest property any joint and survivor annuities that are included in the gross estate and would otherwise be treated as qualified terminable interest property under section 2056(b)(7)(C)? (see instructions)		X —

Part 1.—Property Interests Which Are Not Subject to a QTIP Election

(Note: A marital deduction will NOT be allowed for any terminable interest property (QTIP) that is listed on Part 1 of Schedule M.)

Item number	Description of property interests passing to surviving spouse	Value
1	Schedule D – Item 1 – Life Insurance Proceeds	129,700
2	2 – Life Insurance Proceeds	40,200
3	3 – Life Insurance Proceeds	63,100
4	4 – Life Insurance Proceeds	448,436
5	Schedule E – One-half of jointly owned property	593,711
6	Schedule F – Item 4 – Personal Effects	10,000
7	Schedule I – Item 1 – Individual Retirement Account	929,763
8	Item 2 – Profit Sharing Plan and Trust	450,687
9	Fractional share of residuary estate under article VII (see computation)	– 0 –
10	Fractional share of residuary estate under article VIII (see computation)	1,910,936

Total from continuation schedule(s) (or additional sheet(s)) attached to this schedule . . . .

Total value of property interests not subject to a QTIP election (enter here and on line 1 of Part 3 on the next page) . . . . | 4,576,533

(If more space is needed, attach the continuation schedule from the end of this package or additional sheets of the same size.)
(The instructions to Schedule M are in the separate instructions.)

Schedule M—Page 24

Figure 6.2.   Continued.

Part 2.—Property Interests Which Are Subject to a QTIP Election

(Note: *Listing terminable interest property on Part 2 of Schedule M constitutes the making of a QTIP election for that property under section 2056(b)(7). A marital deduction will not be allowed for any terminable interest property that is not listed on Part 2. If you use a continuation page for Part 2, be sure that it is clearly labeled as Schedule M, Part 2.)*

Item number	Description of property interests passing to surviving spouse (Describe portion of trust for which allocation is made.)	Value
1		
	Total from continuation schedule(s) (or additional sheet(s)) attached to this schedule	

A. Total value of property interests subject to a QTIP election		**A**	

Part 3.—Reconciliation

1	Enter the total from part 1	**1**	4,576,533
2	Total interests passing to surviving spouse (add lines A and 1, above)	**2**	4,576,533
3a	Federal estate taxes (including section 4980A taxes) payable out of property interests listed on Parts 1 and 2	**3a**	
b	Other death taxes payable out of property interests listed on Parts 1 and 2	**3b**	
c	Federal and state GST taxes payable out of property interests listed on Parts 1 and 2	**3c**	
d	Add items a, b, and c	**3d**	
4	Net value of property interests listed on Schedule M (subtract 3d from 2). Also enter on Part 5, Recapitulation, page 3, at item 18	**4**	4,576,533

(If more space is needed, attach the continuation schedule from the end of this package or additional sheets of the same size.)

Schedule M—Page 25

Figure 6.2. *Continued.*

Estate of: John Q. Taxpayer

SCHEDULE S—Increased Estate Tax on Excess Retirement Accumulations

(Under section 4980A(d) of the Internal Revenue Code)

Part I   Tax Computation

1   Check this box if a section 4980A(d)(5) spousal election is being made . . . . ▶ ☐
You must attach the statement described in the instructions.

2   Enter the name and employer identification number (EIN) of each qualified employer plan and individual retirement account in which the decedent had an interest at the time of death:

	Name	EIN
Plan #1	ABC ProfitSharing Plan	13-4567890
Plan #2	ABC Pension Plan	13-0987654
Plan #3		
IRA #1	XYZ Company	None
IRA #2		
IRA #3		

		A Plan #1	B Plan #2	C Plan #3	D All IRAs
3	Value of decedent's interest	450,687	681,436		929,763
4	Amounts rolled over after death				
5	Total value (add lines 3 and 4)	450,687	681,436		929,763
6	Amounts payable to certain alternate payees (see instructions)				
7	Decedent's investment in the contract under section 72(f) .				
8	Excess life insurance amount		496,432		
9	Decedent's interest as a beneficiary				
10	Total reductions in value (add lines 6, 7, 8, and 9)		496,432		
11	Net value of decedent's interest (subtract line 10 from line 5)	450,687	185,004		929,763

12   Decedent's aggregate interest in all plans and IRAs (add columns A–D of line 11) . . . . ▶ | **12** | 1,565,454

13   Present value of hypothetical life annuity (from Part III, line 4) . . . . . . | **13** | 889,401 |

14   Remaining unused grandfather amount (from Part II, line 4) . . . . | **14** | 1,733,108 |

15   Enter the greater of line 13 or line 14 . . . . | **15** | 1,733,108

16   Excess retirement accumulation (subtract line 15 from line 12) . . . . | **16** | –0–

17   Increased estate tax (multiply line 16 by 15%). Enter here and on line 23 of the Tax Computation on page 1. | **17** |

(The instructions to Schedule S are in the separate instructions.)

Schedule S —Page 33

Figure 6.2.   *Continued.*

Part II   **Grandfather Election**

1 Was a grandfather election made on a previously filed Form 5329? . . . . ▶ ☐ Yes ☒ No

    If "Yes," complete lines 2–4 below. **You may not make or revoke the grandfather election after the due date (with extensions) for filing the decedent's 1988 income tax return.** If "No," enter "-0-" on line 4 and skip to Part III.

2 Initial grandfather amount	**2**	1,777,108
3 Total amount previously recovered	**3**	44,000
4 Remaining unused grandfather amount (subtract line 3 from line 2). Enter here and on Part I, line 14, on page 33	**4**	1,733,108

Part III   **Computation of Hypothetical Life Annuity**

1 Decedent's attained age at date of death (in whole years, rounded down)	**1**	59
2 Applicable annual annuity amount (see instructions)	**2**	117,529
3 Present value multiplier (see instructions)	**3**	7.5675
4 Present value of hypothetical life annuity (multiply line 2 by line 3). Enter here and on Part I, line 13, on page 33	**4**	889,401

Figure 6.2. *Continued.*

Estate of John Q. Taxpayer
SS 987-65-4321
Distribution of Residuary Estate Pursuant
to Articles VI, VII, and VIII of Decedent's Will

Computation of Residuary Estate

Gross Estate		$5,714,658
Less:		
Items passing outside of will:		
Life insurance proceeds	$681,436	
One-half of jointly owned property	593,711	
IRA to named beneficiary	929,763	
ABC profit sharing plan and trust	450,687	2,655,597
Specific bequest of tangible personal property per Article IV		10,000
Expenses per Schedule J		13,307
Debts per Schedule K		524,818
Administration expenses not deducted on Form 706		12,500
Residuary Estate (denominator)		$2,498,436*

Share per Will Article VI

Unified credit equivalent	$600,000	
Administration expenses not deducted on 706	(12,500)	
Numerator	$587,500	

Share per Will Article VI
587,500/2,498,436 × 2,498,436 = $587,500

Share per Will Article VII

Gross estate		$5,714,658
Deductions for funeral expenses and debts under sections 2053 and 2054		538,125
Adjusted gross estate		5,176,533
		× ½
		$2,588,267
Less:		
Items passing outside of will:		
Life Insurance Proceeds		$ 681,436
One-half of jointly owned property		593,711
Individual retirement account		929,763
Profit sharing plan and trust		450,687
Specific bequest of tangible personal property		10,000
Numerator		$ 0

Share per Will Article VII
-0-/2,498,436 × 2,498,436 = $ 0

Share per Will Article VIII

Residuary estate		$2,498,436
Less: Share per Will Article VI		587,500
Share per Will Article VII		0
Share per Will Article VIII		$1,910,936

*The residuary estate is used to fund the unified credit bequest to the children per Article VI above, and the marital deduction amount per Articles VII and VIII as reflected on page seventeen.

Figure 6.3. Calculations for Form 706.

Estate of John Q. Taxpayer
SS 987-65-4321
Computation of Beneficiaries' Shares

	Mary Q. Taxpayer	Children	Total
Specific bequest (Article IV)	$ 10,000		
Life insurance proceeds	681,436		
Jointly owned property	593,711		
Individual retirement account	929,763		
Profit sharing plan and trust	450,687		
Share of residuary estate (see computation)	1,910,936	$587,500	
	$4,576,533	$587,500	$5,164,030

Reconciliation of Beneficiary Shares to Gross Estate:	
Beneficiary Shares per above	$5,164,030
Allowable Deductions	538,120
Administration Expenses	12,500
Total Gross Estate	$5,714,650

Estate of John Q. Taxpayer
Index of Exhibits

Exhibit

A   Will

B   Appraisal of Condominium Apartment

C   Form 712

D   Death Certificate

E   Prior Gift Tax Returns

[EXHIBITS OMITTED]

Figure 6.3. *Continued.*

7 GIFT TAX

It is common knowledge that every taxpayer can give away up to $10,000 in any tax year, to any person, without incurring a gift tax. Although the "kiddie tax" has eliminated the income tax benefits of making a gift to children under 14, the significant estate tax rates of up to 55 percent means there can be substantial estate planning benefits from having a gift program. These benefits include not only the reduction of the taxable estate but also possible savings on the generation-skipping transfer tax. Many transfers qualifying for the annual $10,000 gift tax exclusion are not subject to the generation-skipping transfer tax.

You don't have to be altruistic to make a gift. Contrary to the common misconception, there is no requirement for any donative intent on the part of the donor in order to create a potentially taxable gift. The requirement is simply that there be a transfer for less than adequate and full consideration. (This doesn't apply to ordinary business transactions, because then there is adequate consideration paid and the transaction is made at arm's length. For example, a transfer to an employee would probably be characterized as compensation rather than a gift.)

THE ANNUAL $10,000 GIFT TAX EXCLUSION

You can give away up to $10,000 to any one person without incurring a gift tax. There is no limit to the number of such gifts you make during each year—you can give $20,000 or $200,000, as long as you don't give more than $10,000 to any individual. This is an annual exclusion, so you can give away $10,000 every year to the same person. It is available for gifts of a "present interest," an important technical term that is explained below.

Doubling the Value of Your $10,000 Exclusion

A basic, but important, technique in estate planning is gift splitting. This enables either you or your spouse to make a gift and have the other, nondonor, spouse join in the gift. When the other requirements for the annual exclusion are met, gift splitting enables one of you to make a transfer of up to $20,000 per recipient (donee), with the gift being deemed to be made one-half by each spouse, so that each spouse's $10,000 annual exclusion is applied to eliminate any taxable gift. The requirements to qualify for this valuable benefit include the following:

- You're married.
- Both you and your spouse are citizens or residents of the United States.
- The spouse making the gift does not remarry during the remainder of the year.
- You both agree (consent) to this tax treatment for the particular gift and for all gifts made by either of you while married during the calendar year.

The last requirement is fulfilled by signing and filing the annual gift tax return, Form 709. A sample form illustrating gift splitting appears in the "For Your Notebook" section following this chapter.

Don't Forget the Paper Work

Even without gift splitting, a gift tax return, Form 709, may have to be filed. Unfortunately, this requirement is too frequently overlooked, which can be a costly mistake. This is because the statute of limitations won't apply. The statute of limitations generally provides that if the IRS doesn't audit you within three years of the date of any tax return, they can't (if there's fraud, this rule won't apply). If no return has been filed, however, the statute of limitations will remain open forever. In one case, the IRS was allowed to go back to 1977 and assess a gift tax in each succeeding year!

Only individuals are required to file a gift tax return. When a partnership, S corporation, or trust makes a gift, the partners, shareholders, or beneficiaries must report the gifts. When the gifts are made between you and your spouse, filing generally is not required. The Form 709 is an annual tax return. It is filed after January 1 and prior to April 16 of the year following the gift. Extensions of time to file the form, but not to pay the tax, can be obtained.

GIFT TAX RULES AND TRAPS

There are a number of potential tax traps to be aware of when planning year-end, or other, gifts, including the following:

- *$10,000 is really the maximum.* The exclusion is for a total of $10,000 (cash or property) per year. This applies to all gifts during the year. If you write out a check in December for $10,000 to a child or grandchild, the IRS may question the amount of the gift on the basis that most taxpayers give birthday, Christmas, and other gifts throughout the year. IRS Agents have even reviewed taxpayers' checkbooks to find other gifts to the same child. If the $10,000 check exceeds the annual exclusion, it will result in a current gift tax cost or depletion of the unified credit. Consider using an amount somewhat less than the $10,000 amount, perhaps $9,500. This may indicate that consideration has been given to the total amount of annual gifts and the maximum exclusion amount.

- *Gifts to a trust can cause you to exceed the $10,000 exclusion.* Another commonly overlooked matter is that a gift to a trust is really a gift to the beneficiaries of that trust. For example, if you pay $20,000 to an insurance trust that purchases insurance on your life, naming your two children as beneficiaries, you can't then make gifts of $10,000 to each of your children and expect to qualify for the annual exclusion. You will have given more than the maximum $10,000 to each child in that year. The fact that one gift is direct and the other indirect, through a trust, is not relevant.

- *Gifts must generally be of a present interest.* As a general rule, a gift in trust may not qualify for the annual gift tax exclusion if it is not a gift of a present interest. The basic concept is that the recipient must have present use of the gift. For example, any gift of a remainder interest is considered to be a future interest and won't qualify for the annual exclusion.

EXAMPLE: You transfer assets worth $50,000 as a gift to a trust that was established years ago for the benefit of your children and family members. If the children and other family members can't use or benefit from the gift until the money is distributed at some unknown future date (perhaps in the sole discretion of an independent trustee), the gifts will not qualify as gifts of a present interest. Therefore, you won't be able to use the annual exclusion and will have to pay a gift tax on the $50,000 value, or use up a portion of your remaining unified credit (see Chapter 6). This outcome could have been avoided if you had transferred the assets directly to the same beneficiaries instead of indirectly, via the trust.

There are three rules for determining when a gift to a trust qualifies as a gift of a present interest: (1) The trust should generate an income flow. (2) Some portion of the income must go to the trust beneficiaries. (3) The amount of income the beneficiaries will receive must be ascertainable.

There are exceptions to the present-interest requirement. A gift to a special trust for the benefit of a minor child that meets certain requirements can qualify for the annual gift tax exclusion (see Chapter 11). The other alternative is to use a Crummey demand power. This power is named after the tax case in which the court sustained the taxpayer's argument that a gift to a trust, when the beneficiary had an opportunity to withdraw the funds currently but did not elect to do so, qualified as a gift of a present interest and was eligible for the annual gift tax exclusion. This is explained in greater detail in Chapter 11 and is illustrated in the Sample Trust Agreement in the "For Your Notebook" section following that chapter.

- *The stated value of the gift may be challenged.* When gifts of assets such as interests in closely held businesses and real estate are made, valuation questions are critical. Since there is often no ready market for these assets, and since they may be unique and, therefore, difficult to value precisely, the risk of IRS challenge is more significant than for many other types of assets. If you value a gift at $9,800, but the IRS argues successfully that it's worth $16,000, you could face a gift tax cost of more than $3,000.

- *Consider who is really getting the gift.* When a gift is made to a trust, the beneficiaries of the trust are considered to be the recipients and not the trust. When a gift is made to a corporation, the shareholders may be deemed to be the recipients and not the corporation. When the recipients can only enjoy the property upon liquidation of the corporation, no annual exclusion will be available to the donor. When a gift is made to two people as joint tenants, the gift is considered to be made in proportion to the actuarial value of each person's interest. These rules can affect the availability of the $10,000 exclusion and have other important consequences.

- *The gift must be complete in that year.* If a gift is not properly planned, the IRS may argue successfully that the gift was completed in a later year, and in that case, the annual exclusion for the year in which the gift was intended will be lost. A further result could be that in the later year when the gift is deemed to be effective, gifts may exceed the annual exclusion. This will either diminish the donor's unified credit or trigger a taxable gift.

  Even more serious problems can occur. Certain assets given away within three years of death are added back to your estate to determine whether your estate can qualify for certain favorable tax benefits, such as the deferred payment of tax and stock redemption (see Chapter 16). Also, insurance given away within three years of your death can be brought back into your estate (see Chapter 19). If a gift is not properly completed when expected, the results can be disastrous.

  The general concept in establishing completion of a gift is that you must part with sufficient control over the assets so that you cannot retract the gift. The gift must be beyond recall by the donor. The delivery of the gift property should also be completed. It is best to have every technicality met in consummating the gift prior to year-end. A gift of a check has been held to be complete only when the check is cashed, because until that time the donor may be able to revoke (cancel) the check. A gift of stock in a corporation, such as stock in a closely held S corporation, is effective upon the delivery of the properly endorsed stock certificate to the recipient or to his or her agent. Delivery of a gift to your agent may not suffice to constitute a completed gift. In the case of real estate, such as interests in a family limited partnership, or even stock in a closely held corporation, if you retain excessive control over the corporation, it may be arguable whether the gift was ever completed. For example, if you draw all income out of the entity in the form of an unreasonably large salary, or if your child is prevented from realizing any value on the disposition or sale of the ownership interest, it may be deemed that no gift has been completed.

WHAT PROPERTY SHOULD BE GIFTED?

One of the most critical decisions is what property to give away. Once your personal and business needs are adequately addressed, the following suggestions will be helpful:

- Give property that is most likely to appreciate in the future. This will remove the most assets from your estate for the least transfer tax cost.

- Insurance is an ideal asset to give away. Term insurance, for example, may have little if any current value; however, on your death it will balloon to a substantial value. Removing it from your estate can be one of the most important aspects of your gift planning (see Chapter 19).

- Give away property that will help your estate qualify for the estate tax deferral and stock redemption provisions (see Chapter 16).

- When it is appropriate, eliminate joint ownership of assets. When substantial assets are held in joint names, it may be beneficial to restructure the ownership of assets, using the annual gift tax exclusion and the unlimited marital deduction to achieve a more beneficial structure in terms of your unified credit.

- A gift program can be used to take advantage of the graduated estate tax rates. After the use of the $600,000 unified credit, the estate tax rates increase in stages from a 37 percent level to a 55 percent level on amounts over $3 million (actually 60 percent over certain phase-out ranges). The tax on a $3 million estate is $1,290,800. A significant tax savings may be realized by equalizing the estates of you and your spouse so that the estate of the first spouse to die would intentionally incur a tax cost in these lower tax brackets. The savings could exceed $100,000. There is a downside to this planning: You are deliberately incurring an estate tax on the first estate. If the second spouse survives for a long period of time, on a present-value basis, the savings in tax rate on the second spouse's estate could be reduced.

ESTATE FREEZE RULES

When planning for the transfer of interests in family partnerships, closely held corporations, and certain trusts, consideration must be given to the anti-freeze rules. Although these rules are largely related to the gift tax (they attempt to achieve a proper valuation of a transfer at the time it was made), there are important estate tax implications. For example, if required payments aren't made on family debt or other interests in the business retained by you after making a transfer to your children, the value of the assets in your estate can be affected.

When a gift is made of interests in certain corporations, trusts, or partnerships, the value of the gift is determined by subtracting the value of the property retained from the value of the entire property. For example, special valuation rules apply when a gift of stock in a corporation or of partnership interests is made. These rules focus on any liquidation, put, call, conversion right, or certain distribution rights retained by you. If you don't make certain elections, the value of the interests retained by you will be considered to be zero, thus creating a large taxable gift. If payments are supposed to be made on the retained interest, such as cumulative dividends, and these payments aren't made, this can serve to increase the value of the interest you've retained. The result will be a larger gift tax if you eventually transfer the interest, or a larger estate tax if you die owning the interest.

These rules are intended to prevent taxpayers from improperly valuing assets in order to obtain a more favorable estate tax treatment. For example, the value of a business as contained in a buy-sell agreement will be disregarded if it is decided that the buy-sell agreement was intended as a mechanism to transfer property to a family member for less than its fair value (that is, it was not a bona fide business arrangement, comparable to similar arrangements). These provisions also result in certain lapses of right in family partnerships or corporations being treated as gifts. Although these rules were intended to permit business owners who were not abusing the transfer tax rules to consummate intrafamily transactions without costly tax consequences, the rules are unclear in many respects and can result in substantial problems.

CONCLUSION

A properly planned and executed gift program is an essential step for any substantial estate. The judicious use of annual exclusions and other rules can enable you to transfer large assets out of your estate at little or no tax cost. Considering the high gift, estate, and generation-skipping transfer taxes, this type of planning is essential if you wish to pass significant wealth to your heirs.

For Your Notebook:

SAMPLE GIFT TAX RETURN, FORM 709

United States Gift (and Generation-Skipping Transfer) Tax Return

(Section 6019 of the Internal Revenue Code) (For gifts made after December 31, 1989, and before January 1, 1993)

Calendar year 19 _____

► See separate instructions. For Privacy Act Notice, see the Instructions for Form 1040.

OMB No 1545-0020
Expires 8-31-93

Part 1.—General Information

1 Donor's first name and middle initial	2 Donor's last name	3 Social security number
John Q.	Taxpayer	123 45 6789

4 Address (number, street, and apartment number)	5 Domicile
123 Main Street	USA

6 City, state, and ZIP code	7 Citizenship
Anywhere, USA 12345	USA

		Yes	No
8	If the donor died during the year, check here ► ☐ and enter date of death .... , 19		
9	If you received an extension of time to file this Form 709, check here ► ☐ and attach the Form 4868, 2688, 2350, or extension letter.		
10	Enter the total number of separate donees listed on Schedule A—count each person only once . . . . ☐ 2		
11	If you (the donor) filed a previous Form 709 (or 709-A), has your address changed since the last Form 709 (or 709-A) was filed?		X
12	Gifts by husband or wife to third parties.—Do you consent to have the gifts (including generation-skipping transfers) made by you and by your spouse to third parties during the calendar year considered as made one-half by each of you? (See instructions.) (If the answer is "Yes," the following information must be furnished and your spouse is to sign the consent shown below. If the answer is "No," skip lines 13–18 and go to Schedule A.).	X	

13 Name of consenting spouse Mary Q. Taxpayer	14 SSN 001-23-4567		

		Yes	No
15	Were you married to one another during the entire calendar year? (See instructions.)	X	
16	If the answer to 15 is "No," check whether ☐ married ☐ divorced or ☐ widowed, and give date (see instructions) ►		
17	Will a gift tax return for this calendar year be filed by your spouse?		X

18 **Consent of Spouse**—I consent to have the gifts (and generation-skipping transfers) made by me and by my spouse to third parties during the calendar year considered as made one-half by each of us. We are both aware of the joint and several liability for tax created by the execution of this consent.

Consenting spouse's signature ► _____ Date ► _____

Part 2.—Tax Computation

1	Enter the amount from Schedule A, Part 3, line 15	1	0
2	Enter the amount from Schedule B, line 3	2	0
3	Total taxable gifts (add lines 1 and 2)	3	0
4	Tax computed on amount on line 3 (see Table for Computing Tax in separate instructions)	4	0
5	Tax computed on amount on line 2 (see Table for Computing Tax in separate instructions)	5	0
6	Balance (subtract line 5 from line 4)	6	0
7	Maximum unified credit (nonresident aliens, see instructions)	7	192,800 00
8	Enter the unified credit against tax allowable for all prior periods (from Sch. B, line 1, col. C) .	8	0
9	Balance (subtract line 8 from line 7)	9	0
10	Enter 20% (.20) of the amount allowed as a specific exemption for gifts made after September 8, 1976, and before January 1, 1977 (see instructions)	10	
11	Balance (subtract line 10 from line 9)	11	0
12	Unified credit (enter the smaller of line 6 or line 11)	12	0
13	Credit for foreign gift taxes (see instructions)	13	
14	Total credits (add lines 12 and 13)	14	0
15	Balance (subtract line 14 from line 6) (do not enter less than zero)	15	0
16	Generation-skipping transfer taxes (from Schedule C, Part 3, col. H, total)	16	
17	Total tax (add lines 15 and 16)	17	0
18	Gift and generation-skipping transfer taxes prepaid with extension of time to file	18	
19	If line 18 is less than line 17, enter BALANCE DUE (see instructions)	19	0
20	If line 18 is greater than line 17, enter AMOUNT TO BE REFUNDED	20	0

Under penalties of perjury, I declare that I have examined this return, including any accompanying schedules and statements, and to the best of my knowledge and belief it is true, correct, and complete. Declaration of preparer (other than donor) is based on all information of which preparer has any knowledge.

Donor's signature ► _____ Date ► _____

Preparer's signature (other than donor) ► _____ Date ► _____

Preparer's address (other than donor) ► _____

Please attach check or money order here

For Paperwork Reduction Act Notice, see page 1 of the separate instructions for this form.

Form **709** (Rev. 10-90)

Prepared by Goldstein Golub Kessler & Company, P.C., New York, New York

Figure 7.1. Sample Gift Tax Return.

SCHEDULE A   **Computation of Taxable Gifts**

Part 1.—Gifts Subject Only to Gift Tax. *Gifts less political organization, medical, and educational exclusions—see instructions*

A Item number	B Donee's name, relationship to donor (if any), and address and description of gift. If the gift was made by means of a trust, enter trust's identifying number below and attach a copy of the trust instrument. If the gift was securities, enter the CUSIP number(s), if available.	C Donor's adjusted basis of gift	D Date of gift	E Value at date of gift	
1	John Q. Taxpayer, Jr. 123 Main Street Anywhere, USA 12345 Child 100 Shares ABC Corp.	5000	12/1/90	20,000	
2	Mary I. Taxpayer 123 Main Street Anywhere, USA 12345 Child 100 Shares ABC Corp.	5000	12/1/90	20,000	

Part 2.—Gifts Which are Direct Skips and are Subject to Both Gift Tax and Generation-Skipping Transfer Tax. You must list the gifts in chronological order. *Gifts less political organization, medical, and educational exclusions—see instructions.* (Also list here direct skips that are subject only to the GST tax at this time as the result of the termination of an "estate tax inclusion period." See instructions.)

A Item number	B Donee's name, relationship to donor (if any), and address and description of gift. If the gift was made by means of a trust, enter trust's identifying number below and attach a copy of the trust instrument. If the gift was securities, enter the CUSIP number(s), if available.	C Donor's adjusted basis of gift	D Date of gift	E Value at date of gift	
1					

Part 3.—Gift Tax Reconciliation

1	Total value of gifts of donor (add column E of Parts 1 and 2)	1	40,000
2	One-half of items __1 and 2__ attributable to spouse (see instructions)	2	20,000
3	Balance (subtract line 2 from line 1)	3	20,000
4	Gifts of spouse to be included (from Schedule A, Part 3, line 2 of spouse's return—see instructions)	4	NONE
	If any of the gifts included on this line are also subject to the generation-skipping transfer tax, check here ▶ ☐ and enter those gifts also on Schedule C, Part 1.		
5	Total gifts (add lines 3 and 4)	5	20,000
6	Total annual exclusions for gifts listed on Schedule A (including line 4, above) (see instructions) . .	6	20,000
7	Total included amount of gifts (subtract line 6 from line 5).	7	NONE

Deductions (see instructions)

8	Gifts of interests to spouse for which a marital deduction will be claimed, based on items _____ of Schedule A . . .	8		
9	Exclusions attributable to gifts on line 8	9		
10	Marital deduction—subtract line 9 from line 8	10		
11	Charitable deduction, based on items _____ to _____ less exclusions .	11		
12	Total deductions—add lines 10 and 11		12	
13	Subtract line 12 from line 7.		13	NONE
14	Generation-skipping transfer taxes payable with this Form 709 (from Schedule C, Part 3, col. H, Total)		14	
15	Taxable gifts (add lines 13 and 14). Enter here and on line 1 of the Tax Computation on page 1 . . .		15	NONE

(If more space is needed, attach additional sheets of same size.)

Figure 7.1. *Continued.*

United States Gift (and Generation-Skipping Transfer) Tax Return

(Section 6019 of the Internal Revenue Code) (For gifts made after December 31, 1989, and before January 1, 1993)

Calendar year 19 _____

▶ **See separate instructions. For Privacy Act Notice, see the Instructions for Form 1040.**

OMB No. 1545-0020
Expires 8-31-93

1 Donor's first name and middle initial	2 Donor's last name	3 Social security number
Mary Q.	Taxpayer	001 23 4567

4 Address (number, street, and apartment number)	5 Domicile
123 Main Street	USA

6 City, state, and ZIP code	7 Citizenship
Anywhere, USA 12345	USA

Part 1.—General Information

	Yes	No
8 If the donor died during the year, check here ▶ ☐ and enter date of death _____ 19 ____		
9 If you received an extension of time to file this Form 709, check here ▶ ☐ and attach the Form 4868, 2688, 2350, or extension letter. ☐		
10 Enter the total number of separate donees listed on Schedule A—count each person only once		
11 If you (the donor) filed a previous Form 709 (or 709-A), has your address changed since the last Form 709 (or 709-A) was filed?		X
12 Gifts by husband or wife to third parties.—Do you consent to have the gifts (including generation-skipping transfers) made by you and by your spouse to third parties during the calendar year considered as made one-half by each of you? (See instructions.) (If the answer is "Yes," the following information must be furnished and your spouse is to sign the consent shown below. If the answer is "No," skip lines 13–18 and go to Schedule A.).	X	

13 Name of consenting spouse John Taxpayer	14 SSN 123-45-6789

	Yes	No
15 Were you married to one another during the entire calendar year? (See instructions.)	X	
16 If the answer to 15 is "No," check whether ☐ married ☐ divorced or ☐ widowed, and give date (see instructions) ▶		
17 Will a gift tax return for this calendar year be filed by your spouse?		X

18 **Consent of Spouse**—I consent to have the gifts (and generation-skipping transfers) made by me and by my spouse to third parties during the calendar year considered as made one-half by each of us. We are both aware of the joint and several liability for tax created by the execution of this consent.

Consenting spouse's signature ▶   Date ▶

Part 2.—Tax Computation

1	Enter the amount from Schedule A, Part 3, line 15	0
2	Enter the amount from Schedule B, line 3	0
3	Total taxable gifts (add lines 1 and 2)	0
4	Tax computed on amount on line 3 (see Table for Computing Tax in separate instructions)	0
5	Tax computed on amount on line 2 (see Table for Computing Tax in separate instructions)	0
6	Balance (subtract line 5 from line 4)	0
7	Maximum unified credit (nonresident aliens, see instructions)	192,800 00
8	Enter the unified credit against tax allowable for all prior periods (from Sch. B, line 1, col. C) .	0
9	Balance (subtract line 8 from line 7)	0
10	Enter 20% (.20) of the amount allowed as a specific exemption for gifts made after September 8, 1976, and before January 1, 1977 (see instructions)	
11	Balance (subtract line 10 from line 9)	0
12	Unified credit (enter the smaller of line 6 or line 11)	0
13	Credit for foreign gift taxes (see instructions)	
14	Total credits (add lines 12 and 13)	0
15	Balance (subtract line 14 from line 6) (do not enter less than zero)	0
16	Generation-skipping transfer taxes (from Schedule C, Part 3, col. H, total)	
17	Total tax (add lines 15 and 16)	0
18	Gift and generation-skipping transfer taxes prepaid with extension of time to file . . .	
19	If line 18 is less than line 17, enter BALANCE DUE (see instructions)	0
20	If line 18 is greater than line 17, enter AMOUNT TO BE REFUNDED	0

Under penalties of perjury, I declare that I have examined this return, including any accompanying schedules and statements, and to the best of my knowledge and belief it is true, correct, and complete. Declaration of preparer (other than donor) is based on all information of which preparer has any knowledge.

Donor's signature ▶   Date ▶

Preparer's signature (other than donor) ▶   Date ▶

Preparer's address (other than donor) ▶

Please attach check or money order here

For Paperwork Reduction Act Notice, see page 1 of the separate instructions for this form.

Form **709** (Rev. 10-90)

Figure 7.1. *Continued.*

SCHEDULE A   **Computation of Taxable Gifts**

Part 1.—Gifts Subject Only to Gift Tax. *Gifts less political organization, medical, and educational exclusions—see instructions*

A Item number	B Donee's name, relationship to donor (if any), and address and description of gift. If the gift was made by means of a trust, enter trust's identifying number below and attach a copy of the trust instrument. If the gift was securities, enter the CUSIP number(s), if available.	C Donor's adjusted basis of gift	D Date of gift	E Value at date of gift
1				

Part 2.—Gifts Which are Direct Skips and are Subject to Both Gift Tax and Generation-Skipping Transfer Tax. You must list the gifts in chronological order. *Gifts less political organization, medical, and educational exclusions—see instructions. (Also list here direct skips that are subject only to the GST tax at this time as the result of the termination of an "estate tax inclusion period." See instructions.)*

A Item number	B Donee's name, relationship to donor (if any), and address and description of gift. If the gift was made by means of a trust, enter trust's identifying number below and attach a copy of the trust instrument. If the gift was securities, enter the CUSIP number(s), if available.	C Donor's adjusted basis of gift	D Date of gift	E Value at date of gift
1				

Part 3.—Gift Tax Reconciliation

1	Total value of gifts of donor (add column E of Parts 1 and 2)	**1**	
2	One-half of items _____attributable to spouse (see instructions)	**2**	
3	Balance (subtract line 2 from line 1)	**3**	
4	Gifts of spouse to be included (from Schedule A, Part 3, line 2 of spouse's return—see instructions) .	**4**	20,000
	If any of the gifts included on this line are also subject to the generation-skipping transfer tax, check here ► ☐ and enter those gifts also on Schedule C, Part 1.		
5	Total gifts (add lines 3 and 4)	**5**	20,000
6	Total annual exclusions for gifts listed on Schedule A (including line 4, above) (see instructions) . .	**6**	20,000
7	Total included amount of gifts (subtract line 6 from line 5).	**7**	NONE

Deductions (see instructions)

8	Gifts of interests to spouse for which a marital deduction will be claimed, based on items _____ of Schedule A . . .	**8**		
9	Exclusions attributable to gifts on line 8	**9**		
10	Marital deduction—subtract line 9 from line 8	**10**		
11	Charitable deduction, based on items _____ to _____ less exclusions .	**11**		
12	Total deductions—add lines 10 and 11		**12**	
13	Subtract line 12 from line 7		**13**	NONE
14	Generation-skipping transfer taxes payable with this Form 709 (from Schedule C, Part 3, col. H, Total)		**14**	
15	Taxable gifts (add lines 13 and 14). Enter here and on line 1 of the Tax Computation on page 1 . . .		**15**	NONE

(If more space is needed, attach additional sheets of same size.)

Figure 7.1.   *Continued.*

8 GENERATION-SKIPPING TRANSFER TAX

The generation-skipping transfer, or GST, tax, is exceptionally complicated and can be confiscatory in nature in some situations. The purpose of the GST tax is to equalize inter-generational property transfer taxes.

It is only the very wealthy who can afford to substantially endow not one, but two successive generations. This extreme wealth creates an advantage over less wealthy taxpayers. When a less wealthy taxpayer leaves an inheritance to a child, the taxpayer's estate pays an estate tax. On the child's death, the child's estate pays an estate tax. Only after being subjected to two estate taxes will the grandchild's inheritance be received. This is the advantage the GST tax seeks to offset.

EXAMPLE: Grandpa is very wealthy. On his death he leaves $2 million to each of his five children and another $1 million to each of his eight grandchildren. If Grandpa had not been so wealthy, he probably would have left most of his assets to his children. Because Grandpa can leave assets directly to his grandchildren, he effectively avoids the estate tax that would be due on this property if it had gone into his children's estate. The generation-skipping transfer tax attempts to prevent the very wealthy from obtaining this benefit of skipping one (or more if gifts are made to great-grandchildren or even later generations) level of estate taxes.

WHAT IS A GENERATION-SKIPPING TRANSFER?

The simplest example of a generation-skipping transfer is when you give your grandchild property. More technically, the GST tax applies when there is a transfer of property (or income from property) to a person who is considered to be a member of a generation at least two generations below the generation of the person making the gift. For example, if you're generation #1, your child is generation #2, your grandchild is generation #3. If you make a gift to your grandchild, this would be a gift to a member of a generation at least two generations below your generation. A gift to your child would not apply.

This person from generation #3 or below is called a "skip person." A trust established for the benefit of a person from generation #3 is considered a skip person, and a trust is also considered a skip person when no distributions can be made to nonskip persons. A "nonskip person" is someone who is less than two generations below the generation of the person making the gift, such as your child or sibling (no GST tax is charged on a transfer to a nonskip person).

If your child has died and a grandchild survives, your grandchild will not be considered a skip person so that a transfer to your grandchild won't trigger the GST tax.

HOW THE GST TAX WORKS

The GST tax is charged on every generation-skipping transfer. It is calculated as a flat 55 percent tax rate on the taxable amount of a generation-skipping transfer.

EXAMPLE: You become a grandmother and wish to give your grandchild a $1 million gift (cash, an interest in a property, or another asset). The GST tax, assuming you have used up your $1 million lifetime exemption (see below), is in the maximum tax bracket and comes to $550,000! Further, the GST tax paid by you is considered to be a gift to your grandchild as well. So the gift tax to be paid on the $1 million transfer is based on a total gift of $1,550,000 [$1 million actual gift + $550,000 GST tax, which is deemed to be a further gift]. At the 55 percent maximum gift tax rate, you will owe a gift tax of $852,500. To make the $1 million gift you will have had to pay taxes totaling $1,402,500 [$550,000 GST tax + $852,500 gift tax]. Thus, the total cost of making the $1 million gift will have been $2,402,500.

For the GST tax to apply, there must be a generation-skipping transfer, but the tax can apply to a broad range of property transfers. These may include transfers of property in trust (such as a gift to a trust established for a grandchild), life estates (for example, a child has the right to income from the property for life, and on the child's death a grandchild receives the property), and so forth.

This means that the use of a trust in estate and gift tax planning becomes more complex when the beneficiaries are grandchildren instead of children. Suppose a single trust is established for both a child and a grandchild, and the child dies. The death of the child will trigger a direct skip of the trust corpus to the grandchild as the sole remaining beneficiary and thus will trigger the GST tax.

To summarize, there are three events that can trigger the GST tax:

1. *A taxable distribution.* When there is a distribution of property or money from a trust to a skip person, as in a gift, the GST tax may apply. The tax is based on the fair value of the property transferred, reduced by any expenses incurred in connection with determining the GST tax. If the GST tax is paid out of a trust, the amount of tax paid is treated as an additional distribution subject to the tax. The GST tax on a taxable distribution is charged against the property that was given, unless specific provisions are made

for a different treatment. The transferee (your grandchild for purposes of the discussion), however, is liable to pay the GST tax.

2. *A taxable termination.* A taxable termination occurs when the interests of a beneficiary of a trust (the person entitled to receive income from a trust, such as a child) terminate as a result of a death, lapse of time, or release of a power (right). This event will result in a GST tax unless one of the following cases applies:

- Immediately after the termination, a nonskip person (such as a sibling) has an interest in the property.

- No distribution can be made to a skip person (there are no grandchildren). The GST Tax on a taxable termination is payable by the trustee of the trust. The amount of tax is calculated based on the value of all property to which the taxable termination applies, reduced by expenses, debts, and taxes. For example, you establish a trust for the benefit of your child. Upon the child's death, the assets of the trust are held for the benefit of the grandchild. If at the death of the child, there is no person of the same generation as the child, the value of the trust will be considered to have been transferred in a transaction subject to the GST tax.

3. *A direct skip.* A direct skip is a transfer of an interest in property that is subject to the estate or gift tax to a skip person. The GST tax for a direct skip is to be paid by the person making the transfer (probably you). For example, if you transfer property to an irrevocable (cannot be changed) trust for the benefit of your grandchild, since the transfer is a gift for federal gift tax purposes, and a direct skip, it will trigger the GST tax.

Once it's been determined that a gift is a generation-skipping transfer, the GST tax must be calculated. For tax purposes, the property is generally valued at the time the generation-skipping transfer occurred. However, if the transfer was a direct skip and the property was included in your gross estate, the special valuation rules your estate uses will apply to the GST as well. When the transfer also triggers a gift tax, the amount of GST tax paid by the donor is treated as a further gift subject to the gift tax. Once the tax has been calculated, a credit for taxes paid to your state may be available. This will occur when the GST tax occurs by reason of a taxable distribution or a taxable termination at the time of your death. You're also entitled to a $1 million exemption, discussed below.

PLANNING CONSIDERATIONS

A number of planning approaches that can help you avoid the confiscatory GST tax are available:

- *Annual per donee gift tax exclusion.* You can give up to $10,000 of assets ($20,000 if your spouse joins in the gift) in any year to any recipient without triggering the gift tax (Chapter 7). Transfers that are exempt under this $10,000/$20,000 rule may also avoid the GST tax. Over a number of years, this can result in a substantial transfer—without incurring any GST tax.

  It is possible, however, that a transfer would qualify for the annual $10,000 gift tax exclusion but would not be exempt from the GST tax. The $10,000 annual exclusion is only available for GST tax purposes on a direct-skip transfer. This is a gift directly to a grandchild (or later generation) or, in some instances, to a trust for a grandchild. It doesn't apply to a taxable termination or a taxable distribution.

EXAMPLE: Grandparent has one son with two grandchildren. Grandparent gifts $30,000 to a trust for the benefit of all three heirs. He may have a GST problem, depending on the terms of the trust. Each beneficiary should have a Crummey demand power in order for Grandparent to qualify for the annual gift tax exclusion on the entire transfer. After the demand power lapses, the trustee can make distributions to the son and grandchildren. When the trustee has a sprinkling power between generations, there is a GST problem. Even without such a power, if distributions will skip a generation when the interest of the middle generation (the son) terminates (for example, at the son's death or at his attaining age 35, when the trust instrument requires a distribution to the grand-children), a GST tax will be triggered.

- *Transfers for educational and medical benefits.* You can gift unlimited amounts of money to pay for a grandchild's education or medical benefits. Although this provides important planning benefits, it will not help you transfer investment properties or business assets to future generations.

- *Million-dollar exemption.* A once-in-a-lifetime exemption from the GST tax of $1 million is allowed. Under this, you can transfer up to $1 million of property or other assets to grandchildren without triggering a GST tax. This $1 million exemption can be allocated by you or your executor. Many taxpayers plan for this exemption by setting up multiple trusts under their wills and granting their executors the authority to make certain decisions. This provides the maximum amount of planning flexibility. Given the importance of this exemption, a detailed discussion of its use follows.

- *Other exempt transfers.* Transfers are also excluded under any of the following conditions: (1) The property transferred was subject to the GST tax before; (2) the transferee (recipient) in that prior transfer was a member of the same generation as the current transferee; and (3) the transfer does not have the effect of avoiding the GST tax.

ALLOCATING YOUR $1 MILLION GST TAX EXEMPTION

There are some important restrictions on how you use the once-in-a-lifetime $1 million exclusion from the GST tax: (1) This exclusion must be irrevocably allocated to any property transfers you make. (2) This allocation is generally made on your gift tax return. (3) The allocation method used can't be changed. This means the portion of the exclusion used must be designated at the time of the transfer, and, once designated, it cannot be revoked.

To understand the use of the $1 million exemption, another bit of jargon must be introduced, the "inclusion ratio." The GST tax exemption percentage (the inclusion ratio) is set at the time when you make the gift and allocate your exemption. The inclusion ratio is [1 – the applicable fraction]. The applicable fraction, when you make the gift to a trust, is determined as follows:

$$\frac{\text{Amount of GST Exemption Allocated to Trust}}{\text{Value of Property Transferred to the Trust}}$$

EXAMPLE: You set up a $1 million trust fund for your grandchildren and great-grandchildren. You allocate your entire $1 million GST tax exemption to the trust. The assets of the trust appreciate to $10 million before being distributed in a taxable distribution or termination. None of the transfers of the $10 million in trust property to your children and grandchildren is subject to the GST tax, because the applicable fraction is 1, and the inclusion ratio is zero.

Using a Trust

One approach to addressing the potential GST tax is to allocate some portion of the $1 million GST tax exemption to a trust. Deciding how much of your exemption should be allocated is extremely complicated. Any portion that you allocate is considered used, whether or not a GST tax is ever incurred. If no tax is incurred, you've wasted that portion of your exemption. For example, if the trust in the above example declined to $600,000, rather than growing to $10 million, you would have wasted $400,000 of your exemption. All you really can do is to analyze all the relevant factors and estimate the likelihood of the trust's incurring a GST tax. If it appears likely that the trust will incur the tax, then you should wager some of your exemption on the trust. If the likelihood of a GST tax appears small, you should preserve your GST tax exemption for other planning opportunities.

EXAMPLE: Grandparent transfers $100,000 in trust with income to his son for life, the remainder to go to his two grandchildren on the son's death. Assume that Grandparent doesn't allocate any of his GST tax exemption on the gift tax return. Suppose that when the son dies, the trust property will be worth $500,000. The inclusion ratio is 100 percent. The IRS will collect a $275,000 tax, calculated at the flat rate of 55 percent.

Assume a different scenario: If Grandparent allocates $100,000 of his $1 million GST tax exemption against the $100,000 transfer to the trust when he makes the gift, the inclusion ratio will be zero; the entire $500,000 will pass free of the onerous GST tax.

Under a third scenario, assume that Grandparent makes the same gift, but he allocates $50,000 of his exemption against the transfer. The inclusion ratio is 50 percent. If a GST tax is imposed, it will be imposed at 50 percent of the usual rate, because 50 percent of the trust is exempt. On the death of the son, the GST tax will only be $137,500.

Using a Will

Another approach is to set up a GST tax exemption trust (or trusts) under your will. Consider the following options:

- This trust can be set up as a qualified terminal interest property (Q-TIP) trust, which would provide your surviving spouse the right to all of the income, at least annually, from the trust and a limited right to invade the principal for his or her benefit. Any invasions of principal, however, will reduce (and perhaps waste) the maximum GST tax exemption. In a very large estate, it is preferable that principal not be invaded unless it is absolutely necessary in order to preserve your full $1 million exemption.

- You could also provide for the establishment of two GST tax trusts. The first trust would be equal to the amount of the unused unified credit (a credit shelter trust for $600,000 if no unified credit is used prior to death). The executor could then allocate $600,000 of the GST exemption to this trust. This transfer would not trigger any estate tax because of the unified credit. A second trust could be provided under the will to absorb the remaining, or excess, GST exemption amount (most likely $400,000 left of the $1 million exemption, where $600,000 is included in the above trust). This would be a Q-TIP trust, which would avoid any estate tax because of the unlimited marital deduction.

- A third approach is to establish two GST tax trusts, of which one is wholly exempt and one wholly nonexempt. Distributions to children could be made from the nonexempt trust so that none of the GST exemption amount would be wasted. Distributions to children would then only be made out of the wholly exempt trust in an emergency and after depletion of the nonexempt trust.

When planning for the GST tax, your attorney should also consider the tax allocation clause in your will. Taxes should generally be paid out of a portion of the residuary (or other bequests), which won't result in wasting any of your GST tax exemption.

CONCLUSION

The GST tax can have a horrendous impact on your ability to transfer substantial property interests to later generations. Proper use of techniques, such as the judicious use of annual exclusions and the $1 million exemption, and the doubling of these benefits by joining with a spouse in making various transfers, all can help circumvent this tax.

Part Three

PLANNING FOR SPECIAL PEOPLE/BENEFICIARIES

9 SPOUSE

The estate and gift tax laws provide especially favorable treatment to married couples. As a result, every couple can readily avoid any estate tax on the death of the first spouse simply by leaving everything to the second (although it is not always the best approach—see below). The concept behind this favoritism is that married couples are viewed for tax purposes as a partnership, a single economic unit. All assets of the marital economic unit will be subject to the estate tax after the deaths of the two spouses. This same principle is behind the filing of a joint income tax return by a married couple.

While there is logic and equity in this concept, these same benefits are denied to any couple whose relationship is not technically one of marriage. Although these couples may be as much of a single economic entity as a married couple, the tax laws do not recognize this, and nonmarried couples have no access to the marital deduction. As a result, nonmarried couples should use as substitutes, albeit inadequate substitutes, an aggressive gift program and trust arrangements for removing assets from their estates, and to provide for their partner.

HOW THE MARITAL DEDUCTION WORKS

The marital deduction can be explained simply: When your estate makes a transfer to your spouse, or to certain trusts for the benefit of your spouse, the amounts transferred are deducted from the value of your gross estate. However, a number of requirements must be met in order for a transfer to qualify for the estate tax marital deduction.

- The surviving spouse must be a United States citizen (see Chapter 10).
- The amount of the interest involved must be included in your gross estate.
- The property that is intended to qualify for the marital deduction must pass from you to your surviving spouse. For example, if a state death tax must be paid on the property given to your surviving spouse, the amount of this tax won't qualify for the marital deduction because it didn't pass to your surviving spouse.

- The property interest passing to your surviving spouse must be a deductible interest.
- The rights and property transferred to your spouse cannot be what is called a terminable interest. This is an interest that will terminate or fail as the result of the passing of time, the occurrence of an event or contingency, or the failure of an event or contingency to occur. For example, if you transfer property to a trust for the benefit of your spouse but there is a condition that if your spouse remarries the trust will end and all of the property will be distributed to your natural children, this is a contingency that will cause the interests to fail. In such a case, the transfer to the trust won't qualify for the marital deduction.

Exceptions from the Terminable-Interest Rule

There are some exceptions from the terminable-interest rule. One is if the termination would be caused by the death of the surviving spouse within six months of your death, or as a result of a common disaster. A second is if your surviving spouse is given a life estate coupled with a power of appointment in the property. This approach requires that your surviving spouse be given the right to all of the income for life, payable at least annually. In addition, your surviving spouse must have the power, exercisable by him or her alone, to appoint the entire interest in the property as he or she chooses.

The most important exception to the rule denying a marital deduction for property interests that may terminate is provided for Q-TIP property.

The Q-TIP Trust

The value of the Q-TIP technique is that your estate can qualify for the estate tax marital deduction without your having to give complete control over the assets to your spouse. You still will be able to exert important controls over the use and ultimate disposition of the property. But the following requirements must be met:

- Your spouse is given a life estate in particular property.
- Your spouse has the right to all of the income from that property payable at least annually.
- The property must pass from you.
- No person has a power to appoint any part of the property to any person other than the surviving spouse.
- The necessary election is made by your executor to have the property qualify.

On the death of the surviving spouse the entire value of the Q-TIP property is included in his or her gross estate. These assets will be taxed at his or her top marginal tax bracket.

SHOULD THE MARITAL BEQUEST BE MADE OUT RIGHT OR IN TRUST?

To a great extent it is a personal decision whether to make the bequest directly or in trust. The advantages and disadvantages of using a trust generally should be reviewed (see Chapter 4). When there is any concern that the surviving spouse will remarry and deprive your natural children of an inheritance, the Q-TIP approach is ideal. Another reason is if you have children from a prior marriage whom you wish to benefit. The use of a Q-TIP technique to provide for your current spouse will ensure that your children from your previous marriage will inherit assets as well (see Chapter 13). Remember that if the objective is to obtain the marital deduction, any gift in trust must be structured to avoid the terminable-interest rule discussed above.

There is another reason to use the Q-TIP trust: When your estate is very large, and planning is undertaken to use your $1 million exemption from the generation-skipping transfer tax, this exemption can be tied in with your marital deduction. For example, a $1 million Q-TIP trust can be left to your surviving spouse, with the remainder going to your grandchildren and using up your exemption (see Chapter 8).

HOW MUCH OF THE MARITAL DEDUCTION SHOULD BE USED IN THE ESTATE OF THE FIRST SPOUSE TO DIE?

There is no requirement to claim the maximum marital deduction to which your estate is entitled. It is often not the best approach to do so. How much marital deduction should be used depends on a number of considerations, including three basic factors:

1. *The amount of time that will pass between the deaths of the first and second spouse.* When the deaths of the two spouses are not expected to be far apart, there may be an advantage to incurring an estate tax cost in your estate (rather than passing huge assets to your spouse's estate) in order to take advantage of the graduated estate tax rates—37% to 55%. The point to consider here is whether sufficient time will pass from your death to your spouse's death so that enough income can be earned on the extra assets you would pass to the surviving spouse to more than compensate for a higher estate tax due on the death of the surviving spouse.

   If, however, your spouse is much younger than you, so that 20 years could pass before his or her death, it may make sense simply to pass all assets to the surviving spouse. On a present-value basis, any additional tax cost that might be incurred by bunching assets in the surviving spouse's estate will be negligible.

2. *The size of the estate.* If the total marital estate is likely to be less than the $600,000 unified credit on the death of the second spouse for tax purposes, your entire estate can be left directly to the surviving spouse.

NOTE: This does not mean that the gross assets of your surviving spouse (those owned directly and inherited from you) must be less than $600,000. When small children are involved, even a projected estate in excess of $1 million for the surviving spouse may not be expected to trigger a tax in the second estate. Substantial costs may be incurred in raising and educating the children, thus depleting the estate. Further, the surviving spouse can use the annual gift tax exclusion to reduce the assets in the estate.

In most large estates, it's advantageous to utilize the $600,000 unified credit in both spouses' estates. The proper use of the unified credit in the estate of the first spouse to die will keep those assets free of tax in the first estate and ensure that they do not even enter the surviving spouse's estate. In these cases, it is not advisable to use a marital deduction to the extent that it results in a decrease of the unified credit.

The classic zero-tax approach is to establish a credit shelter trust (the assets in it are sheltered from estate tax by the unified credit), or bypass trust (it bypasses the surviving spouse's estate). In this trust are $600,000 of assets. The trustee is given the right to sprinkle income to the surviving spouse and children, and certain principal invasion rights, perhaps limited by an ascertainable standard, are given to the trustee. The remainder of the estate can be given outright or in a Q-TIP trust to the wife. No estate tax will be due.

3. *The nature of the assets.* If the assets already in your surviving spouse's estate are likely to appreciate rapidly, it may prove costly to add more assets to the second estate.

CONCLUSION

For married couples, the marital deduction can be the most important planning technique used to minimize the overall estate and transfer tax burden of the family. However, simply claiming the maximum marital deduction (all property to your spouse on your death, and vice versa) is almost never the optimal approach when you and your spouse have significant assets (in excess of $600,000).

10 NON-U.S. CITIZEN SPOUSE

If your spouse is not a United States citizen (he or she is an alien), there will be important implications to your estate planning.

> **EXAMPLE:** Your wife was born in Australia, and even though she has established permanent residence in New Jersey, she has never given up her Australian citizenship to become a United States citizen. She is considered to be a noncitizen, or alien.

TAX RULES AFFECTING THE NONCITIZEN

If your foreign-born spouse is a United States resident but not a citizen, he or she will be taxed in the same manner as a United States citizen for federal income tax purposes. If your spouse were to make a gift of property abroad (outside of the United States), he or she would be subject to the gift tax like any United States citizen (Chapter 7). Therefore, your spouse also would be entitled to split gifts with you, so that you could make a gift of up to $20,000 in a year to one recipient, which would be treated as a gift by each of you of $10,000, exempted by the annual exclusion. Should your spouse predecease you, his or her estate would be entitled to the marital deduction on bequests and transfers to you. On your spouse's death, his or her entire estate would be taxable, even including property that was disposed of prior to his or her becoming a resident.

ESTATE TAX MARITAL DEDUCTION FOR A NONCITIZEN SPOUSE

The estate tax provides for an unlimited deduction for qualifying transfers and bequests to a surviving spouse. This deduction can be used to eliminate any estate tax on the death of the first spouse to die. Unfortunately, this is not available when the surviving spouse is a noncitizen. If you die, your assets passing by will (or intestacy) to a surviving spouse who is not a citizen of the United States will not qualify for the unlimited estate tax marital deduction that is available to United States citizens.

Some solace for this tax cost is offered through a credit provision. If you bequeath property to your noncitizen spouse, and that property transfer is subjected to the estate tax but would not have been taxed if your surviving spouse had been a citizen, a credit will be available to your spouse's estate on his or her death. This credit will be for the tax paid by your estate on the earlier transfer to your noncitizen spouse, which did not qualify for the marital deduction.

The applicable gift tax provisions specify that the unlimited marital deduction will not be available for a gift to the noncitizen spouse. Since July 14, 1988, however, a gift of up to $100,000 per year can be made to a noncitizen spouse without incurring a gift tax, because the annual per donee gift tax exclusion is increased from $10,000 to $100,000. The gift tax will be imposed in full beyond this point. To qualify, the gift must be one of a present interest. This provision means that substantial assets can be transferred to the noncitizen spouse during your life, if necessary, to effect any estate planning objectives.

There is another restriction on noncitizens that could serve to increase the estate tax cost for you and your spouse. When the surviving spouse is a noncitizen and you own property as tenants by the entirety (the marital residence is usually owned in this manner), your estate (that is, the estate of the citizen spouse) is taxed on the entire value of the jointly owned asset. Your estate can only avoid this taxation if it can be demonstrated that your spouse contributed to the purchase of the house (see Chapter 20).

EXCEPTION FOR ASSETS TRANSFERRED INTO A QUALIFIED DOMESTIC TRUST

An important exception to the above rule exists: When the assets are passed into a qualified domestic trust (Q-DOT), the marital deduction will be available without limit. To qualify, a Q-DOT must meet the following four general requirements:

1. All trustees must be either United States citizens or corporations. This requirement must be noted in the trust documents. Provisions should be made for alternate trustees to assure compliance with this requirement. For example, a final alternate could be a United States bank or trust company.

2. The surviving spouse must be entitled to all of the income from the trust. This income must be payable at least annually. This rule is similar to the rules applicable to a qualified terminal interest trust (Q-TIP) used by many citizens as part of their estate planning.

3. The trust must meet additional requirements, which are to be prescribed by regulations that the IRS will issue in the future. For trusts organized prior to the publication of these regulations, the approach used has been to tailor the trust document to a conservative interpretation of the standards that Congress indicated should apply when it passed this law. The objective of these regulations will be to keep sufficient assets subject to the United States taxing jurisdiction to ensure that the taxes ultimately due will be collected.

4. Your executor must make an irrevocable election on the United States estate tax return with respect to the trust. However, your executor is not required to make the election. The executor's right to make or not make this election should appear in your will or in the Q-DOT trust.

Estate tax will be levied on distributions of principal (corpus) from the Q-DOT. This tax will be calculated as if the amount distributed had been included in the estate of the citizen (and first-to-die) spouse. This calculation adds all prior distributions from the Q-DOT to your taxable estate in order to push the tax on the Q-DOT distributions into the highest federal estate tax brackets. This calculation and tax requirement also will somewhat complicate the administration of the Q-DOT. An exception is provided for certain hardship distributions. In addition, a tax will be assessed on the property remaining in the Q-DOT upon the death of the second spouse. This tax is calculated in the same manner.

PLANNING CONSIDERATIONS

One planning approach is for your spouse and you each to take advantage of your $600,000 unified credits by having each spouse's will transfer up to $600,000 of assets to a nonmarital trust (that is, a trust designed not to qualify for the unlimited marital tax deduction in the case of your spouse, and a trust designed not to qualify as a Q-DOT for your assets). This trust could provide income and certain invasion-of-principal rights to the surviving spouse for life. On the death of the surviving spouse, the assets in the nonmarital trust would go to the children. If the estate is divided evenly (with consideration to the special rule affecting the marital residence), this planning approach could eliminate any estate tax, depending on the size of the estate. If you and your spouse truly are confident that you can live without the assets given, start an annual gift program to transfer assets to your children.

Another consideration should address the couple's insurance assets, and needs. A second-to-die insurance policy could address the issue of an estate tax on the death of the second spouse (see Chapter 19).

CONCLUSION

Planning is imperative to avoid what could be a substantial estate tax when one spouse is not a United States citizen. One route is for the spouse to become a citizen. Otherwise, if you want to avoid United States estate tax beyond the use of the unified credit of $600,000, either a Q-DOT will be necessary for your noncitizen spouse, or a gift tax program will have to be begun to transfer assets via *inter vivos* gifts to the children and your spouse.

11 MINOR CHILDREN

A major focus of estate planning for most people is to provide for their children. This is particularly important when minor children are involved. The planning process involves a number of important decisions. Should assets be given to the children? If so, how much, and when? How should any gifts of assets be structured? The gifts could be made outright to the child (with no strings attached). While this is the simplest approach, it provides no protection in the event that the child is incapable of properly managing the assets. There is no protection from the child's misusing the assets, or from the effects of a potential divorce, or from creditors.

A safer approach is to place the gift in a trust. For example, assets held in a trust for the benefit of your married child may not be subject to equitable distribution (the laws addressing how property should be divided between divorcing spouses in many states). This will help preserve the assets for your family in the event that a child's marriage ends. But trusts have their shortcomings, too, which will be addressed in this chapter.

TO GIVE OR NOT TO GIVE

The first question to address is whether to make gifts to minor children. The parent has a moral, if not always legal, obligation to support the minor child. Above using such amounts as are needed for support, transferring assets directly to the child (or indirectly, for the child's benefit) becomes a personal decision. The natural desire to help your children, reinforced by the high estate tax rates, often provides adequate impetus to make gifts. If gifts are to be made, the next question is whether they should be made before death (*inter vivos*) or after death through your will (testamentary). From a pure planning perspective, lifetime gifts are often preferable, because they afford many more opportunities to minimize transfer taxes (estate, gift, and generation-skipping). Every taxpayer is allowed to give away $10,000 per year to an unlimited number of recipients. Gifts enable you to remove from your estate any increase in value occurring after the gift is made (see Part IV). Other advantages of gifts are illustrated throughout this book.

However, for any of the gift techniques to be effective, you really must part with all control over the assets given away (that is, you cannot count on being able to get back something you've given away, and if you can, you won't qualify for the intended tax benefits). Thus, you have to ask yourself carefully whether you can really afford to part with the assets you're giving away. Gift and estate planning can provide huge tax savings, but they should not be carried out at the cost of putting you, the parents, in financial jeopardy, or even discomfort.

One more question to address, a particularly difficult one, is the potential disinheritance of a child. If you are considering disinheriting a child, a great deal of thought should be given in drafting any provisions in a will or other document to achieve this. A will can be a very final document. If any hope of reconciliation exists, provide some means of recognizing this in your estate plan. It would be truly terrible for a parent to reconcile on his or her deathbed with a disinherited child and have no opportunity to correct the inheritance plan.

HOW MANY STRINGS SHOULD YOU ATTACH?

Once you've made the decision to make gifts to your children during your lifetime, you must consider how those gifts should be made. There are five general possibilities which will be described briefly here and in detail in the rest of the chapter or in other chapters. The five approaches are the following:

1. Make an outright gift with no strings attached, other than the moral responsibility of child to parent. Because the money or other asset will be listed solely in the child's name, the child will be taxed directly on any income earned. You can give unlimited amounts toward your children's medical and educational costs without incurring any gift tax. This type of outright gift has the advantage of not raising concerns about how the child will use the money—that is, you've put it to proper use at the outset.

2. Set up a joint bank account or totten trust (see Chapter 20).

3. Gift the property to your child under your state's Uniform Gifts (or Transfers) to Minors Act. The child will be taxed directly on any income, and the kiddie tax must be considered.

4. Make the gift to a trust established for the benefit of your child. The trust and child (and other beneficiaries) will be taxed on the income of the trust as described in Chapter 4. You must also consider the gift tax consequences of a gift to a trust because it is more difficult to qualify for the annual $10,000 gift tax exclusion (see Chapter 7). Also, if the trust is not properly structured, there is a risk that the property given to the trust will be pulled back into your estate and taxed at the time of your death.

Another point is that to avoid an estate tax, the parent (or other person making the gift) must not have too much control over the trust assets, and should not use the trust funds to meet a parent's legal obligation to support the child. Many state laws require parents to support their children. When monies given to a trust are used for a child's educational, medical, or other obligations that the law requires the parent to meet, the income earned by the trust may be taxed to the parent.

5. Make a no- or low-interest loan to your child.

THE "KIDDIE TAX"—SPECIAL TAX RULES AFFECT CHILDREN UNDER 14

A common tax planning technique had been to give assets to your children that earned interest, dividends, or similar passive income. Because tax rates were progressive (lower percentages for lower income), a parent in a high tax bracket could benefit by transferring CDs, stock, and so forth, to a child and having the income taxed at the child's low tax bracket. Congress became concerned that this technique was being abused to provide a tax shelter for the wealthy. It responded with what became known as the "kiddie tax."

Definition

The kiddie tax assesses the net unearned income of a child under 14 at the parents' tax rate. The unearned income of your child includes income earned on assets (stocks, bonds, and the like) that are listed in your child's name, income earned on certain bank accounts bearing the child's and your name, income on Uniform Gifts to Minors Act accounts, and income distributed from trusts. The child's income is split into two components: earned income (for example, wages from a paper route) and unearned income. The child's earned income is taxed under the regular rules. The unearned income is reduced by the portion of the standard deduction that the child can claim, generally $500. However, if the child has itemized deductions relating to earned income of more than $500, this larger amount is applied to reduce the taxable unearned income. The result of this adjustment of earned income is called net unearned income, and this is the amount subject to the kiddie tax.

The kiddie tax works as follows: The unearned income of all your children is added to your income, and your income tax is recalculated. The difference between the tax figure you derive after the recalculation and the tax due on your return is the additional tax attributable to your children's unearned income. This additional tax is allocated among the children.

EXAMPLE: Parents' tax return shows a tax due of $43,567. Parents have two children, Tom and Jane, who have unearned income of $3,000 and $2,000, respectively. Each child's income above $1,000 can be subject to the kiddie tax, or $2,000 and $1,000 for Tom and Jane. If this additional $3,000 of income is added to Parents' tax return, their tax increases by $930 to $44,497 [$43,567 + $930]. Of this additional tax $620 is allocated pro-rata to Tom and the balance to Jane.

Rules

The kiddie tax rules can be summarized as follows:

- Wages your child may earn by working are not subject to the kiddie tax.
- The first $500 of your child's unearned income is offset by the child's standard deduction. The child is not permitted a personal exemption ($2,050 in 1990, and adjusted annually for inflation) if claimed as a dependent on the parents' tax return.
- The next $500 of unearned income is taxed to the child at his or her tax rate (probably 15 percent).
- Unearned income above this first $1,000 is taxed at the top tax rate of the parents, 31 percent, and perhaps higher.

A couple of scenarios illustrate how the kiddie tax operates:

EXAMPLE: Father gives Child $10,000 of stock, which generates dividends of $975. The first $500 is offset by the Child's $500 personal exemption. The next $475 is taxed at 15 percent. Child's tax can be calculated on Form 1040A.

In a different scenario, Mother also gives Child $10,000 of stock, which generates an additional $952 in dividends. Child's income now totals $1,927 [$975 + $952]. Child must file Form 8615, Computation of Tax for Children Under Age 14 Who Have Investment Income of More Than $1,000. The first $500 is not taxed as a result of Child's standard deduction. The next $500 is taxed at Child's tax rate, presumably 15 percent. The remaining income of $972 is taxed at the parents' tax rate.

Planning for the Kiddie Tax

When estate planning involves gifts to a child under age 14, the selection of an appropriate investment strategy can minimize the burden of the kiddie tax. Any assets are appropriate until the $1,000 income level is reached. After that point, you should give assets that will appreciate rather than generate current income. These can include growth stocks, raw land, and Series EE United States bonds. After the child reaches age 14, when the kiddie tax will no longer apply, these assets can be traded for income-producing assets. Gifts of tax-exempt bonds also avoid the kiddie tax. It may even be possible to employ the child in a family business because the child's standard deduction can be applied to offset earned income.

There is an election that can save the cost and paperwork of preparing a separate tax return for the child. In certain circumstances, a parent can simply report the child's income on the parent's tax return. To qualify for this treatment, the child's income must not be more than $5,000 and must consist only of interest and dividend income. Further, the child cannot have made estimated tax payments or be subject to the backup-withholding rules. A special form must be filed by the parent, Form 8814, Parent's Election To Report Child's Interest and Dividends. The parent will incur an additional $75 in tax to make this election. The election can have some valuable tax benefits—for example, when the parent has incurred interest expense that is subject to the investment interest limitation. This rule limits a taxpayer's current deduction for interest incurred to buy or carry investments to income generated by investment-type assets. If the child's interest and dividend income is added to the parent's, this additional deduction may be available to eliminate any tax on the income.

There are additional regulations when the child has a net loss from self-employment, claims a net-operating-loss deduction, or is subject to the alternative minimum tax. In such cases, you should consult your tax adviser.

UNIFORM GIFTS (TRANSFERS) TO MINORS ACT

One of the most commonly used "trust-type" arrangements is to make a gift to a child under the Uniform Gifts (or Transfers) to Minors Act (it's not a real trust because the child has title). Uniform Transfers to Minors Acts are similar to the Uniform Gifts to Minors Acts, but they are likely to be more recently enacted and broader in scope, permitting investments in real estate and other assets. These acts are often referred to by the acronyms UGMA or UTMA. In the following discussion reference will be made only to the Uniform Gifts to Minors Act; however, your lawyer can tell you which act your state has adopted, and advise you on any nuances.

No matter which of these approaches is used, it costs nothing and it's easy. To give a gift under your state's version of UGMA or UTMA, simply open a brokerage account or bank account and tell your broker or bank teller that you want the account name to reflect that the gift is being made under the Uniform Gifts (or Transfers) to Minors Act, with your name as guardian. You then administer the account for the child's benefit. When the child reaches the age of majority in your state (the age at which the child is considered to be an adult in financial matters), the assets will belong to the child.

CAUTION: Check with an attorney in your state for details concerning your state's laws.

Giving gifts to your children under the Uniform Gifts to Minors Act has a number of drawbacks that should be carefully considered. While this approach is often the preferred method for small transfers, as the size of assets placed in your child's name increases, a regular or traditional trust approach, described below, may be preferable. The time to switch is when the assets under consideration become large enough to justify the legal cost and formality of setting up a trust, as well as the filing of tax returns for the trust each year.

The following summary of rules of the Uniform Gifts to Minors Act highlights some of the shortcomings of this approach:

1. The effect of a gift made under a Uniform Gifts to Minors Act is to irrevocably transfer the property to the child and to indefeasibly vest legal title to the property in the child. This means you have to give up the property for keeps. Even if you're the child's guardian and the custodian for the account, you won't have any rights with respect to the property, except as specifically provided in the Uniform Gifts to Minors Act. As the custodian for the account, the powers you have may include the following: to collect, hold, manage, invest, and reinvest the custodial property; and to pay to your children, or to expend for their benefit, the amount reasonably advisable for their support, maintenance, education, and benefit.

2. There are a number of important restrictions on the custodian's rights. After reaching age 14, the minor can petition the court to have an accounting of the money, stock, or other assets in the UGMA account. After reaching age 14, the minor can petition the court to require the custodian to make payments for his or her support, maintenance, or education. This is a nuisance and cost to which few parents would knowingly subject themselves. To the extent that the custodial property isn't distributed for the benefit of the child as provided above, all of the property must be turned over to the child at age 18. Few, if any, parents willingly decide to turn over trust assets to a child at age 18. In fact, most parents tend to use trust agreements that spread the distribution of assets over a number of years, with the children receiving a certain percentage of the trust at ages 25 and 30, and the remainder at age 35. Many parents try to tie up assets even longer.

EXAMPLE: At 16, Child dropped out of school, moved away from home, and was cultivating a lifestyle that greatly worried her parents. When Child turned 18, the age of legal majority, she called her parents and insisted that they send her the entire balance of her Uniform Gifts to Minors Act account. Through fortunate stock investments in the 1980s, the once-modest holdings had reached a significant value. The parents were concerned because the money would enable Child to continue for a number of years unemployed and thus prolong her present lifestyle. Unfortunately, there was little the parents could do; the money was legally Child's, and she was entitled to it. If the assets had been invested in a trust, the trustee assuredly would have retained control beyond Child's 18th birthday and would have been able to spend the money in a manner that would be more helpful to Child. The only control the parents were able to exert was to pay for certain medical and other expenses that Child had incurred, which reduced the amount sent to her.

---

3. In order to designate a successor, a custodian must execute and date a written designation and have the document witnessed. This is a formality few parents bother with. In a trust agreement, by contrast, most lawyers insist that one or more alternate trustees be named in case the parents can no longer serve. This can be extremely important if the parent or other named guardian should become disabled or die while the child is still too young to handle his or her own financial affairs.

USING TRUSTS FOR MAKING GIFTS TO MINOR CHILDREN

By establishing a trust for your children while they're young, you can see how the trust works. If you don't like what you see, you can create a different trust for future gifts, or try a different approach altogether.

Requirements

Generally, to meet the estate planning objective of removing the gifted assets from your estate, the trust will have to meet two main requirements:

1. It has to be irrevocable. This means that if you're not fully pleased with its operation, you'll have to create a new trust to effect a change. Assuming that the trust provisions and operations are satisfactory, assets given (bequeathed) to your children under your will could be given (poured over) into the same trust. Further, stock in a family business (Chapter 16) or interests in a family real estate partnership (Chapter 15) could be gifted to the trust to accomplish your planning objectives for a family business or real estate asset, while providing the control and other benefits of a trust.

2. You cannot have any prohibited rights and powers over the trust assets. For example, you can't retain a right to appoint the trust assets to anyone at your discretion (a general power of appointment).

General Considerations

Besides making sure the assets given to the trust stay out of your estate to avoid the estate tax, there are a number of other points to consider when establishing a trust for your children:

- Careful consideration should be given to the choice of trustees and successor trustees. Should you name the same persons who are named the guardians of your children under your will? On the plus side, this provides complete control and avoids any conflict between the guardian's need for money for your children and a trustee's opinion of what is appropriate to spend. However, many parents prefer to separate these functions so that some check-and-balance system is built into the arrangement. Also, serving as a guardian requires personal skills, while serving as a trustee requires financial skills. Different people may have different attributes and should be picked accordingly.

- A trust can contain a spendthrift provision to limit the rights creditors of your children may have to the assets of the trust.

- Successor trustees and other arrangements can be detailed. If trustee number one is unable or unwilling to serve, your second choice named in the trust can take over, and so on.

- The trustee can be authorized to distribute income from the trust among your children based on their need (a sprinkling power). This can be very important, because it is often impossible to determine what the needs of each child will be in the future. Similarly, a right for the trustee to spend the principal (not just income) can be provided for in the event of emergencies.

- You must decide at what ages your children should be given the assets from the trust. A common approach is for one-third to be given at ages 25, 30, and 35. The idea is to accustom the child to receiving money over a period of time so that if the child is irresponsible at the first distribution, there will be two more opportunities to learn responsibility.

- You must determine whether to have one trust for all of your children or separate trusts for each child. When you have a common trust, you can use the sprinkling power described above to give the most money to the child with the most need. Typically, when a common trust is used, the money and assets are distributed equally when the youngest child reaches a certain age, say 21. Distributions can be made at earlier dates, but they would reduce the amount available to meet emergencies of the youngest child. You may want to designate what expenses should be paid out of this common trust. For example, college expenses may be paid but postgraduate expenses excluded. Single trusts create additional legal, tax-filing, and administrative costs, but they assure each child of the amount designated for that child. A single trust also enables an older child to receive assets earlier.

NOTE: Great care should be used in making the above decisions because they can have a dramatic affect on your children's lives. Don't simply assume that a "standard agreement" is appropriate. These are personal decisions and can easily be reflected in any trust arrangement you use.

TYPES OF TRUST ARRANGEMENTS COMMONLY USED FOR MINOR CHILDREN

There are a number of different trust arrangements, each with somewhat different tax consequences, that can be used. An important factor in all of these trusts is the effort to qualify for the annual $10,000 gift tax exclusion. This exclusion permits every taxpayer to give away up to $10,000 per year to any person without incurring a gift tax, and without using up any of their once-in-a-lifetime $600,000 exclusion. To qualify for this benefit, a gift must be of "a present interest." This means that a gift in trust will only qualify when your child, or the other beneficiary, is entitled to use all the income currently, or to withdraw up to the $10,000 (or lesser amount) which was given to the trust, or the special rules of section 2503(c) are met. Note that whenever a $10,000 gift can be made, you can join with your spouse and together give $20,000 per year (see Chapter 7).

Income-Only Trust (Section 2503(c) Trust)

This trust must specify that the income be distributed annually to your child or other beneficiary. This will permit you to make a gift of up to $10,000 per year and qualify for the annual gift tax exclusion. The child then will be taxed on all of the income earned by the trust. If the child is under 14, the kiddie tax described above will apply. The income can be distributed to a Uniform Gift To Minors Act trust without disqualifying you from the benefits of the annual exclusion. The assets in the trust will have to be income producing for the IRS to respect the arrangement (for example, raw land that isn't leased won't work). This type of trust offers additional flexibility over the section 2503(c) special minor's trust described below because the remainder beneficiary (the person who gets the trust property after the trust ends) doesn't have to be the same person who gets the trust income while the trust is in existence.

When different beneficiaries are named, take great care in how the trust agreement is worded. If the child beneficiary receiving certain income during the existence of the trust has an emergency, should the trustee be permitted to dip into the trust principal for this child? If this is done, it will reduce the amount available to the person receiving the assets when the trust terminates. Clear rules advising what the trustee should do are important.

Right to Withdraw Under Crummey Power

With the exception of a special trust for minor children discussed below, if a trust can accumulate income, you will not qualify for the annual $10,000 gift tax exclusion on gifts to the trust. However, if a gift to a trust can be characterized as having a present interest, you may qualify for the annual exclusion up to the amount that the child can withdraw each year from the trust. This situation is achieved by means of a Crummey power. This power is named after a famous tax case in which the court sustained the taxpayer's argument that when the beneficiary had an opportunity to withdraw the funds currently but did not elect to do so, a gift to a trust still qualified as a gift of a present interest, and hence was eligible for the annual gift tax exclusion.

By this technique, the money can remain in the trust, and the parent can avoid any gift tax. However, there are a host of complications associated with this type of planning, which should be reviewed carefully with your attorney. The following discussion merely highlights some of the concerns.

- For the Crummey power to be effective, the trust must give the child beneficiary a reasonable opportunity to withdraw the money. This is accomplished by having the trustee give written notice to the child that the withdrawal right for monies contributed exists and that the child has some period of time, say 30 to 60 days, to send in a written request that the money be distributed. This period should end before year's end. Also, it's best to send the notice by certified mail, so that you can prove it was sent.
- Care must be taken that the right of the child beneficiary to withdraw funds doesn't create a problem called a secondary gift-over. This can be illustrated by an example with a typical trust.

EXAMPLE: You set up a trust for the benefit of your son and daughter. Any monies not paid out or withdrawn are to be accumulated until the younger child reaches age 35; then the monies are to be distributed equally to each child. A Crummey power is provided, giving each child the right to withdraw one-half of the amount contributed each year, up to a maximum of the $10,000 annual exclusion. However, the demand power that your son has could also be considered as a power to appoint the amount not withdrawn to your daughter. When the son fails to exercise this power, he is deemed to make a gift. If the total gift you made to the trust for the year was $20,000, then your son will be deemed to have made a gift back to your daughter of the $10,000 he does not elect to withdraw from the trust under his power. This is called a "gift-over," and can be a taxable gift for your son (and similarly, for your daughter).

- One solution to the gift-over problem is to limit the annual gifts to 5 percent of the trust principal, or $5,000, so that the gift-over problem can be avoided under the special exclusion. This special rule provides that the end (lapse) of a power that is limited to the lesser of 5 percent or $5,000 won't create any gift tax implications. When the child beneficiary's right to withdraw exceeds this amount, a technique called a hanging power is used. A hanging power permits the child's power to withdraw to lapse only when it won't create a gift under the 5 percent or $5,000 rule. Under this approach, the beneficiaries' unexercised rights to withdraw $10,000 of trust property each year will lapse at the rate of $5,000 per year. The name "hanging power" is a result of the fact that the child's withdrawal right may continue to "hang" until future years and lapse at the rate of $5,000 per year long after you've stopped making contributions to the trust.

- Another solution is to have separate trusts for each child. When this approach is used, the failure of the child to exercise his or her right to withdraw money will be a gift to the trust and not to a sibling. Therefore, no gift-over can be created.

Special Trust for Children Under Age 21 (Section 2503(c) Trust)

There is a rule that permits you to transfer $10,000 per year to a special trust, and even though the trust accumulates income, you still can qualify for the annual gift tax exclusion. The criteria are as follows:

- The trust must be set up to benefit a minor child.
- The trustee must have the ability to use the income for the benefit of the minor child without restriction.
- The trust must be invested in income-producing assets (stocks, bonds, and CDs, but not raw land).
- When the child reaches age 21, the trust must be distributed to the child. To offset this requirement, the child can be given the right to receive the assets of the trust when he or she reaches age 21 but can voluntarily choose not to take the money. Giving the child the right to take the money may increase the risk of the child's obtaining the assets of the trust earlier than with a trust using a Crummey power, but it can be a safer approach for assuring the benefits of the annual exclusion.
- If the child dies prior to age 21, the trust assets must be distributed to the child's estate, or in a manner that the child appoints. This type of trust is commonly used in planning for minor children. A sample Section 2503(c) trust, with explanations and planning suggestions, appears in the "For Your Notebook" section following this chapter. For income tax purposes, note that the trust will pay

income tax on income it keeps, and the child will pay income tax on income distributed to him or her.

USING TRUSTS VERSUS GIVING UNDER THE UNIFORM GIFTS TO MINORS ACT

Having your children hold assets under a Uniform Gifts to Minors Act does not provide the maximum flexibility and protection and can result in costly and public intrusions by the courts. Trusts can minimize these problems to some extent. However, trusts can also be challenged in court, putting personal matters into the public record. Forming a trust will incur legal and accounting fees and require that various filings and other formalities be addressed. Overall, if funds are sufficient to pay the extra costs, a trust is clearly preferred.

What if you've already made substantial transfers to your children under a Uniform Gifts to Minors Act and now realize that you would prefer more control? The answer isn't easy, because the assets have already been transferred to your children's names. A possible solution may be to have your children transfer the assets that they own into revocable trusts to provide for the administration and management of those assets. It may even be possible to name a parent as trustee to administer the funds, although it is preferable that it not be the parent if a parent made the original gifts. The obvious limitation of this approach is that the children can always revoke a revocable trust they have set up. The benefit would merely be psychological. Be certain to review this carefully with an attorney before proceeding. You may be able to put some of the funds in your children's Uniform Gifts to Minors Act accounts into a family real estate partnership or family business. As long as these are legitimate investments and don't violate state law, this approach may provide you with some measure of control through your control of the real estate or business.

NO- OR LOW-INTEREST LOANS

A technique used in the past has been for a parent to make a no- or low-interest loan to a child. The child then could invest the money and earn income that otherwise would have been taxed at the parent's higher tax rate. It also permitted the child to accumulate assets. The tax laws, however, have restricted this technique since 1984, by requiring that a fair interest rate be imputed on such loans.

If parents lend money to their children and decide to give the children a break by only charging them a low or nominal interest rate, complicated tax consequences may ensue. These rules don't apply for small loans. If all of the loans between parents and children don't exceed $10,000, there won't be any complications, providing that the children use the money to buy a house or any other non-income-producing asset. If the loan exceeds this amount and the interest rate is too low, the IRS may find that the parents have made a gift loan.

If a gift loan is made, the IRS will impute an interest charge, using a realistic market rate of interest, which the children as borrowers should have paid to the parents, and which the parents as lenders should have reported as income. The amount of this imputed interest charge will be treated as a gift made from the parents to the children, possibly creating a gift tax cost (if the amount exceeds the annual $10,000 exclusion).

Term Loan

The gift tax consequences of a no- or low-interest loan will depend on whether the loan is a term loan (due in a certain number of years) or a demand loan (must be repaid whenever the parents say). For a term loan, the excess of the amount lent by the parents over the present value of all the payments required to be made by the children is treated as a gift made by the parents to their children.

EXAMPLE: Parents loan Daughter and Son-in-Law $50,000 to use as a down-payment on their first home. Parents want to give the kids a break and only charge them 5 percent interest. The children must pay interest on December 31 of each year and repay the $50,000 in 10 years. The children will pay the parents $2,500 in interest [5% × $50,000]. Assume, however, that the proper interest rate to charge would have been 9 percent, so that the children should have paid $4,500 [9% × $50,000]. It's as if the $2,000 of interest the children won't be paying is being given to them as a gift.

The children will actually be making two types of payments to the parents. The first type is the annual interest payment of $2,500. The second is the repayment of the $50,000 after 10 years. The interest payments for the 10 years will total $25,000 [10 years × $2,500 per year]. The present value of the $2,500 payments for 10 years, using a 9 percent interest rate, is $16,044. The present value of the $50,000 payment to be made in 10 years is $21,120. The sum of these two present values is $37,164 [$16,044 + $21,120]. The total amount of the gift is $12,836 [$50,000 − $37,164].

The amount of the term loan in the above example will not result in a gift tax to the parents if both have made the loan or the loan was to both children. If only one parent made the loan, or if the loan amount were larger, or the interest rate charged were lower, the parents would have to pay a gift tax for lending money to their children.

Demand Loan

In the case of a term loan, the gift is treated as made in the year the loan was made. For a demand loan, the rules are different. Since it isn't possible to know when the loan will be repaid until it actually is repaid, the gift will be calculated at the end of every year in which the loan remains unpaid. The amount deemed to be a gift is based on interest calculations for the amount of unpaid imputed interest for each day in the year.

Income Tax Considerations

In addition to the gift tax consequences of a no- or low-interest loan, there are also income tax consequences. For income tax purposes, foregone interest may have to be treated as if it were transferred from the parents/lenders to the children/borrowers. Since this transfer is a gift, there will be no income tax consequences to the parents or children from this stage of the transfer. This foregone interest (based on interest rates set monthly by the IRS) is then considered as if it were retransferred by the children/borrowers to the parents/lenders. The children will be able to deduct this interest deemed paid to the parents if they meet the regular tax rules for interest deductions. The parents, unfortunately, may have to report the imputed interest as income.

There is an exception that will limit the impact of these rules for many parental loans. When the total gift loan is less than $100,000, the amount treated as interest transferred from the children to the parents (and to be reported as income by the parents) will be limited to the amount of the children's net investment income for that year. Net investment income is income from stock dividends, bond interest, savings account interest, and so forth, less expenses incurred in earning this income. If the children's net investment income is less than $1,000, it will be assumed to be zero. If the parents make the loan for the purpose of avoiding taxes, this *de minimis* rule will not apply.

To have any family loan transaction respected by the IRS, the loan must be treated like a bona fide loan by both parties. It is, therefore, important to have a legally binding loan agreement drafted by an attorney and signed by all the parties involved. The children must carefully make all of the payments they are required to make according to the loan agreements. If this is not done, the IRS may claim that the transfer of money by the parents to the children was really a gift and not a loan, which could result in a gift tax.

Estate Tax Considerations

From an estate tax perspective, if the parents have a substantial estate, an outright gift may make more sense than a loan. The loan will be treated as an asset in the parents' estate and will be subject to estate tax on their eventual death. If the parents are not comfortable making an outright gift, a compromise solution may be for them to make a loan to the children and each year forgive some portion of the loan. Great care must be exercised in using such a plan, so that it will not appear as if the parents never intended for the children to repay the loan.

One of the most important estate planning considerations when you are making a gift or a loan is the fairness to the other children involved. Parents often prefer to treat all of their children approximately equally. If this is the case, and you give one child a loan at a favorable interest rate, you may want to provide some additional benefit to your other children in your will. Your estate adviser may be able to assist you in planning an overall gifting program that will eventually equalize the benefits conferred on each child or other intended beneficiary.

Another estate planning consideration connected with a loan is this: What happens to the loan if you die before it is repaid. You could provide nothing in your will about this and leave it up to the administrator of your estate to handle the matter, but doing nothing can be a mistake. While you may assume that the administrator of your estate will handle affairs as you would have, problems can arise.

EXAMPLE: In one situation an estranged older brother was serving as the executor. His wife, jealous over perceived favoritism of the other siblings, convinced her husband, acting in his capacity as executor, to call the demand loan the parents had made to a younger brother. This created a substantial hardship for the younger brother, all to the delight of the older brother's wife.

A safer approach is either to provide in your will when the loan should be required to be repaid, or to give additional consideration to a situation in which the note would be enforced by your estate when your lawyer drafts the loan documents. You could even provide in your will that the loan will be forgiven as part of the inheritance of the child who borrowed the money. Consult your tax adviser concerning the consequences of this.

OTHER METHODS OF GIVING

The general gift tax planning ideas suggested in Chapter 7 should be considered when evaluating all of the gift strategies discussed in this chapter. Other gift approaches to consider in providing for your children, or in planning to minimize your estate tax, are the following: real estate partnerships (see Chapter 15), stock in a family business (Chapter 16), stock in a family S corporation (Chapter 17), naming the children beneficiaries of a life insurance trust (Chapter 19), and so forth. Any of these approaches should be carefully discussed with your tax adviser before taking any steps to implement your estate plan.

GIFTS TO GRANDCHILDREN

When you can afford to make gifts to both your children and grandchildren, you will face rules similar to those described above. There is, however, an important tax benefit to be derived from a regular gift program for grandchildren. Gifts that qualify for the annual $10,000 gift tax exclusion can also escape the clutches of the expensive generation-skipping transfer tax. Thus, when planning gifts for grandchildren, these rules should be considered (see Chapter 8).

CONCLUSION

Ensuring the welfare of your children, particularly minor children, is often the most important estate planning objective. There are a number of different approaches that can be used. They should all be considered carefully in light of the tax, financial, and emotional background of your family.

For Your Notebook:

SAMPLE TRUST FOR INDIVIDUAL UNDER THE AGE OF 21
(WITH COMMENTS)

FOR DISCUSSION WITH YOUR LAWYER ONLY—DO NOT USE AS A TRUST

THIS AGREEMENT dated as of MONTH DAY, 1991, between GRANTOR'S NAME, who resides at GRANTOR'S ADDRESS (the "Grantor"), and TRUSTEE'S NAME, who resides at TRUSTEE'S ADDRESS (the "Trustee").

NOTE: The person named as trustee should not be given (or retain) sufficient powers of ownership that the trust assets will be included in the trustee's estate on the trustee's death. The grantor (the person setting up the trust) should not also be the trustee.

WITNESSETH:

WHEREAS, the Grantor desires to create this trust (the "Trust"), the terms of which are hereinafter set forth, and the Trustee has consented to accept and perform said Trust in accordance with such terms;

NOW, THEREFORE, in consideration of the premises and mutual covenants herein:

I. ESTABLISHMENT OF TRUST; TRUST ESTATE

A. The Grantor assigns and transfers to the Trustee, and the Trustee, by executing this Agreement acknowledges receipt from the Grantor of the property described in Schedule "A" attached. This property, together with any other property that may be later transferred to the Trustee by the Grantor or by the legal representatives of the Grantor's estate pursuant to Grantor's last will, or by any other person (if said property is acceptable to the Trustee), including the proceeds of such property and the securities or other property in which such proceeds may be invested, shall constitute the "Trust Estate."

NOTE: A detailed description of the assets being transferred to the trust should be labeled "Schedule A" and attached to the trust agreement. If the property is real estate, give a full legal description (not merely an address). If securities are involved, be sure to list the CUSIP number and other identifying information.

B. The Grantor retains no right, title, or interest of any nature in any of the property in Schedule A and shall not retain any right, title, or interest of any nature in any property transferred to this Trust after the execution of this Agreement.

NOTE: It is important that the grantor (typically a parent, but it could be a grandparent or any other person) have no further rights to the assets in the trust to avoid having those assets brought back into the grantor's estate (see Chapter 6).

II.   PURPOSE AND USE OF THE TRUST ESTATE

A. The Trustee shall hold the Trust Estate for the following purposes and subject to the terms and conditions of this Trust:

B. The Trustee shall collect and add to the Trust Estate:

1. Any amounts payable under the Grantor's employee benefit plans in which the Trustee has been designated as beneficiary;

2. Any amounts payable under insurance policies on the life of the Grantor held in the Trust;

3. Any amounts payable under insurance on the life of the Grantor in which the Trustee has been designated as beneficiary;

4. Any property payable to the Trustee by the legal representatives of the Grantor's estate pursuant to the provisions of the Grantor's last will;

5. Any property payable by any other person, whether pursuant to the provisions of such person's last will or otherwise; and thereafter the Trustee shall deal with and dispose of the Trust Estate as hereinafter provided.

C. The Trustee shall hold the Trust Estate, in trust, for the following purposes:

1. To pay to or for the benefit of CHILD'S NAME, the Grantor's child (the "Beneficiary"), net income and principal of the Trust as the Trustee, in the exercise of his or her absolute discretion, may determine to be desirable for the comfort and welfare of the Beneficiary.

2. To accumulate any of the Trust's net income not paid out and to add it to the principal of the Trust Estate at least annually, and then to hold, administer, and dispose of such income as a part the Trust Estate.

3. The Grantor requests, but does not require, that the Trustee not pay the Trust Estate to discharge either the Grantor's or the Trustee's legal obligation under the laws of the State, if any, to support the Beneficiary. This request shall not create a binding limitation on the Trustee, and shall not limit the broad discretion given to the Trustee to pay funds for the benefit of the Beneficiary in the Trustee's sole and absolute discretion.

NOTE: When the income of a trust is used for the support of a minor child whom the grantor is legally obligated under state law to support, it may be taxable to the grantor for income tax purposes. For example, when monies were used for school tuition for a private day school, or to meet expenses for the home where the family resided, the grantor was taxed. When the grantor does not have an obligation under state law to support the minor beneficiary of the trust, this provision can be removed.

III.   APPLICATION OF TRUST ESTATE WHEN BENEFICIARY ELECTS NOT TO RECEIVE TRUST ESTATE UPON ATTAINING AGE 21

A. The Beneficiary may make a binding election to have this Trust continue beyond the date of his or her Twenty-First (21st) birthday by providing the Trustee with a written election statement to such effect. This provision shall be limited so as not to violate any of the provisions of Code Section 2035(c), or the regulations or cases thereunder.

NOTE: In many, if not most, cases, parents (or others) establishing a trust for a minor child will not want to turn over what could be substantial amount of money to a 21-year-old. Unfortunately, if the trust is required to be continued beyond this age, the favorable tax benefits of the annual exclusion will not be available. A solution is for the child to elect not to terminate the trust. This objective can be accomplished in one of two ways. First, the child can be given the right to require that the assets of the trust be distributed when he or she reaches age 21. The second approach, which is used in the sample trust, is to permit the trust to continue after the beneficiary reaches age 21 only upon an affirmative act by the beneficiary to do so. This approach may increase the risk of the beneficiary's obtaining the assets of the trust, but it seems to be a safer approach to ensuring the benefits of the annual exclusion.

B. The Trustee shall pay the net income of the Trust to or for the benefit of the Beneficiary in annual or more frequent installments. When the Beneficiary reaches Twenty-Five (25) years, the Trustee shall pay to the Beneficiary One-Third ($1/3$) of the Trust Estate. When the beneficiary reaches Thirty (30) years, the Trustee shall pay to the Beneficiary One-Half ($1/2$) of the Trust Estate. When the Beneficiary reaches Thirty-Five (35) years, the Trustee shall pay to the Beneficiary the balance of the Trust Estate.

NOTE: When the beneficiary permits (or affirmatively elects) to let the trust continue after age 21, the trust should provide for the assets of the trust to be distributed at some future date. The distribution of one-third of the trust at ages 25, 30, and 35 is a typical approach. Most parents feel that this gives the child a chance to gradually learn responsibility for the money that may be available.

C. If the Beneficiary should die prior to the distribution of the entire Trust Estate as provided herein, the Trustee shall transfer and pay over the Trust Estate as provided in Section IV.B., below.

IV.   PROVISIONS WHEN THE BENEFICIARY ATTAINS AGE 21

A. Upon the Beneficiary reaching Twenty-One (21) years, the principal of the Trust Estate and any net income then remaining in the hands of the Trustee shall be paid to the Beneficiary.

B. Upon the death of the Beneficiary before reaching Twenty-One (21) years, the principal of the Trust Estate and any net income then remaining in the hands of the Trustee shall be paid over to or for the benefit of such persons, including the estate of the Beneficiary, to such extent and in such amounts, and in such lawful interests or estates, whether absolute or in trust, as the Beneficiary may by his or her Last Will appoint by a specific reference to this power. If the power of appointment is for any reason not validly exercised in whole or in part by the Beneficiary, the principal of the Trust Estate and any net income remaining in the hands of the Trustee, to the extent not validly appointed by him or her, shall, upon his or her death, be transferred, conveyed, and paid over to ALTERNATE NUMBER ONE, if any then living, in equal shares; if none of such persons is then living, to ALTERNATE NUMBER TWO, if any then living, in equal shares; if none of such persons is then living, to the heirs and assigns of ALTERNATE NUMBER TWO.

NOTE: To qualify for the $10,000 annual exclusion for monies held in trust, the assets of the trust that are not spent for the benefit of the minor child must pass to the child at age 21, or if the minor dies before age 21, to the estate of the child, or to a person the child designates.

V. GENERAL PROVISIONS AFFECTING THE TRUST ESTATE

A. The Trustee of this Trust, or any trust created under this Agreement (collectively the "Trust") is authorized and empowered, at any time and from time to time, with respect to any person eligible to receive the net income of the Trust, to pay to or for the benefit of such person, part or all of the principal of the Trust, as the Trustee, in the exercise of his or her absolute discretion, may consider desirable for such person's comfort and welfare, and without regard to such person's income and other resources, or the duty of anyone to support such person, and without regard to any other funds that may be available for such purposes. However, the Trustee is directed to consider the Grantor's objective as stated in Section II.C.3., above.

B. Notwithstanding anything to the contrary contained in this Agreement, if the Trustee shall determine that the aggregate value or the character of the assets of any Trust created under this Agreement makes it inadvisable, inconvenient, or uneconomical to continue the administration of such Trust, then the Trustee, in the exercise of his or her absolute discretion, may pay over the Trust Estate, equally or unequally, to or among one or more persons then eligible to receive the net income of that Trust.

C. Whenever pursuant to the provisions of this Agreement any property shall become distributable to a Person Under a Disability (as defined in Section XVI, below), title to Donee Property shall vest in such a person, but the payment may be deferred until the disability ceases. In such cases the Donee Property shall be held by the Trustee, who shall apply any portion, or all, of the principal and income from the Trust, as the Trustee in the exercise of his or her absolute discretion may determine. This determination may be made without regard to the income and other resources of such person, and without regard to the duty of anyone to support such person, and without regard to any other funds which may be available for the person under a disability, or of his parents or spouse. However, the Trustee is directed to consider the Grantor's objective as stated in Section II.C.3., above. The Trustee shall pay such amounts for the comfort and welfare of the Person Under a Disability, and when such disability ceases, the Trustee shall deliver to the person formerly under a disability any Donee Property remaining, together with the accumulations, if any, of income. If the Person Under a Disability should die, the Trustee shall pay the Donee Property, and any accumulations of income, to the legal representatives of the estate of the Person Under a Disability. Income accumulations, if any, shall be added to and accounted for as part of the principal of the Trust.

D. The exercise by the Trustee of the discretionary powers granted under this Agreement with respect to the payment of principal or income of any Trust shall be final and conclusive upon all persons and shall not be subject to any review whatsoever. It is the Grantor's intention that the Trustee shall have the greatest latitude in exercising all discretionary powers granted under this Agreement, and that any persons entitled to receive any portion, or all, of the principal of any Trust shall upon the termination of such Trust be entitled only to such principal as may remain after the last exercise of the Trustee's continuing discretionary powers. However, under no circumstances shall any person who may be acting as a Trustee participate in the exercise of any power with respect to any discretionary payment to himself of any principal or income of any Trust.

E. For convenience of administering any Trust, the Trustee, in the exercise of his or her absolute discretion, may administer as one trust the assets of any Trust created under this Agreement and any property held pursuant to the provisions of this Agreement, provided that the Trustee keep a separate record of all transactions, investments, payments, expenses, and distributions for any Trust and for property held pursuant to this Agreement.

VI. SPENDTHRIFT PROVISION

Except as may be otherwise provided in this Trust, no charge, distribution, or encumbrance on the net income or principal of any Trust, or any part of any Trust, by any Beneficiary by anticipation shall be valid or binding on the Trustee. No Beneficiary shall have the right to assign, transfer, encumber, or otherwise dispose of any part, or all, of the income or principal of the Trust until the same shall be paid to that Beneficiary by the Trustee. No income or principal shall be subject to any claim of any creditor or claimant of any type of any Beneficiary.

NOTE: The intent of this paragraph is to help preserve the trust for its intended purposes by making it clear that no beneficiary can pledge any part of the trust. The effectiveness of this provision will depend, in part, on state law.

VII. ACCOUNTING

The Trustee may render an accounting upon termination of any Trust and at any other time as the Trustee, in the exercise of his or her absolute discretion, deems advisable. The written approval or assent of all persons, other than a Person Under a Disability, entitled at that time to receive the net income of any Trust, and also all persons then presumptively entitled to the principal of such Trust, exclusive of any Person Under a Disability, as to all matters and transactions shown in the account, shall be final and binding on all persons who may at any time be entitled to all, or any part of, the income or the principal of any Trust. However, if the Trustee is accounting to another fiduciary, then the written approval of the other fiduciary shall be final and binding on all persons beneficially interested in the estate or trust estate represented by the other fiduciary. The written approval of the persons specified in this section shall have the same force and effect in discharging the Trustee as a decree of a court of competent jurisdiction. However, any such written approval shall not change the beneficial interest of any Beneficiary of any Trust. Notwithstanding anything herein to the contrary, the Trustee, in the exercise of his or her absolute discretion, may submit the account to a court for approval and settlement.

VIII. TRUSTEE COMPENSATION

Each Trustee acting hereunder, except for NAME OF TRUSTEE NOT ENTITLED TO COMPENSATION, shall be entitled to withdraw from the Trust Estate, without obtaining court or other approval, the compensation that is allowed to a trustee under the laws of the State that govern compensation to the trustee of a testamentary trust, computed in the manner and at the rates in effect at the time the compensation is payable.

IX. POWERS OF THE TRUSTEE

The Trustee shall have in addition to, and not in limitation of, the powers granted elsewhere in this Agreement, or the powers allowed by law, the following powers:

A. To invest and reinvest any assets comprising the Trust Estate in any securities or other property, whether real or personal, of any class, kind, or nature (including an undivided interest in any one or more common trust funds), as the Trustee may deem advisable without regard to any restrictions of law on a Trustee's investments.

B. To exercise voting rights in person or by proxy, rights of conversion or of exchange, or rights to purchase or subscribe for stocks, bonds, or other securities or obligations that may be offered to the holders of any asset, and to accept and retain any property that may be acquired by the exercise of any such right with respect to any stocks, bonds, or other securities or obligation included in the Trust Estate, in the Trustee's absolute discretion.

C. To employ or retain accountants, custodians, agents, legal counsel, investment advisers, and other experts as the Trustee shall deem advisable. To rely on the information and advice furnished by such persons. To fix the compensation of such persons, and in the case of legal counsel who may also be acting as a Trustee hereunder, to take payments on account of legal fees in advance of the settlement of the Trustee's account without applying to or procuring the authority of any court.

D. To the extent permitted by the laws of the State, the Trustee may hold securities in the name of a nominee without indicating the trust character of such holdings, and may hold unregistered securities, or securities in a form that will pass by delivery.

E. To retain and continue for any period deemed appropriate by the Trustee, in exercise of his or her absolute discretion, any asset, whether real of personal, tangible or intangible, included in the Trust Estate, constituting the Trust Estate.

F. To sell at public or private sale and to exchange or otherwise dispose of any stocks, bonds, securities, personal property, or other asset constituting the Trust Estate at such time, price, and terms as the Trustee deems advisable.

G. To grant options for the sale or exchange of any asset comprising the Trust Estate, at times, prices, and terms that the Trustee deems advisable, without applying to or procuring the authority of any court.

H. To sell, exchange, partition, convey, and mortgage, and to modify, extend, renew, or replace any mortgage that may be a lien on all, or any part, of any interest in real property included in the Trust Estate.

I. To lease any real or personal property, whether or not for a term beyond the period of time fixed by statute for leases by a trustee, and whether or not extending beyond the termination of any Trust, and upon such terms as the Trustee deems advisable, without obtaining the approval of any court.

J. To foreclose mortgages and bid in property under foreclosure and to take title by deed in lieu of foreclosure or otherwise.

K. To extend the time of payment of any bond, note, or other obligation or mortgage included in the Trust Estate, or of any installment of principal thereof, or of any interest due thereon. To hold such instrument after maturity, as a past due bond, note, or other obligation or mortgage, either with or without renewal or extension. To consent to the modification, alteration, and amendment of any terms or conditions of such instrument, including those regarding the rate of interest, and to waive any defaults in the performance of the terms and conditions of such instrument.

L. To compromise, adjust, settle, or submit to arbitration upon terms the Trustee deems advisable, in his or her absolute discretion, any claim in favor of or against the Trust Estate. To release, with or without consideration, any claim in favor of the Trust Estate.

M. To participate in any refunding; readjustment of stocks, bonds, or other securities or obligations; enforcement of obligations or securities by foreclosure or otherwise; corporate consolidation by merger or otherwise; or reorganization that shall affect any stock, bond, or other security or obligation included in the Trust Estate. To participate in any plan or proceeding for protection of the interests of the holders of such instruments. To deposit any property under any plan or proceeding with any protective or reorganization committee and to delegate to such a committee the discretionary power with respect thereto. To pay a proportionate part of the expenses of a committee. To pay any assessments levied under such a plan, and to accept and retain any property that may be received pursuant to any such plan.

N. To borrow money for the purpose of raising funds to pay taxes or for any other purpose deemed by the Trustee, in his or her absolute discretion, to be beneficial to the Trust Estate, and upon such terms as the Trustee may determine. To pledge as security for the repayment of any loan any assets included in the Trust Estate.

O. To make any distribution under any Trust, in cash or in property, or in any combination of cash and property. To make non-pro rata distributions of cash and property then included in the Trust Estate.

P. To exercise for the benefit of the Trust Estate, and for any property included in the Trust Estate, all rights, powers, and privileges of every nature that might or could be exercised by any person owning similar property absolutely and in his or her own right. In connection with the exercise of any or all of such rights, powers, and privileges, the Trustee may take any other action that is reasonable and necessary to the exercise of any such right, powers, and privileges, even when such right, power, or privilege may not have been specifically mentioned in this Trust. To negotiate, draft, enter into, renegotiate, or otherwise modify any contracts or other written instruments that the Trustee deems advisable, and to include in them the covenants, terms, and conditions as the Trustee deems proper, in the exercise of his or her absolute discretion.

NOTE: Although state law may provide substantial power and authority to the trustee, it is customary to enumerate broad powers and authority so that the trustee will not be hampered by legal constraints in achieving the grantor's objectives. When reviewing a trust with your attorney, don't be lulled into skimming or ignoring this provision by a comment that it's "boiler-plate" (the same in every agreement). Read and understand the provisions. You may wish to prohibit the trustee from investing in certain speculative types of investments, for example, while making advance payments through retainers is common, you may want to limit the scope of this.

Remember, however, that no grantor has a crystal ball to gaze into the future. Exercise restraint in restricting the broad powers given to the trustee, since at the time the trust is established there can be no way to know what will be required in order to best achieve the grantor's objectives.

X. TRUSTEE EMPOWERED TO ENTER TRANSACTIONS WITH GRANTOR'S ESTATE

The Trustee is authorized and empowered, at any time, to do the following:

A. To purchase at fair market value from the legal representatives of the Grantor's estate any property constituting a part, or all, of the Grantor's estate.

B. To lend for adequate consideration to the legal representatives of the Grantor's estate such part, or all, of the Trust Estate, upon such terms and conditions as the Trustee in the exercise of his or her absolute discretion deems advisable.

NOTE: Giving the trustee authority to purchase assets in the grantor's estate can provide important flexibility. It can help solve any liquidity problem that the grantor's estate may have, and it can permit the trust to purchase assets from which the beneficiary can benefit—for example, the remaining shares outstanding of a family business.

XI. RELIANCE OF THIRD PARTIES ON THE TRUSTEE

No person, bank, trust company, corporation, partnership, association, or firm dealing with the Trustee or holding or keeping any assets, whether funds, securities, or other property of the Trust Estate, shall be required to:

A. Investigate the authority of the Trustee for entering into any transaction involving assets of the Trust Estate;

B. See to the application of the proceeds of any such transaction;

C. Inquire into the validity, expediency, or propriety of any transaction;

D. Be under any obligation or liability whatsoever, except to the Trustee; and any such person, bank or trust company, corporation, partnership, association, or firm shall be fully protected in making disposition of any assets of the Trust Estate in accordance with the directions of the Trustee.

XII.   RIGHTS OF THE TRUSTEE; LIMITATIONS ON TRUSTEE LIABILITY

A. The Trustee shall not be personally liable for any loss to or other decline in the value of the Trust Estate occurring by reason of (i) the exercise or nonexercise of the powers granted to the Trustee under this Agreement; or (ii) a mistake or error in judgment in the purchase or sale of any investment or the retention of any investment, so long as the Trustee shall have been acting in good faith.

B. Every action taken, power exercised, or obligation assumed by the Trustee in accordance with the terms of this Agreement, shall be considered to have been done, exercised, or assumed by the Trustee acting in the Trustee's fiduciary capacity and not otherwise.

C. Every person contracting, or otherwise dealing, with the Trustee shall look solely to the assets comprising the Trust Estate for payment of any money that may become due or payable under any obligation arising under this Agreement, in whole or in part. The Trustee shall not be individually liable therefor, even though the Trustee did not exempt itself from individual liability when entering into any contract, obligation, or transaction in connection with or growing out of the Trust Estate.

D. No bond or security of any kind shall be required of any Trustee acting hereunder.

E. Any Trustee hereunder may resign at any time without obtaining prior judicial approval. Such resignation shall be deemed complete upon the delivery of an instrument in writing declaring such resignation to the Grantor, or if the Grantor shall then be deceased, to the remaining Trustee, or if there shall be no remaining Trustee, to the successor Trustee. Such resigning Trustee shall promptly deliver the assets of the Trust Estate to the remaining or successor Trustee. The resigning Trustee shall, at the request of the remaining or successor Trustee, promptly deliver such assignments, transfers, and other instruments as may be reasonably required for fully vesting in such remaining or successor Trustee all rights, title, and interest in the Trust Estate.

F. Any discretion or power granted to or conferred upon the Trustee by this Agreement may be exercised by any number of them, or one of them, acting under this Agreement, or by any one of them who is designated in a written instrument delivered to all of the Trustees.

G. No Trustee acting hereunder shall be under a duty to render a judicial accounting at any time, including, but not limited to, resignation.

H. The Trustee may consult with legal counsel (who may be counsel to the Grantor) concerning any matter that the Trustee deems appropriate, and the opinion of such counsel shall be considered full and complete authorization and protection in respect of any action taken or suffered by the Trustee, if taken in accordance with the opinion of such counsel and in good faith.

XIII. SUCCESSOR TRUSTEES

A. In no event shall the Grantor serve as a successor Trustee of this Trust.

B. If the above-named Trustee shall fail or cease to act as Trustee, the Grantor hereby appoints SUCCESSOR TRUSTEE as Trustee in his or her place and stead.

NOTE: It is vitally important to provide a mechanism for designating a successor trustee in case the initial trustee will no longer be willing or able to serve as trustee. The simplest approach is to name one or more successors when the trust is first established.

C. In the event that there shall be no Trustee acting under this Agreement for a period of Thirty (30) days, the Grantor hereby appoints as successor Trustee such one or more individuals (other than the Grantor) or such bank or trust company as shall be designated by an instrument in writing signed by NAME OF GRANTOR'S LAW FIRM, doing business at LAW FIRM'S ADDRESS, or any successor firm, and delivered to the Grantor, or if he or she shall then be deceased, to the legal representatives of the estate of the Grantor or a court of competent jurisdiction.

D. The acceptance of the position of trustee by any Trustee who is not a party to this Agreement shall be evidenced by an instrument in writing delivered to the remaining Trustee, or if there shall be no remaining Trustee, to the Grantor, or if he or she shall then be deceased, to the legal representatives of the estate of the Grantor or a court of competent jurisdiction.

XIV. ADDITIONS TO THE TRUST ESTATE

A. The Grantor or any other person may at any time assign or transfer to the Trustee securities or other property, whether real or personal, acceptable to the Trustee, to be added to the Trust Estate. If at anytime additional securities or other property acceptable to the Trustee shall be assigned or transferred by any person, whether by will or otherwise, and delivered to the Trustee to be added to the Trust Estate, the Trustee shall hold and dispose of such assets as part of the Trust Estate subject to the terms and conditions of this Agreement.

B. Subject to the provisions of this Agreement, the Trustee shall accept and hold hereunder all policies of insurance upon the life of the Grantor, or other persons, that may be assigned to the Trustee by the Grantor or by any other person.

NOTE: In most cases contributions will be made to the trust on an annual basis. This provision permits the trustee to accept future contributions, but no commitment is required for future years. If the parent, or other grantor, ever becomes unhappy with the trust, no further contributions have to be made. See Chapter 19 for a discussion of life insurance in trusts.

XV. IRREVOCABLE TRUST; NOT A GRANTOR TRUST

A. The Grantor has been advised of the differences between a revocable and an irrevocable trust, and Grantor hereby declares that this Agreement and the Trust Estate created under this Agreement, and any other Trusts, are to be irrevocable. However, the Trustee may modify or amend this Agreement to facilitate the administration of the Trust Estate or to conform this Agreement to laws or regulations affecting inter vivos trusts as those laws may be amended. In no event shall any modification or amendment affect the possession or enjoyment of the Trust Estate.

B. Notwithstanding anything in this Trust to the contrary, this Trust shall not be interpreted in a manner that would make this Trust a Grantor trust. The Grantor shall not be permitted to reacquire the property set forth in Schedule A attached hereto, or any other property transferred to this Trust after the execution of this Trust. This restriction shall apply notwithstanding the Grantor's offer to pay fair market value and full and adequate consideration for such property, or to offer replacement property therefor.

XVI. DEFINITIONS

The following terms, if and when used in this Agreement, shall be defined as follows:

1. "Issue" is a descendant in any degree, whether natural or adopted.

2. "Donee Property" is any net income of any trust created hereunder, or all or any part of the Trust Estate distributable to a Person Under a Disability to be held by the donee of a power to manage during disability.

3. "Person Under a Disability" is either a person under age Twenty-One (21) years or a person who, for a period determined by the Trustee, is classified by the Trustee, in

the exercise of his or her absolute discretion, to be physically or mentally incapable of managing his or her affairs, whether or not a judicial declaration may have been made with respect to such disability.

4. "Per stirpes" is a disposition of property in which issue take a portion thereof in representation of their deceased parent, with division to be made into the number of equal shares at each degree of relationship from the common ancestor, so that there shall be one share for each person of the same degree living at the time of the distribution, and one share for the issue collectively then living of each person of the same degree who is then deceased. The division is to be made even though there may not then be any person living within that degree.

5. "State" is the State of NAME OF STATE.

6. "Trustee" is the trustee named in this Agreement or appointed by a court or pursuant to the terms of this Agreement and any and all successors, and may be masculine, feminine, or neuter, and singular or plural, as the sense requires.

7. To hold "in trust" is to manage, invest, and reinvest the principal of a trust and to collect the income thereof.

8. "Child" is an issue in the first degree.

9. "Trust Estate" is the remaining principal of any trust, as then constituted, and any accrued and undistributed income existing upon the termination of such trust.

XVII. CONSTRUCTION; MISCELLANEOUS

A. The validity, construction, and effect of the provisions of this Agreement shall be governed by the laws of the State.

B. This Agreement shall extend to and be binding upon the executors, administrators, heirs, successors, and assigns of the Grantor and the Trustee.

C. This Agreement may be executed in one or more original counterparts, but all taken together shall be deemed to be the same instrument.

D. All references in this Agreement to chapters or sections of the Internal Revenue Code are to the Internal Revenue Code of 1986, as amended, and shall be deemed to refer to corresponding provisions of any subsequent federal tax law.

E. Captions, titles, and section numbers (and letter designations) are inserted for convenience only and shall not be read to broaden or limit the scope of any provision.

F. The words "Trustee" and "Trustees" shall mean and include the persons originally designated herein and any person appointed as a Co-Trustee or as a successor in accordance with the provisions of this Trust and shall be construed as masculine, feminine, or neuter, or in the singular or plural, as the sense requires.

G. For purposes of this Trust, masculine terms shall be read as the feminine or neuter equivalent, singular terms as the plural equivalent, and vice versa, all as required for proper interpretation of the applicable provision.

H. This Trust has been formed with the express intent that it qualify as a trust under Code Section 2035(c). Notwithstanding anything in this Agreement to the contrary, if any provision contained in this Trust, or any action hereafter taken by the Grantor or Trustee, shall violate such provision, then such provision or action shall be interpreted and modified to the extent necessary to comply with the requirements of Code Section 2035(c) and the regulations thereunder.

IN WITNESS WHEREOF, the undersigned Grantor and Trustee have executed this Agreement as of the date first-above written.

_____ (L.S.)
GRANTOR'S NAME, Grantor

_____ (L.S.)
TRUSTEE'S NAME, Trustee

For Your Notebook:

SAMPLE KIDDIE TAX RETURN, FORM 8615

Facts and Comments

The kiddie tax, as explained above, can affect anyone doing estate planning who has small children. The Form 8615 will have to be filed with your tax return if you elect to report your children's tax on your return, rather than having them file separately.

The sample tax return is based on the following fact pattern: Junior Taxpayer, age 13, received $6,750 of investment income. He has no earned income and no itemized deductions. His sister, age 9, had $4,700 of investment income. Each of the children qualified as a dependent of the parents, John and Mary Taxpayer. Therefore, each of their exemption amounts was zero. Each of the children is entitled to a $500 standard deduction. The children's parents had $91,500 of taxable income and filed a joint tax return for 1990.

Form 8615

Tax for Children Under Age 14 Who Have Investment Income of More Than $1,000

Department of the Treasury
Internal Revenue Service

► See Instructions below and on back.
► Attach ONLY to the Child's Form 1040, Form 1040A, or Form 1040NR.

OMB No. 1545-0998

1990

Attachment
Sequence No. 33

General Instructions

Purpose of Form. For children under age 14, investment income (such as taxable interest and dividends) over $1,000 is taxed at the parent's rate if the parent's rate is higher than the child's rate.

Do not use this form if the child's investment income is $1,000 or less. Instead, figure the tax in the normal manner on the child's income tax return. For example, if the child had $900 of taxable interest income and $200 of wages, Form 8615 is not required to be completed and the child's tax should be figured on Form 1040A using the Tax Table.

If the child's investment income is more than $1,000, use this form to see if any of the child's investment income is taxed at the parent's rate and, if so, to figure the

child's tax. For example, if the child had $1,100 of taxable interest income and $200 of wages, complete Form 8615 and attach it to the child's Form 1040A.

Investment Income. As used on this form, "investment income" includes all taxable income other than earned income as defined on page 2. It includes income such as taxable interest, dividends, capital gains, rents, royalties, etc. It also includes pension and annuity income and income (other than earned income) received as the beneficiary of a trust.

Who Must File. Generally, Form 8615 must be filed for any child who was under age 14 on January 1, 1991, and who had more than $1,000 of investment income. If neither parent was alive on December 31,

1990, do not use Form 8615. Instead, figure the child's tax based on his or her own rate.

Note: The parent may be able to elect to report the child's investment income on his or her return. If the parent makes this election, the child will not have to file a return or Form 8615. For more details, see the Instructions for Form 1040 or Form 1040A, or get Form 8814, Parent's Election To Report Child's Interest and Dividends.

Additional Information. For more information about the tax on investment income of children, please get Pub. 929, Tax Rules for Children and Dependents.

(Instructions continue on back.)

Child's name shown on return	Child's social security number
Junior Taxpayer	000 : 00 : 0000

A Parent's name (first, initial, and last). (Caution: See instructions on back before completing.)	B Parent's social security number
John & Mary Taxpayer	000 : 00 : 0000

C Parent's filing status (check one):

☐ Single, ☒ Married filing jointly, ☐ Married filing separately, ☐ Head of household, or ☐ Qualifying widow(er)

D Enter number of exemptions claimed on parent's return. (If the parent's filing status is married filing separately, see the instructions.) ► | 4 |

Step 1 — Figure child's net investment income

1	Enter the child's investment income, such as taxable interest and dividend income (see the instructions). (If this amount is $1,000 or less, stop here; do not file this form.)	1	6,750
2	If the child DID NOT itemize deductions on Schedule A (Form 1040 or Form 1040NR), enter $1,000. If the child ITEMIZED deductions, see the instructions	2	1,000
3	Subtract the amount on line 2 from the amount on line 1. Enter the result. (If zero or less, stop here; do not complete the rest of this form but ATTACH it to the child's return.)	3	5,750
4	Enter the child's taxable income (from Form 1040, line 37; Form 1040A, line 22; or Form 1040NR, line 35).	4	6,250
5	Compare the amounts on lines 3 and 4. Enter the smaller of the two amounts here ►	5	5,750

Step 2 — Figure tentative tax based on the tax rate of the parent listed above

6	Enter the parent's taxable income (from Form 1040, line 37; Form 1040A, line 22; Form 1040EZ, line 5; or Form 1040NR, line 35). But if the parent transferred property to a trust, see the instructions	6	91,500
7	Enter the total, if any, of the net investment income from Forms 8615, line 5, of ALL OTHER children of the parent. (Do not include the amount on line 5 above.)	7	4,200
8	Add the amounts on lines 5, 6, and 7. Enter the total	8	101,450
9	Tax on the amount on line 8 based on the parent's filing status	9	25,340
10	Enter the parent's tax (from Form 1040, line 38; Form 1040A, line 23; Form 1040EZ, line 7; or Form 1040NR, line 36)	10	22,057
11	Subtract the amount on line 10 from the amount on line 9. Enter the result. (If no amount is entered on line 7, enter the amount from line 11 on line 13; skip lines 12a and 12b.)	11	3,283
12a	Add the amounts on lines 5 and 7. Enter the total ... 12a 9,950		
b	Divide the amount on line 5 by the amount on line 12a. Enter the result as a decimal (rounded to two places) .	12b	x .58
13	Multiply the amount on line 11 by the decimal amount on line 12b. Enter the result ►	13	1,904

Step 3 — Figure child's tax

Note: If the amounts on lines 4 and 5 are the same, skip to line 16.

14	Subtract the amount on line 5 from the amount on line 4. Enter the result . 14 500		
15	Tax on the amount on line 14 based on the child's filing status	15	77
16	Add the amounts on lines 13 and 15. Enter the total	16	1,981
17	Tax on the amount on line 4 based on the child's filing status	17	941
18	Compare the amounts on lines 16 and 17. Enter the larger of the two amounts here and on Form 1040, line 38; Form 1040A, line 23; or Form 1040NR, line 36. Be sure to check the box for "Form 8615". ►	18	1,981

For Paperwork Reduction Act Notice, see back of form.

Form **8615** (1990)

Prepared by: Diamond, Kerbis & Weinstein, P.C., Certified Public Accountants, New York, New York

Figure 11.1. Sample Kiddie Tax Return.

Form 8615.

Paperwork Reduction Act Notice. We ask for the information on this form to carry out the Internal Revenue laws of the United States. You are required to give us the information. We need it to ensure that you are complying with these laws and to allow us to figure and collect the right amount of tax.

The time needed to complete and file this form will vary depending on individual circumstances. The estimated average time is:

Recordkeeping	13 min.
Learning about the law or the form	11 min.
Preparing the form	37 min.
Copying, assembling, and sending the form to IRS . . .	17 min.

If you have comments concerning the accuracy of these time estimates or suggestions for making this form more simple, we would be happy to hear from you. You can write to both the IRS and the Office of Management and Budget at the addresses listed in the instructions of the tax return with which this form is filed.

Incomplete Information for Parent. If a parent or guardian of a child cannot obtain the necessary information to complete Form 8615 before the due date of the child's return, reasonable estimates of the parent's taxable income or filing status and the net investment income of the parent's other children may be made. The appropriate line of Form 8615 must be marked "Estimated." For more information, see Pub. 929.

Line-by-Line Instructions

We have provided specific instructions for most of the lines on the form. Those lines that do not appear in these instructions are self-explanatory.

Lines A and B. If the child's parents were married to each other and filed a joint return, enter the name and social security number of the parent who is listed first on the joint return. For example, if the father's name is listed first on the return and his social security number is entered in the block labeled "Your social security number," enter his name on line A and his social security number on line B.

If the parents were married but filed separate returns, enter the name and social security number of the parent who had the higher taxable income. If you do not know which parent had the higher taxable income, see Pub. 929.

If the parents were unmarried, treated as unmarried for Federal income tax purposes, or separated either by a divorce or separate maintenance decree, enter the name and social security number of the parent who had custody of the child for most of the year (the custodial parent). **Exception.** If the custodial parent remarried and filed a joint return with his or her spouse, enter the name and social security number of the

person who is listed first on the joint return, even if that person is not the child's parent. If the custodial parent and his or her spouse filed separate returns, enter the name and social security number of the person with the higher taxable income, even if that person is not the child's parent.

Note: *If the parents were unmarried but lived together during the year with the child, enter the name and social security number of the parent who had the higher taxable income.*

Line D. If the parent's filing status is married filing separately and the parent claimed an exemption for his or her spouse, write "Spouse" in the space above the box on line D.

Line 1. If the child had no earned income (defined below), enter the child's adjusted gross income (from Form 1040, line 32; Form 1040A, line 17; or Form 1040NR, line 31).

If the child had earned income, use the following worksheet to figure the amount to enter on line 1. However, if any of the following applies, use the worksheet in Pub. 929 instead of the one below to figure the amount to enter on Form 8615, line 1:

● The child files **Form 2555**, Foreign Earned Income.

● The child had a net loss from self-employment.

● The child claims a net operating loss deduction.

Worksheet (keep for your records)

1.	Enter the amount from the child's Form 1040, line 23; Form 1040A, line 14; or Form 1040NR, line 23, whichever applies . .	6,750
2.	Enter the child's **earned income** (defined below) plus any deduction the child claims on Form 1040, line 28, or Form 1040NR, line 27, whichever applies . .	0
3.	Subtract the amount on line 2 from the amount on line 1. Enter the result here and on Form 8615, line 1 . .	6,750

Earned Income includes wages, tips, and other payments received for personal services performed. Generally, earned income is the total of the amounts reported on Form 1040, lines 7, 12, and 19; Form 1040A, line 7; or Form 1040NR, lines 8, 13, and 20.

Line 2. If the child itemized deductions on Schedule A (Form 1040 or Form 1040NR), enter on line 2 the **greater** of:

● $500 plus the portion of the amount on Schedule A (Form 1040), line 27 (or Schedule A (Form 1040NR), line 10), that

is directly connected with the production of the investment income on Form 8615, line 1; OR

● $1,000.

Line 6. Enter the taxable income shown on the tax return of the parent identified on line A of Form 8615. If the parent's taxable income is less than zero, enter zero on line 6.

If the parent filed a joint return, enter the taxable income shown on that return even if the parent's spouse is not the child's parent.

If the parent transferred property to a trust which sold or exchanged the property during the year at a gain, include any gain that was taxed to the trust under Internal Revenue Code section 644 in the amount entered on line 6. Write "Section 644" and the amount on the dotted line next to line 6. Also, see the instructions for line 10 below.

Line 7. If the individual identified as the parent on this Form 8615 is also identified as the parent on any other Form 8615, add the amounts, if any, from line 5 on each of the other Forms 8615 and enter the total on line 7.

Lines 9, 15, and 17. Figure the tax using the Tax Table or Tax Rate Schedules, whichever applies.

Line 10. Enter the tax shown on the tax return of the parent identified on line A of Form 8615. If the parent filed a joint return, enter the tax shown on that return even if the parent's spouse is not the child's parent.

If line 6 includes any gain taxed to a trust under Internal Revenue Code section 644, add the tax imposed under section 644(a)(2)(A) to the tax shown on the parent's return. Enter the total on line 10 instead of entering the tax from the parent's return. Write "Section 644" on the dotted line next to line 10.

Line 18. Compare the amounts on lines 16 and 17 and enter the **larger** of the two amounts on line 18. Be sure to check the box for "Form 8615" on the appropriate line of the child's tax return even if the amount on line 17 is the larger of the two amounts.

Amended Return. If after the child's return is filed, the parent's taxable income is changed or the net investment income of any of the parent's other children is changed, the child's tax must be refigured using the adjusted amounts. If the child's tax is changed as a result of the adjustment(s), file **Form 1040X**, Amended U.S. Individual Income Tax Return, to correct the child's tax.

Alternative Minimum Tax. A child whose tax is figured on Form 8615 may be subject to the alternative minimum tax. Get **Form 6251**, Alternative Minimum Tax—Individuals, and its instructions to see if the child owes this tax.

Figure 11.1. *Continued.*

12 SPECIAL CHILD

Most of the same techniques and caveats stressed throughout this book apply in planning for the special child. However, when a child has special needs as a result of a disability, the importance of proper estate planning is even more accentuated. A critical factor from the outset will be the total assets available to provide for the special child, other children, and you and your spouse. This amount should take into account all sources of funding, including life insurance and government benefits for your special child.

TRUSTS FOR THE SPECIAL CHILD

When planning gifts or bequests for a special child, the use of a trust rather than an outright gift will always be recommended as long as the funds are sufficient (see Chapters 4 and 11). The use of an insurance trust, if there are not sufficient direct funds is an excellent alternative (see Chapter 19). The following are the central considerations in setting up a trust for a special child:

- One of the important advantages a trust offers over any other type of arrangement is that it enables you to name a trustee to manage the assets, as well as naming a number of alternates to serve as backups for your first choice. As recommended elsewhere, your attorney's law firm, or a particular bank or trust company, should be empowered to name a trustee when none of the individuals you've named is available. This approach will ensure that adequate management will continue for as long as necessary.

- A similar approach was suggested in Chapter 4 concerning the choice of a guardian, if a guardian is necessary (the presence of a trustee to manage financial matters may be sufficient protection without a guardian). With a special child, even greater care must be made in selecting a guardian and the alternates. Also, a particular social agency or specialized organization might be appropriate to name as the final choice of guardian in the event that all previously named guardians cannot serve.

- When a minor child reaches the age of majority, in order for the guardian to continue, the guardian's appointment may have to be confirmed by the court. When the child's abilities warrant and your state's laws permit, a partial or limited guardian may be more appropriate. Although the court is not obligated to recognize your choice of guardian, it probably will in the absence of unusual circumstances. Another alternative, depending on state law, is to have the parent's guardianship confirmed by the court. This might permit the parents to name successor guardians without the successor guardians having to go through the same judicial process.

- A trust for your special child could be established as a funded irrevocable insurance trust, or even a funded, or unfunded, living trust. Alternatively, a trust could be set up under your will. The sample will contained in the "For Your Notebook" section in Chapter 3 provides for such a trust; however, specific changes must be made to accommodate the needs of a special child.

  The sample will does not contain a specific provision for allowing a trustee to defer the distribution of assets to any beneficiary who is disabled. (To find such a provision, see the sample life insurance trust in the "For Your Notebook" section following Chapter 19.) The trustee under the testamentary trust (contained in the sample will) is given the power to sprinkle trust income to the beneficiaries most in need. This provision, however, is only present for the bypass or credit shelter portion of the estate. Under the Q-TIP trust established for the spouse in the sample will, on the spouse's death, the trust is divided into individual trusts for each child, but this approach would be inappropriate when a special child is involved. A single trust with a sprinkle power would provide the trustee greater flexibility to meet the special child's needs and to avoid jeopardizing government benefits.

- A spendthrift provision should be included in any trust. This provision attempts to prevent creditors of a child beneficiary from seizing trust assets, although the effect of a spendthrift clause will depend on state law. Such a clause is illustrated in all of the trusts in this book.

- The sample will and sample trusts in this book all authorize a trustee to distribute money "to or for the benefit of" the beneficiary. The trustee should be authorized to distribute funds for the benefit of the special child (for example, to service providers), as well as directly to the child, at the trustee's discretion. Depending on your state's laws, however, and the rules of the particular benefits program your child may qualify for, the typical language permitting the trustee to make such transfers could be too broad and open the way to a claim against trust property for reimbursement by a creditor or by the government agency providing aid. One safeguard is to provide language authorizing the trustee to distribute any amount to the guardian of the beneficiary (see the sample insurance trust). Alternatively, the trustee is empowered to add any trust income to the principal.

Depending on the nature of your child's disability and the likelihood of improvement, you might wish to provide that some portions of the principal of the trust, or some percentage of the annual income, be distributed directly to your child. This type of distribution, however, is likely to be inappropriate when your child qualifies for government benefits. A common approach is to have the language in the trust track the applicable statutes and regulations that identify what assets a disabled person can have without affecting his or her government benefits.

- A general statement should be included in the trust expressing your concern and objectives for your child. This can provide substantial guidance to a trustee, and to the court in the event of a change in law or other problem. Similarly, included with the general provisions permitting a trustee to make payments for the benefit of the beneficiary should be a list of specific types of expenditures the trustee is personally likely to incur in connection with the care and maintenance of your child (for example, reimbursement of the trustee's costs to visit the child to ascertain the quality of care being given).

GOVERNMENT AND AGENCY FUNDING

Designating multiple alternates for both trustee and guardian, coupled with the adequate funding of the trust, is the cornerstone combination in planning for the special child. However, all planning must be conducted in light of any special federal, state, or other agency funding for which your child may be eligible. Government benefits may be an important element in financing your child's care, and any trust arrangement will have to be coordinated so that it doesn't cause reduced government assistance or result in dissipating your estate in lieu of government funding. If the government can charge your child's assets for his or her care, the extra amount of money you worked so hard for and intended to have provide care and comfort above the amounts provided by benefit programs, could be depleted quickly.

The provisions that should be included in any trust agreement—the trustee's powers to sprinkle income among beneficiaries and to accumulate income and add it to principal, the spendthrift clause, and so forth—should help avoid this problem. Some agreements add a specific provision stating that if the assets of the trust are required to meet basic living expenditures of the special child, which otherwise would be met by government benefit programs, the trust will terminate and the assets will be distributed to other beneficiaries. Such a provision should be reviewed carefully with an advocate or attorney familiar with the benefit programs your child is currently using to be sure that the provision won't somehow taint future government benefits.

CONCLUSION

When a special child is involved, the basic estate planning documents and approaches will continue to be used. However, important changes are necessary. Although this chapter has highlighted some of them, careful attention must be paid to your state's laws, and to the specific benefit programs for which your special child might qualify.

13 DIVORCED TAXPAYERS

When negotiating a divorce settlement, aside from a possible provision in your separation agreement requiring each spouse to maintain life insurance with a designated beneficiary, estate planning is often ignored. This can be a considerable mistake, because there are several legal, tax, and personal matters that should be considered. Once the divorce has been concluded, your entire estate plan must be reviewed. This will extend from the reformulation of investment strategies through a complete revision of all legal documents (except for irrevocable trusts, which cannot be changed).

PRENUPTIAL AGREEMENTS

The preferred method for estate planning with regard to divorce is to consider the possibility (of divorce) prior to the marriage. A binding prenuptial agreement, in which you and your fiancée agree to place limitations on the rights to each other's estate and assets in the event of divorce, is the best approach.

Another approach is to keep assets out of your marital estate, thus limiting your spouse's claim to them in the event of a future divorce. Suppose you receive a gift from your family of an interest in a rental property, placed in trust. If you are not the trustee and will not participate in the leasing or management of the rental property, the asset may not be included in the marital property and should not be subject to a claim by your spouse (or ex-spouse).

ESTATE PLANNING AND THE DISCOVERY PROCESS

One of the most important aspects of many divorces is the process of discovering, and then valuing, all of the marital assets. In many situations, one of the spouses hides or undervalues assets. In the process of investigation, remember to look for documentation that may be important for estate planning. Although a spouse who is hiding assets is unlikely to leave such a paper trail, a request for documentation can yield valuable insight.

For example, if one spouse made a substantial transfer to the children (or to a third party) and filed a gift tax return, by requesting that return, you will obtain a description of the assets transferred and their valuation. Trusts or wills may occasionally be drafted by one spouse without the other's knowledge. The specific bequests contained in a will and the property used to fund any trust should be carefully reviewed for assets the other spouse was not aware of.

REVISION OF DOCUMENTS FOLLOWING DIVORCE

Will

Many divorced spouses fail to quickly revise their wills. You must revise your will—preferably, as soon as divorce appears imminent—so that your soon-to-be ex-spouse won't continue as your executor or trustee. Although state law may automatically affect the rights of an ex-spouse, these provisions are not always sufficient. For example, you may also want to remove your ex-spouse's family members from positions as guardian, trustee, or executor.

The nature of your dispositions may change as well. Many wills simply leave everything outright to the surviving spouse, or when there is no surviving spouse, to the children. With a divorce in process, it isn't likely that you will want the same distribution of assets that you had prescribed in the marriage's better days. The use of a trust can help assure that your remaining assets will be disposed of for your natural children, rather than going to your ex-spouse.

Power of Attorney

Any powers of attorney should be revised as soon as a separation occurs, or divorce seems possible (that is, before it is imminent). This is because powers of attorney for spouses often are not springing powers (those which become effective on your disability) but are effective when signed. This means that your estranged spouse may have in hand a document giving him or her authority to sign your name for a broad range of financial transactions.

CAUTION: Contact your attorney immediately and have any powers of attorney revoked. Many states have a form you can fill out to revoke a power of attorney when you can't be sure you've destroyed all the originals. If you know that form powers of attorney have been left with your bank or brokerage firm, contact them in writing (use certified mail) advising them that the documents they have are void.

You will need to prepare new powers of attorney to be certain you have someone to act in your behalf in case you become ill or disabled (see Chapter 2).

Living Will and Other Documents

If you have a living will and named your spouse as the agent to carry out your wishes, you may want to revise the form to name a new agent (see Chapter 5). Discuss the matter with your attorney.

Review any other legal documents for possible amendment. For example, if you own a closely held corporation, you may have made your spouse a director or officer. You will need to have the appropriate actions taken by the corporation to replace him or her. Often, this will require no more than a brief statement (a unanimous consent of all shareholders and directors) signed by you and perhaps the other shareholders or directors. But be certain these actions won't prejudice your divorce action or conflict with any separation agreement you may have signed.

CORRECTION OF OWNERSHIP OF PROPERTY

Another common oversight is the failure to retitle property and change names of beneficiaries. You must take the necessary legal steps to change the names and ownership of your bank and securities accounts, real estate, and other assets. It is common for many married couples to take title to property as joint tenants. The marital residence, bank accounts, brokerage accounts, and bonds are common examples of property held as joint tenants. When the marriage terminates the joint ownership of property must be divided and the right of survivorship in the jointly owned property ended. To do this, you and your spouse have to cooperate to transfer the property from yourselves as joint tenants to each of you as tenants in common. If the proportional interests each of you owns is maintained, the transfer will not be taxable. If the division of joint property takes place prior to divorce there will not be any gift tax consequence.

Consult your lawyer to learn what steps must be taken to change title to your individual name for these and other assets. Without these steps, the revisions of your will may not be effective, because property held in joint name won't pass under your will. Consider the tax consequences of these changes (see Chapter 20).

CAUTION: If your divorce is in process, be certain to discuss any proposed change to the title of any property with your lawyer before taking any action, because it will have implications for your divorce negotiations and tax implications.

STATE LAW AND ELECTIVE-SHARE RIGHTS

Revising your will may not accomplish your estate planning objectives for another reason—state law. Under the laws of most states, a spouse has a right to demand a specified portion (the "elective share") of the assets in your estate upon your death. So depending on the status of your divorce if you revise your will to exclude your spouse, the changes may not be effective. In your state, the surviving spouse may be entitled to take one-third of your estate instead of what is provided for in your will. The rules vary by state, and often by whether the marriage had children. If there are no children, the surviving spouse may be entitled to one-half of your estate.

You should revise your will in any case, because it may not be certain that your spouse will be entitled to the elective share. Further, you still will accomplish other objectives of naming new executors, trustees, and reducing your spouse's share to no more than that required under state law.

The amount of your "estate" to which your spouse is entitled may be much larger than you have anticipated. Certain assets that generally are not considered to be part of your estate may be added to your estate for purposes of the calculation of your spouse's elective share. Assets added into your estate may include gifts made just prior to your death, bank accounts set up in trust for your children, a buy-sell agreement changed just prior to death, and trusts established for your benefit if you had the sufficient control and rights in the trust (these are known as "testamentary substitutes"). In addition to the elective share, your spouse may be entitled to such other assets as the family car, a limited amount of cash, and certain personal property.

Some states provide a few exceptions from this rule. For example, if your spouse is deemed to have "abandoned" you (as defined under state law), this right may have been forfeited. Some states provide for an alternative to the elective share. You may be able to leave assets in a trust for your surviving spouse and eliminate the spouse's right to the elective share. To achieve this, the assets in the trust will have to meet a number of requirements, including the following: (1) the value of the assets must at least equal the amount your spouse would be entitled to as an elective share; (2) the spouse must be entitled to all of the income generated by the assets; and (3) the principal of the trust cannot be invaded other than for the benefit of the surviving spouse. The advantage of using a trust approach is that the trust can provide for the disposition of the assets to your natural children on your surviving spouse's death. These trusts can be similar to the Q-TIP trusts commonly used in estate planning (see Chapter 9 and below).

CAUTION: State laws can vary considerably. Be sure to confer with an attorney in your state to ascertain exactly what steps you must take and what nuances of your state's law you must be aware of.

PLANNING FOR CHILDREN'S EDUCATION

An important issue is planning to finance the education of the children of divorced parents. The kiddie tax, which taxes the unearned income of a child under age 14 at the parents' tax rate, must be considered. (See Chapter 11 for details on the taxes, acts, and trusts referred to in this section.) If the parent's are no longer married, it is the tax rate of the custodial parent that applies. The use of trusts to fund education is restricted by the grantor trust rules, which include any trust in which the transferor retains more than a 5 percent reversionary interest. As a result, if you and your ex-spouse set up a trust to fund your child's education and there is a possibility of having the money revert to you, you may be taxed on the income earned by the trust.

Education costs can be planned for by using outright gifts or gifts made under the Uniform Gifts (Transfers) to Minors Act. (If the child is under age 14, however, the kiddie tax must be considered.) Use of a Code Section 2503(c) trust, which can accumulate income until the child reaches age 21 while still qualifying for the annual $10,000 per donee gift tax exclusion, is another alternative. A trust for the child can offer the following advantages: (1) provide a future college fund; (2) provide an emergency fund; and (3) provide for the management, investment, and control over the funds placed in the trust to ensure their use for your child's benefit. An illustrative clause requiring the spouses to set up such a trust is included in the "For Your Notebook" section following this chapter.

USE OF A Q-TIP TRUST IN DIVORCE

A common goal for divorced couples is to make sure that their natural children receive some inheritance. There are a number of ways to go about this. Gifts can be made directly to your children, or in trust for their benefit. However, you may also wish to preserve assets for your own use for retirement, and often for the support of your spouse in a second or later marriage. The most common and effective means of accomplishing all these objectives is to set up a Q-TIP trust (also see Chapter 9).

"Q-TIP" is an abbreviation for qualified terminable interest property. A Q-TIP trust arrangement can best be illustrated by an example.

EXAMPLE: Husband is married to Second Wife. Husband has children from his prior marriage with First Wife. Husband's objectives are to provide generously for Second Wife for her life so that she should want nothing. However, on Second Wife's death, he wants his estate to go to the natural children of his prior marriage and not to the children of Second Wife. Husband also wants to minimize the estate tax costs.

The solution is for Husband to include a Q-TIP trust in his will, giving all his assets in trust to Second Wife upon his death, and specifying that on her death, the remaining assets will go to the children of his first marriage. When properly structured, the Q-TIP bequest qualifies for the unlimited estate tax marital deduction, which means that on Husband's death, the full amount of assets placed in the Q-TIP trust will be available for Second Wife's support.

To qualify, all income from the Q-TIP trust must be paid, at least annually, to the second wife. No person can have any right to appoint any of the assets in the Q-TIP trust to anyone other than the second wife during her lifetime. The husband's executor must elect to have this bequest to the Q-TIP trust qualify for the marital deduction. Upon the death of the second wife, the Q-TIP trust can provide all the remaining assets to the husband's children from his first marriage. If the children are minors at that time, the assets should be held in trust for their benefit at least until they reach the age of majority. Most parents choose to retain assets in trust until the children are even older and more likely to be mature enough to handle the assets.

NOTE: When planning for a second marriage, review the status of your divorce from your first spouse with your attorney, the need for a pre-nuptial agreement, and all of your estate planning documents.

ESTATE AND GIFT PLANNING AFTER DIVORCE

Estate Tax

Divorce raises several estate tax issues. The property you're required to transfer to your ex-spouse by the settlement agreement still may have to be included in your gross estate. This result occurs in the following situations:

- Transfers in which you retained a life estate. "Life estate" means you reserved for your life, or for a period that does not end before your death, the use, possession, right to income, or other enjoyment of the property transferred to your ex-spouse.

- The value of any transfers made during your lifetime that don't take effect until your death.

- Transfers in which you retained a power to alter, amend, or revoke.

These provisions can be triggered by a number of events. Suppose as part of the divorce settlement you are required to transfer certain of your property to a trust, with the income going to your spouse for his or her life and the remainder to your children. If you retain any interest in the trust property in violation of the provisions discussed above—for example, the power to appoint the remainder interest—the value of the trust will be included in your estate. The only exception may be when the transfer was supported by adequate consideration.

A common situation in divorce is for the husband to be required to make alimony payments to the wife for a period of years, which is to last until the wife dies or remarries. If the husband dies before all of the required alimony payments are made to the wife, his estate generally will be obligated to complete them. The payment of these claims to the wife by the husband's estate will be a deductible expense for the estate. There is a limitation on deductions for claims against an estate that requires the claims to have been made in good faith and for adequate consideration. If the payment of alimony is pursuant to a written agreement, if the divorce occurred within one year before or two years following the date of the agreement, and if the payments were in settlement of the decedent's marital or property rights, the claim will be deemed to have been made for adequate consideration.

Gift Tax

Gift taxes sometimes can be an important factor in a settlement. Most transfers of marital property pursuant to a divorce will be exempt from gift taxation. Be certain, however, that your accountant handles the appropriate filing and reporting requirements. You and your spouse may take advantage of gift splitting, the technique by which you and your spouse agree to split a gift so that each of your $10,000 annual exclusions can be used and the gift can have double the value (see Chapter 7). For gift splitting to be effective, a joint gift tax return must be filed. If a divorce occurs prior to the filing, provisions addressing each spouse's willingness to file should be included in the separation agreement.

The basic tax rule concerning property settlements in a divorce is that no gain or loss is recognized for tax purposes as a result of transferring property between spouses or former spouses as a result of a divorce settlement. There is an exception to this general rule that is easy to overlook. When the liabilities to which the property is subject exceed the tax basis in the property transferred, the nonrecognition rule won't apply. There is a cost for not having to incur an immediate tax cost. In that case, the tax basis (cost plus improvements, minus depreciation) will carry over from the transferor spouse to the recipient spouse. This can have important tax consequences and should be considered in the context of any gift planning.

EXAMPLE: Husband owns a vacation home at the shore that he bought 15 years ago, before the marriage, for $45,000. Prices skyrocketed so about four years ago, when the vacation home was worth $125,000, the couple refinanced and took out a new mortgage of $90,000. The house is now worth $142,000. Depreciation on the vacation home, totaling $21,000, had been claimed over the years. Husband's tax basis in the vacation home (figured for the example as cost minus depreciation) is only $24,000.

If a property settlement is agreed to in which Husband transfers his interests in the vacation home to Ex-Wife, the transfer won't trigger the significant tax cost to him. This general rule of nonrecognition of gain on property transfers comes at a price. Ex-Wife will now have a tax basis in the vacation home equal to Husband's $21,000 tax basis. If Ex-Wife is forced to sell the property to raise cash, she will have an income tax cost of $42,350 [($142,000 value − $21,000 tax basis) × 35% tax rate].

Consider the potential for built-in tax costs when planning what to do with any property and when planning a gift program. If a substantial gain may be triggered, it may be more advantageous to give the property to your children than to sell it.

CONCLUSION

Divorce creates a host of gift and estate planning problems. Although there will be many other personal and financial matters to address during and following a divorce, the estate planning issues should not be overlooked.

For Your Notebook:

SAMPLE CLAUSE FOR SEPARATION AGREEMENT REQUIRING CHILD'S TRUST
(WITH COMMENTS)

FOR DISCUSSION WITH YOUR LAWYER ONLY—DO NOT USE IN ANY AGREEMENT

I. The Husband and Wife shall establish a trust ("Trust") for the benefit of the Child. This trust shall be used primarily as a future college fund for the Child, a secondarily to provide an emergency fund in the event of any health or other matters for which the Child would require funds that are not provided for under the general provisions of the Separation Agreement.

II. The parties shall execute and fund a trust agreement, and take any other steps reasonably necessary to implement the intent of this provision, not later than Thirty (30) days from the execution of this Separation Agreement.

III. The terms of such trust shall provide for the management, investment, and control over the trust funds for the purpose of assuring that both the principal and income of the Trust are used for the benefit of the Child as provided herein. Said Trust shall be drafted so as to conform with the provisions of Internal Revenue Code of 1986 Section 2053(c).

NOTE: Have your tax adviser review the options available to you in addition to the Section 2053(c) minor's trust (discussed in Chapter 11). Use the approach most appropriate for your needs.

IV. All funds contributed to the Trust shall be invested in money market accounts, certificates of deposit, municipal bonds, obligations of, or insured by, the United States government, mutual funds, and other investments reasonably suited to meet the objectives of the Trust. The Trust funds, both principal and interest, may be retained after the Child attains the age of 21, with his or her permission, and in compliance with the applicable tax laws. If monies are so retained they shall be accumulated and then applied for the Child's postgraduate study, to the extent available.

NOTE: The investment standard suggested in this paragraph is much more restrictive than the powers granted to the trustees under any of the trusts illustrated in this book. In some divorce situations, this more conservative and specific approach may be appropriate to prevent future arguments or problems. In other instances, the broad language contained in the sample trusts, granting the trustees the authority to invest as they determine, may be acceptable.

V. The Trust shall be jointly administered by the Husband and Wife as co-trustees. In the discretion of Husband and Wife, a neutral third party may be named as a third trustee to cast deciding votes in the event of a disagreement by Husband and Wife in their capacities as trustees of the Trust.

NOTE: A third-party tiebreaker is very important. In an acrimonious divorce, it should be mandatory. The best approach is to agree on who should serve in this capacity when negotiating the settlement agreement. Deferring the decision until the trust is adopted at a later date may prevent the trust from ever being implemented.

VI. The Trust shall be funded by mandatory annual contributions by the Husband and Wife each as follows:

A. Four percent (4%) of each of their respective gross wages in excess of Twenty Thousand Dollars ($20,000) for each calendar year, commencing with the calendar year in which the Child attains the age of Five (5) years and extending until, but not including, the calendar year in which the Child attains the age of Eleven (11) years.
B. Six percent (6%) of each of their respective gross wages in excess of Twenty Thousand Dollars ($20,000) for each calendar year, commencing with the calendar year in which the Child attains the age of Eleven (11) years and extending until, but not including, the calendar year in which the Child attains the age of Sixteen (16) years.
C. Eight percent (8%) of each of their respective gross wages in excess of Thirty-Five Thousand Dollars ($35,000) for each calendar year, commencing with the calendar year in which the Child attains the age of Sixteen (16) years and extending until, and including, the calendar year in which the Child attains the age of Twenty-One (21) years.

NOTE: There is no recommended formula. The objective is to accumulate enough money to properly care for the child, and to avoid having payments that are an excessive burden on you and your ex-spouse. Consideration should be given to the earnings of each spouse, the likely changes in such earnings, the type of education you both want for your children, and any other relevant factors. It's also advisable to have your accountant make various projections of the payments from each spouse and the funds that will be available in the trust.

D. The following rules shall govern the operation of these payments:
   1. If either the Husband or Wife ceases working for any reason other than disability, the payments shall continue to be made and the "gross wages" for said spouse shall be defined as his or her average earnings for the three calendar years preceding the calendar year in which said spouse ceased working.

NOTE: This should not be done unless each spouse has assets or other income sources. The purpose of this provision is to deter either spouse from simply quitting work and ignoring his or her responsibility for funding the child's trust.

   2. If either the Husband or Wife becomes employed as a sole proprietor, then for the purposes of this section his or her "gross wages" shall be defined as net income from self-employment, adjusted as follows: (i) add back depreciation and similar noncash expenses; (2) subtract the cash paid for long-lived assets or equipment subject to depreciation (however, no adjustment shall be made for structural improvements to a principal residence used in such business); (3) add back Eighty percent (80%) of all travel and entertainment expenses.

NOTE: Whether this provision is appropriate will depend on your specific circumstances. The key point is that the attorney drafting the separation agreement and trust must make provisions for as many possible work situations as you and your spouse reasonably can anticipate. The trust may be funded over a long period of time, and circumstances can change. The last thing either of you should want is to have to go back to court years from now to address the payment provisions in the trust.

---

   3. If any spouse does not make the contribution required hereunder, such funds shall accrue interest at the federal midterm interest rate as determined under Internal Revenue Code Section 1274, and the regulations thereunder, plus Two percent (2%).
   4. The payments under this provision shall cease upon the substantial disability or death of a spouse.
   5. In no event shall any payments be made on gross wages in excess of One Hundred and Fifty Thousand Dollars ($150,000).

NOTE: The purpose of this clause is to limit the amount that will be put into trust.

---

14 CHARITIES

The first question to ask yourself regarding charity is, should you really make a substantial charitable contribution? To help answer that, the second question is, do you meet the following four tests: (1) Your estate is very substantial; (2) you're confident that the needs of your heirs are safely provided for; (3) you have a charitable intent; and (4) you can afford to transfer significant assets to charity. In spite of the hoopla some financial columns have created about charitable giving, be wary of committing to any major charitable program unless the answer to all four of these questions is a resounding yes.

TIP: Charitable planning is often combined with the purchase of a life insurance policy to replace the estate value lost through the contribution. The purchase of the life insurance probably should be arranged through an irrevocable life insurance trust in order to protect the insurance and keep it out of your estate (Chapter 19). If this technique is considered, be sure to review all of the costs and investment aspects with your insurance adviser and financial planner before making any commitments. Also, make sure you're insurable.

GENERAL CONSIDERATIONS IN CHARITABLE GIVING

Charitable gifts can be made in a number of different ways. They can take effect currently (a present gift) or after a specified number of years (a future gift). Gifts of assets can be made during your lifetime, or through a bequest under your will. The timing and nature of the gift will affect the amount and type of charity tax deduction to which you, and your estate, will be entitled. If you make a charitable contribution that will be effective at your death, your estate may be entitled to a deduction for the value of the property donated to charity. If the contribution is effective during your lifetime, you may be entitled to a contribution deduction for income tax purposes.

With some of the common charitable contribution techniques, you may obtain both an income tax deduction during your life (based on a mathematical valuation of the amount the charity will receive at some future date) and an estate tax deduction for the value of the asset included in your estate and donated to the charity. When a gift of only a future interest is given, the value of the charitable contribution deduction is limited to the present value of the donation. Present value is a mathematical approach to considering the time value of money and perhaps your life expectancy in estimating the value today of a charitable gift that will only be effective after some number of years, or after your death.

Charitable contributions can consist of cash or property, and can be wholly donated or given as a bargain sale (you sell the property for, say, half its value, so the transaction is partly a sale and partly a donation). A contribution can also take the form of what is called a split interest. This is when you and the charity each have use of the donated property for a certain time period. Included in this category are charitable remainder trusts, charitable lead trusts, and pooled-income funds, all of which are discussed below. Finally, you can gift a remainder interest in your house or farm to a charity (see Chapter 18).

Generally, except for certain transfers in trust, there is no deduction permitted for a charitable contribution of less than an entire interest in a property. For example, a contribution of the right to use property is a contribution of less than an entire interest, which will not qualify for a deduction.

EXAMPLE: A taxpayer permits a local art museum to use her vacant land for overflow parking. Even though the value of this use can be readily estimated from prices of nearby parking facilities, no deduction is permitted because this is a nonqualifying partial interest in property.

This exception does not apply when the partial interest contributed is the entire interest you own—for example, a donation of 40 percent of a property when you only own a 40 percent interest. In that case, a charitable deduction is permitted. A remainder interest in a personal residence or farm may qualify (see Chapter 18).

CHARITABLE REMAINDER TRUST

If you want to make a charitable contribution but don't want to part with the property or its income immediately, a deferred-giving program may be appropriate. You could create a remainder interest in the property in favor of a charitable organization. "Remainder" simply refers to the value that is left in the asset after you have finished using it, after which the property is transferred to a charity.

NOTE: If have no need for current income, an outright gift to a charity may be preferable because a larger contribution deduction will be available. Legal and other fees will be almost nil.

The technique works as follows. You donate the asset (property, stock, and so forth) to a charity for future use and receive a tax deduction in the year of the donation, limited to the present value of the donation (see below). For example, you can reserve an income interest in the charitable remainder trust for a specified number of years (not more than 20), or for your life and the life of your spouse as the income beneficiaries. This means that the income generated from the donated property would be paid to you for life and thereafter to your spouse for life. Both of you are taxed on the income as you receive it, but the trust itself is generally tax free. After the deaths of you and your spouse, the charity will obtain full use and benefit of the donated property.

The amount of the charitable contribution is calculated as the fair market value of the property at the time of the donation to the charitable remainder trust, less the present value of the income interest retained by you and your spouse.

In addition to the current income tax deduction, there is an important estate tax benefit. If you are one of the income beneficiaries of the charitable trust (which is almost always the case), the value of the trust will be included in your estate. However, since the interest will pass to the charity, there will be an offsetting estate tax charitable contribution deduction. This creates a wash, effectively removing the value of the property from your estate. The savings in income, estate, and inheritance tax, plus probate and administrative costs, can be substantial.

With the exception of gifts of a remainder interest in a personal residence or farm property, you can only get an income, gift, and estate tax deduction for a donation to a remainder trust when the trust qualifies as either an annuity trust or a unitrust (you cannot use a hybrid of the two). The trust must be irrevocable—you can't change it once you've set it up. Also, the trusts must comply with complex requirements to qualify. The IRS has provided sample forms, and it is generally best to have your attorney use modifications of these.

Annuity Trust

An annuity trust provides a fixed annuity to its income beneficiaries. This return, which must be a fixed or determinable amount, but not less than 5 percent, is calculated once, based on the fair market value of the property at the time of the donation. Once the trust is established, no further contributions can be made to it. If the trust income is insufficient to meet the required annual return, principal must be invaded.

Unitrust

A unitrust provides a form of variable annuity benefit to its income beneficiaries. The minimum rate of return to the income beneficiaries must be 5 percent. This rate of return is calculated on the fair market value of the property, determined on an annual basis. This means an annual appraisal is necessary. While this is a simple matter for securities, it can be quite costly when real estate or art is involved; therefore, for these assets, an annuity trust is more appropriate. The trust may provide that if the annual income of the trust property is insufficient to meet the required distribution to the beneficiaries, principal may be invaded; if principal is not required to be invaded, the deficit must be made up in later years. Once a unitrust is established, additional contributions may be made in later years under certain conditions.

CHARITABLE GIFT ANNUITIES

When a charitable gift annuity is used, money or property is transferred to a qualified charitable organization in exchange for a payment of an annuity by the charity. When appreciated property is donated, you will recognize any gain as the annuity payments are received. The deduction for a charitable contribution will be based on actuarial calculations.

CHARITABLE LEAD TRUST

If you don't need the money now, but want it to be used later to provide for your heirs, a charitable lead trust may be appropriate. A charitable lead trust is the opposite of a charitable remainder trust: The charity receives the income from a property for a specified period of years, and then the property is transferred to designated beneficiaries, such as your children. Obviously, the estate tax benefits are minor because only the income accumulation from the years of the trust is removed from the estate.

POOLED-INCOME FUND

Under this type of arrangement, you contribute property and in exchange receive units of participation in an investment pool (like a mutual fund) managed by the charity. The trust pays you a pro rata share of the income from the pooled trust. On your death, the charitable organization gets your share of the trust assets.

INCOME TAX RULES

By using any of the above techniques, an income tax deductible charitable contribution is created. It is important to understand the basic rules affecting these deductions, because they will be an important part of any benefit you realize.

Qualifying Organizations

When a cash contribution is made to a qualified charitable organization, the amount of the cash is generally deductible. Most qualified charitable organizations are listed in IRS Publication No. 78, "Cumulative List of Organizations," and include the following: the United States, a state, a U.S. possession, or a political subdivision of the above, when the contribution is made for a public purpose; also, a community chest, corporation, trust, fund, or foundation organized or created under the laws of the United States, a state, or a political subdivision. The organization must exist for charitable, religious, educational, scientific, or literary purposes; for the prevention of cruelty to animals or children; or to foster amateur sports competition. War veterans organizations qualify, as do domestic fraternal societies where the contribution is used solely for charitable, religious, scientific, literary, or educational purposes, or to prevent cruelty to animals or children.

The 30 Percent and 50 Percent Rules

Charity deductions are limited to specified percentages of your income. You generally can deduct the fair market value of property that has increased in value even if this amount exceeds your tax basis. This is one of the most valuable benefits of donating property—you can get a tax deduction without paying tax on the gain. Your deduction will be subject to a limitation, however. The general rule is that if you donate appreciated capital gain property, you will be entitled to deduct the full fair market value of the donated property up to a limit of 30 percent of your adjusted gross income.

If you elect to reduce the amount of the contribution deduction by the appreciation in the property, you can deduct a contribution of up to 50 percent of your adjusted gross income. The following factors should be considered before making this election: (1) How much has the property appreciated? (2) What impact on the tax calculation does each option have? (3) Will you be subject to the alternative minimum tax (AMT) as a result of donating assets with long-term appreciation (special rules apply for 1991)?

The AMT might be triggered if the property has appreciated substantially. If you are subject to the AMT, the appreciation in the gift will generally be included in the AMT base (some exclusions apply) but if you make this 50 percent election, no deduction is being claimed for the appreciation in the property donated, so the AMT implications disappear. This is because the appreciation not recognized on the contribution creates an AMT adjustment. The AMT tax rate is 24 percent, not substantially less than the maximum 31 percent rate for purposes of the regular tax. Therefore, when the 24 percent AMT rate is applied against your taxable income increased by the unrecognized appreciation, the tax is likely to exceed your regular tax calculated at a 31 percent rate.

When appreciated property is donated, your charitable deduction for that property is limited to 30 percent of adjusted gross income; when a special election is made to exclude the appreciation from the contribution deduction, so that you can use the 50 percent limitation, the AMT issue becomes moot.

The following steps may be considered in planning to avoid the AMT (which could affect whether you should make the special election): (1) stagger gifts of property among different tax years to avoid triggering AMT; (2) carefully select (and time) gifts based on the amount of appreciation in each property in order to avoid triggering AMT; (3) consider bargain sales for a sufficient amount of property to avoid the AMT and achieve an overall better tax result.

Non-Capital-Gain Property

If you donate property that would have generated ordinary income (inventory) or short-term capital gain if sold, the contribution deduction is limited to the fair market value of the property reduced by the ordinary income or short-term capital gain portion.

Gifts of non-capital-gain property made to qualifying charitable organizations (generally public charities, characterized as 50 percent limit organizations) can be deducted up to but cannot exceed 50 percent of your adjusted gross income. Other contributions are limited to 30 percent or 20 percent of your adjusted gross income. Contributions that cannot be deducted because of these limitations may be deducted in later years.

Reporting Rules

How you report your donations on your tax return is also important. There are three stages of rules:

- For deductions not exceeding $500, only a reliable written record and a receipt from the charitable donee setting forth the name of the organization, the date and location of the contribution, and a description of the property is required.

- For deductions that exceed $500 but are less than $5,000, Form 8283, Noncash Charitable Contributions, must be filed.

- For deductions involving properties that exceed $5,000 in value, the IRS requires you to obtain a qualified appraisal. When donations of two or more similar properties are made in the same tax year, they will be aggregated for purposes of applying this test.

NOTE: These rules will always apply when setting up a charitable remainder or lead trust, because the amounts will be large. Carefully review the requirements with your accountant before making the gift to help ensure the intended tax results. Special penalties can be assessed if the value of donated property is overstated.

Special rules apply in the case of a donation of securities. If the securities are publicly traded, no appraisal is required. If the securities are not publicly traded, an appraisal is required only when the claimed market value of the contribution is greater than $10,000. Make sure the appraiser is familiar with the requirements of making an appraisal for tax purposes and provides all of the information you will need to claim the deduction on your tax return. The appraiser's compensation cannot be set as a percentage of the appraised value. The appraisal may not be provided by the charity or by the person who sold you the property.

CONCLUSION

For those who are charitably inclined, there are multiple advantages to making a charitable contribution of property: You can benefit a wide range of charitable organizations; you can often achieve substantial tax savings; and you can even provide a secure income stream for yourself or your family. These techniques are quite complicated, however, and should only be undertaken after a careful review of some of the caveats noted in this chapter, and after meetings with your tax, legal, and investment advisers.

TIP: While it's essential to have your own attorney review all aspects of any major charitable transaction, discuss the necessary legal work with the charitable organization first. Many of the larger organizations have very sophisticated attorneys on staff, who can assist you with many of the issues and documents you need, at no cost.

For Your Notebook:

ILLUSTRATION OF PLANNING WITH A CHARITABLE REMAINDER TRUST

FACTS AND COMMENTS

You own all the shares of stock in a C corporation that owns real estate worth $1 million (a selection was never made). The property was bought many years ago, has been fully depreciated, and thus has only a nominal tax basis. If you were to sell the property, given that the real estate is owned by a corporation, you would face a double tax: The corporation would have to pay a substantial tax on the gain on the property, and then you, as sole shareholder, would have to pay a substantial personal income tax on receiving the distribution from the corporation. Further, there could be significant transfer costs and taxes.

A charitable trust arrangement could save the day. You could give a remainder interest in the stock of the corporation to a designated charity. The charity could take the stock, liquidate the corporation, sell the property, and invest the proceeds (all without incurring any tax) and pay income to you and your spouse for life. After the death of the later of you or your spouse the charity would receive the remaining proceeds.

During your lifetime, the income tax deduction for a charitable contribution could be substantial. Assuming that the charity would sell the apartment house and invest the proceeds, you could receive an annual income that exceeds the income you have been receiving from the real estate involved. The charitable contribution deduction could eliminate any income tax liability for five years. Further, the charity could invest in a diversified portfolio, providing you with much less risk than you had through your ownership of a single parcel of real estate. The gift of the stock, and hence the property, could also eliminate a substantial management burden. Finally, by making the donation while you're alive, you would be better able to arrange for this, as well as to enjoy the community kudos for your philanthropy.

You could use one of the following approaches: an annuity trust arrangement, which would give them a fixed annuity for life; a unitrust arrangement, which would provide a fluctuating payment based on the fair market value of the portfolio held by the charity; or a pooled-income fund. If you and your advisers decide that the unitrust approach should be used, with payments going to you (age 62) and your spouse (age 58), and that you want 10 percent of the value of the portfolio paid to you quarterly, you will be entitled to a charitable deduction of $107,120. If you're in a 40 percent federal and state tax bracket, this deduction will be worth almost $43,000. This is the situation illustrated in the first chart. If you decide to be a bit more conservative and only require an 8.125 percent payout, their contribution deduction would increase to $156,820 (see second chart). This would be worth almost $63,000.

```
┌──────────────────────────────────────────────────────────────────┐
│        C H A R I T A B L E   R E M A I N D E R   U N I T R U S T   │
├──────────────────────────────────────────────────────────────────┤
│  Two Lives                          Wednesday February 13, 1991    │
├──────────────────────────────────────────────────────────────────┤
│     Transfer Date: 1/1990   10.0%   9.8%   9.6%  Table Rate:10.00% │
│                                                                    │
│     FMV of Trust:  $1,000,000.00     Percentage Payout:10.000%     │
│                                                                    │
│     Payment Period: 4    Months Valuation Precedes Payout: 2       │
│                                                                    │
│            First Age: 58    Second Age: 62                         │
├─────────────────────── Calculation Results ═══════════════════════┤
│  Payout Sequence Factor ...........................    0.950021    │
│  Adjusted Payout Rate .............................      9.500%    │
│  Interpolation: Factor at 9.4% at Ages 58 and 62 .....  0.10936    │
│                Factor at 9.6% Ages 58 and 62 ........   0.10489    │
│                Difference ...........................   0.00447    │
│  (9.500% - 9.4%) / 0.2% = X / 0.00447; Therefore X ...  0.00224    │
│  Two-Life Factor = Factor at 9.4% less X ............   0.10712    │
│  Charitable Deduction for Remainder Interest ........ $107,120.00  │
└──────────────────────────────────────────────────────────────────┘
```

```
┌──────────────────────────────────────────────────────────────────┐
│        C H A R I T A B L E   R E M A I N D E R   U N I T R U S T   │
├──────────────────────────────────────────────────────────────────┤
│  Two Lives                          Wednesday February 13, 1991    │
├──────────────────────────────────────────────────────────────────┤
│     Transfer Date: 1/1990   10.0%   9.8%   9.6%  Table Rate:10.00% │
│                                                                    │
│     FMV of Trust:  $1,000,000.00     Percentage Payout: 8.125%     │
│                                                                    │
│     Payment Period: 4    Months Valuation Precedes Payout: 2       │
│                                                                    │
│            First Age: 58    Second Age: 62                         │
├─────────────────────── Calculation Results ═══════════════════════┤
│  Payout Sequence Factor ...........................    0.950021    │
│  Adjusted Payout Rate .............................      7.719%    │
│  Interpolation: Factor at 7.6% at Ages 58 and 62 .....  0.16093    │
│                Factor at 7.8% Ages 58 and 62 ........   0.15402    │
│                Difference ...........................   0.00691    │
│  (7.719% - 7.6%) / 0.2% = X / 0.00691; Therefore X ...  0.00411    │
│  Two-Life Factor = Factor at 7.6% less X ............   0.15682    │
│  Charitable Deduction for Remainder Interest ........ $156,820.00  │
└──────────────────────────────────────────────────────────────────┘
```

Note: These examples were prepared using the Charitable Financial Planner software published by Commerce Clearing House, Inc., Chicago, Illinois.

Figure 14.1.   Illustration of planning with a charitable remainder trust.

Part Four

PLANNING FOR SPECIFIC ASSETS

15 REAL ESTATE

For many Americans, real estate (whether in the form of a home, investment property, or business property) is one of the most significant components of their estate. Real estate presents a number of unique problems and opportunities, all of which should be considered in your estate planning. Fortunately, real estate investors have a lot of planning techniques to choose from.

CHARACTERISTICS OF REAL ESTATE THAT AFFECT PLANNING

Three important factors govern the estate planning needed for real estate. They are appreciation, lack of divisibility, and lack of liquidity. Until recently, a major focus of estate planning for real estate owners has been to remove appreciable assets from their estates in order to mitigate the gift or estate tax costs. A long-term time horizon is typical for estate planning. In spite of the recent declines in real estate values in many parts of the country, it is still likely that real estate will continue to appreciate, although more slowly than in the 1980s. Therefore, the removal of future appreciation is still a cornerstone of estate planning for real estate assets.

In fact, a low point in the market may be the ideal time to transfer real estate assets, because lower valuations should be justified and gift taxes minimized. However, the recent weaknesses in the real estate markets point to another concern—properties may decline in value. There is no point in using your unified credit (Chapter 6) or incurring a current gift tax cost (Chapter 7) for property that declines in value. This is because the property will be worth less when you die at some future date and thus will cost less to transfer then. Therefore, greater care is required than ever before in choosing which real estate assets should be given to your family.

The second issue is that real estate, unlike stocks, is not readily divisible. Divisibility is important when you want to give real estate assets to more than one benefactor, and you want to use the annual $10,000 gift tax exclusion ($20,000 with gift splitting). If a rental building is worth $450,000, how can you give each of your three children a

$20,000 interest in the building? Ways to address this problem are discussed below.

Finally, real estate is not considered to be a liquid asset. Unlike stocks, real estate cannot be sold within moments by a telephone call to a broker. The estate tax is generally due within nine months of death (some state death taxes are due earlier), and this is not a lot of time in which to raise money.

EXAMPLE: You have an office building worth $1.6 million. You're in the maximum 55 percent estate tax bracket; therefore, your estate will owe $880,000 in federal estate tax on just this building. The net cash return (excess of rental income over expenses) may only be about $100,000, leaving a substantial tax burden.

This liquidity problem can be addressed in a number of ways. A funded insurance trust can provide liquidity without increasing your estate taxes (Chapter 19). If you own the property with partners, a buy-out agreement can be a valuable means of gaining some liquidity (but don't count on it to provide enough money to pay the entire estate tax when due). Buy-outs are discussed below, and a sample buy-out agreement designed especially for partners in a real estate investment is included in the "For Your Notebook" section following this chapter. If the property is not highly leveraged, nine months may be a sufficient amount of time to refinance the mortgage to raise money. Or your estate may qualify for a special provision that permits a deferral and payout of the estate tax over a number of years (see below).

VALUATION AND APPRECIATION ISSUES

The Appraisal

One of the most important aspects of estate planning for a real estate asset is the valuation of the interests either given away or included in your estate. Everyone argues for the lowest valuations possible. The correct approach is to obtain a fair appraisal to use as the value of any gift. The appraisal should be made by a qualified appraiser. It should consider all relevant factors that could affect the value of the property, including the strength or weakness of the local real estate market, asbestos problems, rents per square foot, vacancy rates, minority discount (the sale of less than a controlling interest in an investment or business is arguably worth less than a strict proportional value—50 percent of a $1 million business is worth less than $500,000), and so on.

NOTE: A written appraisal prepared by a qualified appraiser (one who has recognized credentials in the industry) is essential. The appraisal report must address the recent sales prices of comparable properties (or contain an explanation of why there are no comparables). A one-line statement from a broker that a property is worth some amount is unlikely to be of any use if the IRS questions your valuation.

Valuation as a Planning Tool

Valuation issues can present estate planning opportunities. The time to consider giving away real estate to children or a family trust may be the very time it is least thought about—a major anchor just closed up; asbestos was just discovered; and so forth. If these events substantially reduce the value of the property, you may be able to give away a substantial interest in the property with little or no transfer tax cost. After the gift is completed, you can pursue the resolution of the problems. Then, when a new anchor is found, or the asbestos abated, the increase in value will inure to the benefit of your heirs and not the tax collector.

Should You Use Your Unified Credit Now?

In many situations, estate planners try to avoid using up a taxpayer's once-in-a-lifetime $600,000 unified credit. This credit permits taxpayers to give away during their lives, or through their wills upon death, property worth up to $600,000 without incurring any transfer taxes (see Chapter 6). With property values currently very low relative to historical prices in many parts of the country, consideration should be given to making a large gift now of an interest in a property that is likely to appreciate. If a gift can be consummated when the value of the underlying real estate can be demonstrated to be very low, substantial future appreciation can be removed from your estate at minimum current tax cost. If the property is really at a low point (in terms of value) and appreciation is likely, it may pay to give more than $600,000 of property—no tax on the first $600,000 and some tax beyond that.

CAUTION: State tax laws may differ dramatically so that a sizeable state gift tax cost may be due even if the unified credit eliminates any federal gift tax. New York is an example.

In addition, the cash used to pay the gift tax cost will be deducted from the estate if you live for three years after the transfer.

A Gift Tax Program for Real Estate Assets

Although the $10,000 annual limit on tax-free gifts is very small compared to the value of real estate assets included in many estates, your gifts can be increased dramatically to increase the amount given by increasing the number of donees (gift recipients) and taking other steps. A few common techniques are used in the form "Sample General Partnership Agreement For Small Family Real Estate Transactions," which appears in the "For Your Notebook" section of this chapter. First the husband and wife joined in giving a gift to their daughter. This increased the annual exclusion from $10,000 to $20,000. Next, they included their daughter's husband and child (their grandchild) in the gift program. This increased the amount that could be transferred free of a gift tax (and without using their unified credits) to $60,000. Finally, the program to gift a rental property was planned over a number of years. Over time, substantial amounts can be transferred to a younger generation with significant tax savings, solely by using the annual exclusion. As demonstrated in the form, about $180,000 of value was transferred in just a few more days than one year (for example, December 31, 1991, January 1, 1992, and January 1, 1993).

DEALING WITH THE DIVISIBILITY PROBLEM

How can you give one piece of real estate to five children and six grandchildren in pieces small enough so that they don't exceed your annual $10,000 gift tax exclusion ($20,000 if you join with your spouse)? This is the divisibility problem presented by real estate assets. Several approaches can be used:

1. If the property you want to give away is not worth more than $600,000 ($1.2 million if your spouse joins in the gift), you could give the entire property away and use up your unified credit (lifetime exemption). The benefits of this approach include the following:

   - Simplicity
   - All future appreciation in the value of the property removed from estate
   - No current tax cost
   - Only one deed (transfer) of the property needed (this can save legal and recording fees, and in some places expensive transfer taxes)
   - Only one appraisal needed

   The big drawback of this approach is that you will have used up some, or all, of your lifetime credit so that it won't be available to your estate on your death.

2. You could give away small interests, none greater than the annual $10,000 per donee exclusion. Giving away interests is a simple and direct method but requires considerable paper work. Each year an appraisal must be completed and a deed for each child prepared reflecting his or her new interest in the property. In many places, a special "gift deed" is used for this purpose, which may provide savings on filing fees or transfer taxes. A potential problem is that a minor child may not be permitted under local law to own real estate. The solution then is simply to gift the interest in the property under the state's Uniform Transfers to Minors Act or to use a trust (see Chapter 11).

3. When the outright gift approach isn't used, the most likely alternative is to use a family partnership. This can range from a simple co-ownership arrangement (illustrated in the "For Your Notebook" section) to a complex family limited partnership arrangement. Because this method is so common, it is addressed at greater length in the next section.

    The remaining two methods are generally less preferable.

4. You could sell the property outright to your children and take back notes and a mortgage on the property. These notes could be collected, or forgiven, at your discretion. This method would provide a mechanism to transfer some of the value of the property over a period of time using the annual $10,000 gift tax exclusion (the property itself is transferred at the date of sale). All future appreciation in the value of the property will also be removed from your estate.

    Unfortunately, this approach has substantial tax problems. The notes must charge interest and the interest must be fair to comply with the imputed interest rules (see Chapter 11). If the transaction isn't handled as if it were made between independent parties, the tax benefits will be lost. Even exercising this much care won't guarantee that the IRS won't challenge the transaction by claiming that you really gave away the property at the beginning (when the purported sale occurred).

    Integral to this approach is your forgiving some or all of the notes, which raises several unpleasant tax issues. You may have taxable income if your tax basis (cost less depreciation, plus improvements) in the property was less than the fair value of the property when you sold it to your children. Further, your children could have a tax cost, because the amount of obligation you forgive could be treated as income. If this approach is used, you ought to include in each installment note a provision canceling the notes upon your death. Otherwise your executors may have to enforce the payments of the notes, possibly creating extreme hardship for your children. This cancellation provision, however, could result in an additional gift tax cost. If no premium is charged for the self-destructing feature, the seller may be deemed to have made a part-gift, part-sale.

5. Combining a gift of part of the property with a sale to your children of the rest of the property is another alternative. This hybrid approach minimizes both the drawbacks of a sale described above, and the problem of an outright gift, involving the use of your unified credit.

6. You could use a nominee corporation. The purpose of the nominee is to convert the real estate into an asset that is divisible to permit annual transfers equal to the maximum annual exclusion of $10,000. To apply this approach, you would transfer title to the property by deed to a corporation. This transfer would be a

tax-free transaction. As a precautionary measure, the corporation could elect to be taxed as an S corporation.

The way it works is that the corporation would hold title to the real estate as a nominee for you, and later for your family members, but you and your children would be the actual owners. This is critical, because actual ownership of the property by a corporation would have adverse tax consequences. You would have an appraisal completed for the property. Based on the value of the appraisal, you would gift shares of stock (representing the equivalent value of interest in the property) to your children equal to the amount of the annual gift tax exclusion. Each year additional shares of stock would be issued in amounts equal to the annual gift tax exclusion.

USING FAMILY PARTNERSHIPS TO OWN AND TRANSFER REAL ESTATE

When planning to gift rental real estate to family members, a critical issue for smaller properties requiring active management is how to retain management control. An ideal structure for this purpose is a family general partnership, with you serving as the managing partner. For larger transactions, where the income generated can warrant the extra fees and costs you can use a family limited partnership, with you serving (preferably through a controlled corporation) as the general partner and assuming all responsibility for management. Your children or other heirs can be given partnership interests each year worth $10,000 ($20,000 if your spouse joins in). This would accomplish three major planning goals: use the maximum annual gift tax exclusion, avoid any current tax cost, and preserve your unified credit for future use.

Family General Partnership

When the transaction is small and the risk of liability exposure (for example, being sued by an injured tenant) is not great, a family general partnership can be used. Forming the partnership is simple; it should only require filing an inexpensive certificate with the county clerk (but check with your lawyer, since the requirements vary). A partnership agreement should be prepared setting forth the relationships of everyone involved and the responsibilities and rights that each person has. The property should be appraised, and then you can assign partnership interests each year to your children.

PLANNING TIP: The sample forms in the "For Your Notebook" section following this chapter explain many of the issues to be decided. Review these forms, noting what you agree and don't agree with, and take your notes when you meet with your attorney to set up the partnership. This advance preparation will help you decide many of the issues before your lawyer's clock even starts running. It will also provide you with a number of alternatives and planning ideas to discuss with your attorney.

Family Limited Partnership

For a more complicated property or one that presents greater liability exposure, a family limited partnership should be considered. The advantage is that a limited partner can only be held liable for the amount invested in the partnership, whereas in a general partnership, each partner is fully liable for any suit or debt (if a tenant slips, he or she can sue each partner personally).

Every limited partnership must have at least one general partner. You should not serve personally as a general partner, exposing yourself to potential liability. Instead, an S corporation controlled by you should serve as the general partner. This will limit your personal liability to the amount invested in the S corporation. The basic legal documents necessary to establish, operate, and gift the limited partnership interests include a certificate of limited partnership to be filed in accordance with state law, a limited partnership agreement, and assignment forms for the annual transfer of limited partnership interests by gift. The agreement of limited partnership would be amended annually in order to reflect the varying partnership interests.

CAUTION: A limited partnership must comply with a number of requirements in order to be respected as a partnership for tax purposes. These should be discussed with your tax adviser. Your tax adviser should also review the partnership agreement.

Switching from General to Limited

Because of the advantages a limited partnership offers over a general partnership, you may want to convert an existing general partnership into a limited partnership. Several issues should be reviewed by your tax adviser before doing so: Will the switch cause a termination of the partnership for federal income tax purposes? Will the IRS recognize the transaction as a tax-free contribution by the old general partnership to the new limited partnership? Will the conversion reduce any partner's share of partnership liabilities by an amount greater than the basis of his or her partnership interest, requiring a taxable gain to be recognized?

Mechanically, the transaction could be structured in a couple of ways. There could be a constructive distribution from the current general partnership to its partners. These assets would then be recontributed to the new limited partnership. This would result in a transfer by the current partners of their respective shares of partnership assets to the new limited partnership in exchange for their interests in that new limited partnership. Alternatively, the transaction could be structured as a contribution of existing partnership interests for different interests in the new limited partnership. This is a complex matter that involves several legal and tax issues and should be carefully reviewed with lawyers with expertise in tax and partnership law.

Partnership Tests

Whether you use a general or limited partnership, a number of tests must be met by a family partnership in order for the gift to be respected by the IRS.

- Capital must be a material income-producing factor in the partnership. This requirement is readily met for most real estate properties, because the real estate capital is the primary income generator and usually is the sole asset of the partnership.
- Your children (or other heirs) must be the real owners of the capital interests given to them. They must have genuine interests in the partnership and must be entitled to receive a portion of the assets on withdrawal from the partnership. They must be able to transfer their interests in the limited partnership without financial detriment.
- In your capacity as general partner of a limited partnership or managing partner of a general partnership, you should not have unrestricted authority to establish reserves, pay yourself fees, or otherwise impede the proper flow of income to the children.

BUY/SELL PROVISIONS

The buy-out provision in any partnership or joint-venture agreement, which governs what happens when a partner dies or becomes disabled, is critically important to estate planning. Buy-out agreements must be considered when analyzing the liquidity of an estate and when determining the value of real estate interests for gift and estate tax purposes.

If you were a small investor in a very large limited partnership comprised of passive investors, your death would not cause a disruption or have significant business implications. Your spouse or other heirs would receive your partnership interest and simply continue to own the interest and collect any distributions. However, in a closely held general partnership, where partners can exert control over important decisions, the issue of what happens to your partnership interest on your death or disability is significant. At the partnership's inception, when the buy-out provisions are being negotiated, the partners will be concerned about providing for their spouses or heirs in case of an untimely death or disability. They will insist on having certain controls over who can succeed to any deceased partner's interests. They will be concerned about liquidity, because an improperly drafted buy-out provision could force the untimely liquidation of real estate assets. A surviving spouse (who is not a partner and is not active in the business) may deserve special consideration, because he or she could be at a disadvantage in negotiating a buy-out with the remaining active partners, who are intimately familiar with the business.

Typically, an agreement for a real estate general partnership or a joint venture will include one or a combination of the following buy-out provisions:

1. *Right of first refusal.* If any partner, such as the estate of a deceased partner, wants to sell an interest in the property, the other partners have an opportunity to buy that interest on the same terms.

2. *Appraisal.* If any partner wants to sell the property, the property must be appraised, and the other partners must buy out the selling partner's interests for the appropriate proportion of the price so set. Many investors disfavor the appraisal approach because of concern that appraisals can be arbitrary, costly, and time consuming. But when a spouse with limited real estate experience inherits an interest in a real estate partnership, an appraisal can be an important option, because the surviving spouse or heirs may not have the experience or resources to negotiate another type of sale/buy-out transaction.

3. *The three-appraiser method.* First, the selling partner hires an appraiser to value his or her interest. The other partners can buy at that price or hire their own appraiser. If the two appraisers don't agree, a third appraiser is brought in, whose opinion is binding. Payment terms should be set forth in the partnership agreement along with certain agreed-upon constraints on the appraiser.

4. *Dutch auction.* The auction method can be illustrated as follows: "We have agreed that the price is X dollars per unit or per percentage interest. Either you buy me at that price, or I'll buy you." A problem with this approach is that it can give one partner an unfair opportunity to take advantage of a temporary financial setback of another partner.

5. *The advanced Dutch auction.* Mr. A can offer to buy out Mr. B for X dollars. Mr. B can accept the offer of X dollars or counter Mr. A's offer with an offer of Y dollars. Mr. A can then sell to Mr. B at the counteroffer amount of Y dollars, or buy Mr. B's interest at that amount. If Mr. A agrees to sell to Mr. B at the counteroffer amount of Y dollars and Mr. B is unable to close, Mr. A gets to buy out Mr. B at 75 percent (perhaps 50 percent) of the original offer of X dollars. This keeps Mr. B's counteroffer real.

6. *Third-party/Dutch auction.* A third-party bona fide offer can be treated as the price to start a Dutch auction or advanced Dutch auction.

7. *Fixed price.* A less frequently used approach than the others is for the partners to meet at regular intervals, perhaps every six months, and set a value for the partnership. Although this approach is simple to use, if partners fail to meet regularly the result will be useless old values, and one of the other methods will still be needed. Important changes—the announcement of a new road or development, for example—can quickly obsolete any value that has been set.

The "For Your Notebook" section contains sample language illustrating one possible application of these methods.

DEFERRING ESTATE TAXES TO ADDRESS THE LIQUIDITY ISSUE

The federal estate tax is generally required to be paid within nine months after death. An important exception to this rule permits the payment of the estate tax attributable to interests in certain closely held business interests to be deferred for four years and then paid over a 10-year period, for an overall deferral of 14 years (also see Chapter 16). The term "closely held business" can include real estate owned by you directly, or through partnerships or corporations in which you own an interest. Some portion of the estate tax on the first $1 million of the estate may also qualify for interest to be paid at a very low rate on the amount of tax deferred.

To be eligible for the deferral, more than 35 percent of your adjusted gross estate must be comprised of interests in qualifying real estate. Your adjusted gross estate is the resulting amount after the fair market value of all the assets in the estate has been reduced by funeral and administrative expenses, claims against the estate, certain mortgages and other debts, and losses arising during the settlement of the estate.

The key phrase above is "qualifying real estate." Your ownership of real estate assets must be able to be characterized as an active business. Although real estate ownership and management *can* qualify as an active trade or business, the IRS takes an extremely restrictive view. Your overall activities of managing, developing, trading, leasing, and otherwise dealing in various real estate assets that are presently owned, or have been owned in the past, will be considered, as will any brokerage and consulting services and other real estate activities of yours that are clearly active businesses. The more active and integrated the overall real estate and ancillary activities are, the more likely the pure real estate assets will qualify. The idea is that, whether directly or through an agent, you must have materially participated in the active management of the property.

EXAMPLE: One taxpayer owned stock in S corporations that engaged in building homes on land owned by other entities that he controlled. The IRS agreed that the raw land and home-building businesses all qualified as active businesses, and the estate tax deferral benefits could be used for everything.

Another taxpayer wasn't as lucky. His estate wasn't allowed to treat all his real estate assets as qualifying simply because most qualified.

Before he died, the second taxpayer owned an S corporation that built homes on his land, a sole proprietorship that sold and developed real estate, a real estate business office, a warehouse, and eight rental houses. Everything except the rental houses was considered to be active business and was eligible for the estate tax deferral. The IRS position on the eight houses was that the mere holding of net leased rental property is an investment and not an active business.

The level of your activity before your death is very important in determining whether real estate assets will qualify. Negotiating leases, advertising for tenants, maintaining buildings, and collecting rents may be sufficient evidence of an active business. If you only directed the management and operations of the real estate by contract, your estate probably won't qualify for estate tax deferral benefits. The IRS also considers whether the real estate assets you own are in the same entity (corporation, partnership, and so forth) in which the activities occur. Suppose real estate is owned by you personally, and your business, which uses the real estate, is a corporation. The IRS may test whether your activities qualify at the real estate level—ignoring your corporation's activities.

If immediate payment of the estate tax would force a sale of the real estate, the IRS is more inclined to allow the deferral to avoid the disruption of your business.

PLANNING TIP: A number of steps can be taken to improve the opportunities for qualifying for the deferred tax payment. First, document your activities of managing properties. Second, the more properties you own, the greater the likelihood of qualifying; so, if you're planning to give away or sell real estate, try to keep some small interest in as many properties as you can. Third, leases should not be net leases. You should be responsible for as many costs and services as you can.

MISCELLANEOUS PLANNING STRATEGIES

The Ground Lease as an Estate Planning Tool

A properly structured ground lease can be a valuable planning tool by turning non-income-producing land holdings into a productive investment. When you no longer have the desire to actively subdivide or develop the property, leasing the land rather than selling it can provide a steady income stream for your estate, spouse, and children, and may enable you to avoid expensive transfer costs, brokerage fees, and capital gains.

EXAMPLE: You own raw land that is ripe for development in the form of a small office building, which would cost $1 million. You are getting on in years and don't want to go through the development process, however. You are also concerned about providing for your children. You could sell the property and gift the cash, of course, but this approach would result in substantial tax and other costs. Also, there would be no assurance that the children wouldn't squander such a large sum. A better solution would be to negotiate a ground lease with an active real estate developer. This approach should provide a secure income stream for your family for many years to come. If you retain the land in your estate, it will get a step up in basis on your death (so if your children sold it they would not have any income tax cost). You will have provided some additional liquidity for your estate.

Gift-Leaseback Transactions and Estate Planning

Gift-leasebacks have been a popular income and estate planning tool for wealthy taxpayers for many years.

EXAMPLE: You're a successful physician with a private practice that you operate out of a medical building you own. You have substantial current income and a substantial estate. Depreciation deductions on the building are almost exhausted. You give the medical building to your children (or to a trust for their benefit). You then lease the medical building from them or the trust and continue to use it in your practice.

Through a gift-leaseback transaction such as the one above, you may realize the following tax benefits:

- If your children are in a lower income tax bracket than you, there may be an income tax savings for the family unit (see Chapter 11).
- You can deduct the rental payments made to your children or a trust for the use of the building (they will report this rental income, net of expenses such as depreciation, on their tax returns).
- The value of the building will be removed from your estate, and any future appreciation of the building will be removed as well.
- If you paid a gift tax on the transfer, the tax paid may also be removed from your estate.

The IRS has attacked the deduction of rental payments in these transactions (the second item above), claiming a lack of business purpose. Not all courts have approved this argument. In order to deduct the rents, the following requirements should be met: (1) the rental payments must be required for the continued use of the property; (2) the continued use of the property is for the purpose of your business; and

(3) you (the seller and then the tenant) have not taken or kept any ownership of the property.

PLANNING TIP: The gift-leaseback provides tax planning benefits, but care and advance planning is required to ensure such benefits. Use the following techniques to support your gift-leaseback transactions:

- Document all aspects of the transaction.
- Make sure the executed lease gives your children powers typically held by a landlord.
- File a gift tax return.
- If the tenant is a corporation, draft minutes supporting the business purpose of the transaction.
- Obtain a real estate agent's letter supporting fair rental value.
- Distinguish the donor (you or your practice) from the tenant (for example, if you personally made the gift, a medical corporation or other entity should be the tenant).
- Use the same terms in the transaction that unrelated people would use.
- Abide by the lease terms, and act in all respects as landlord and tenant would.

Mortgaging Property Prior to Making a Gift

A simple planning technique is to place a mortgage on property prior to making a gift. This permits you to give a larger percentage interest in the property, using the annual $10,000 gift tax exclusion or your unified credit. If there is likely to be substantial future appreciation in the property over its current value, this approach will permit the transfer of larger portions of that future appreciation from the estate. Be certain to review this with your tax adviser because debts can result in unexpected and unfavorable tax consequences.

EXAMPLE: Parents bought undeveloped land for $90,000, which is now worth $100,000. If Parents give gifts to Child each year, it would take five years at the maximum $20,000 per year (assuming that Congress doesn't lower the annual exclusion and that there is no appreciation in the land) to complete the gift. Instead, Parents place an $80,000 mortgage on the land. The net equity, or value, of the land is now only $20,000 [$100,000 value − $80,000 mortgage], and it can be given away entirely in one year (assuming that the lender consents).

Additional Planning Opportunities

Remember that real estate can also be used as part of a charitable gift program (see Chapter 14). Special rules apply when the real estate is a farm or ranch property (Chapter 18). As you will see, life insurance is sometimes the best solution to solve the liquidity problems of real estate assets (Chapter 19).

CONCLUSION

Real estate is a significant asset in many estates. Careful planning, begun as early as possible, can help you to overcome many of the problems peculiar to planning for real estate and enable you to take advantage of some of the unique opportunities this asset offers.

For Your Notebook:

SAMPLE GENERAL PARTNERSHIP AGREEMENT FOR SMALL-FAMILY REAL ESTATE TRANSACTIONS
(WITH COMMENTS)

FOR DISCUSSION WITH YOUR LAWYER ONLY— DO NOT USE AS A PARTNERSHIP AGREEMENT

FAMILY PARTNERSHIP ASSOCIATES AGREEMENT

AGREEMENT MADE and entered MONTH DAY, YEAR, by and between GRANTOR'S NAME, an individual who resides at GRANTOR'S ADDRESS ("Grantor"); CHILD'S NAME, an individual who resides at CHILD'S ADDRESS ("Child"); SON-IN-LAW'S NAME, an individual who resides at CHILD'S ADDRESS ("Son-In-Law"); CHILD'S NAME as custodian for GRANDCHILD'S NAME ("Grandchild") under the STATE'S NAME Uniform Transfers to Minors Act, an individual who resides at CHILD'S ADDRESS (collectively the "Co-Owners").

RECITALS:

WHEREAS, the Co-Owners desire to provide for the ownership and management of the building and land located at ADDRESS OF INVESTMENT PROPERTY, County of COUNTY'S NAME, State of STATE'S NAME, more fully described as Lot ____ of Tract ____, and more fully described in Exhibit A (the "Property");

WITNESSETH:

In consideration of the mutual covenants set forth herein, and intending to be legally bound and for other good and valuable consideration, the parties agree as follows:

I. THE INVESTMENT

A. The Co-Owners have entered into this arrangement as co-owners of the Property for the limited purposes and scope set forth herein (the "Investment"). The Co-Owners intend this Agreement to govern their Investment from the date of this Agreement. The affairs of the Investment shall be conducted solely under the name Family Partnership Associates.

NOTE: A certificate may have to be filed in the county where the property is owned in order for your family to use a partnership name. This certificate may be called a "Doing Business As" form, or a "Fictitious Name Certificate," or something similar. Your county clerk's office may be able to guide you, or check with your lawyer. The filing fees are usually nominal and the form simple. Since the partnership is a new taxpayer, it must obtain a federal tax identification number (simply complete Form SS-4 available from your nearest IRS office).

B. The purpose of the Investment is to maintain the Property as Co-Owners for investment purposes and, if necessary, to lease, mortgage, own, and sell, as a single asset, the real and personal property comprising the Property.

C. Except for the rights of the Co-Owners as set forth herein, nothing in this Agreement shall be deemed to restrict in any way the freedom of any Co-Owner to conduct any other business or activity whatsoever at any location.

D. Except as otherwise expressly provided in this Agreement, no Co-Owner shall have any authority to act for, or assume any obligations or responsibility on behalf of, any other Co-Owner or the Investment. Nothing herein shall be construed to authorize any of the Parties to act as general agent for any other Party, or to permit any Party to bid for or to undertake any other contract for any other Party.

E. The principal place of business of the Investment shall be: Family Partnership Associates, c/o GRANTOR'S NAME, GRANTOR'S ADDRESS. Copies of any mail or notices received at such address shall be forwarded to the other Co-Owners at the addresses provided for above, unless notice of a different address is given in accordance with the notice provision below.

II.   TAX STATUS OF FAMILY PARTNERSHIP ASSOCIATES AND THE CO-OWNERS

For accounting and federal, state, and local income tax purposes, all income, deductions, credits, gains, and losses of the Investment and Family Partnership Associates shall be allocated between the Co-Owners as provided for in this Agreement and Exhibit B attached. Each Co-Owner shall report his or her respective share of any items of income, expense, gain, or loss on his or her own tax return. Each Co-Owner's pro rata share shall be computed in accordance with each Co-Owners percentage interest in Family Partnership Associates as set forth on Schedule B attached, as amended. The Co-Owners shall not make an election not to be taxed as partners.

NOTE: This election is not appropriate, or allowable, in all cases. Its purpose is to eliminate the requirement for the family partnership to file its own tax return, thus saving annual accounting fees. (The election is made by attaching a required statement to the partnership tax return filed for the first year the partnership does business.) As the investment becomes larger or more complicated, this approach becomes less appropriate. Discuss your options with your accountant.

III.   MANAGEMENT

A. The overall management and control of the affairs of the Investment, including but not limited to the sole right to determine whether the Property should be leased or sold, and whether Family Partnership Associates should repurchase any interests of a Selling Co-Owner (as defined below) shall be vested in a manager (the "Manager"). The Manager, within the scope of authority granted to him or her under this Agreement, shall have full, complete, and exclusive discretion to manage and control the Investment and affairs of Family Partnership Associates for the purposes herein stated. The Manager shall make all decisions affecting the Investment. The Manager shall manage and control the affairs of Family Partnership Associates to the best of his or her ability and use his or her best efforts to carry out the purposes of the Investment. In so doing, the Manager shall take all actions necessary or appropriate to protect the interests of the Co-Owners as a group and of the Investment. Except as expressly provided to the contrary herein, all decisions with respect to the management and control of the Investment shall be made in the reasonable discretion of the Manager and shall be binding on the Investment and on the other Parties. The Manager shall devote such time as he or she deems necessary to the affairs of the Investment but shall not receive compensation therefor.

B. GRANTOR'S NAME shall be the Manager. Should he or she be unable or unwilling to serve as Manager, then CHILD'S NAME shall serve as the Manager. Should she be unable or unwilling to serve as Manager, then SON-IN-LAW'S NAME shall serve as the

Manager. Should he be unable or unwilling to serve as Manager, then GRANDCHILD'S NAME shall serve as the Manager. Should he or she be unable, for reasons of minority, to serve as Manager, then the legal guardian for GRANDCHILD'S NAME shall serve as the Manager.

C. The Manager may be removed by the other Co-Owners only for gross negligence, willful misconduct, complete and total disability, or other material violation of the terms of this Agreement.

D. All Co-Owners agree that they shall maintain the Property, and conduct the affairs of Family Partnership Associates, or cause such affairs to be conducted by others under their supervision, in accordance with, and limited by, the terms of his Agreement, including the following:

1. They shall protect and preserve the titles and interests of Family Partnership Associates and the Co-Owners with respect to the Investment and any other assets owned.

2. They shall keep, or cause another to keep under their supervision, all books of account and other records required by the Investment in accordance with good accounting principles and procedures applied in a consistent manner. They shall keep statements, receipted bills and invoices, and all other records covering all collections, disbursements, and other data in connection with the Property and Family Partnership Associates. Any Co-Owner, or any person designated in writing by any Co-Owner, may at any reasonable times during regular business hours, and upon reasonable advance notice, review such books, records, and accounts.

3. They shall deliver to each Co-Owner a statement containing the information necessary for preparation of each Co-Owner's tax returns (state, federal, and local) as soon as reasonably practicable after the close of each calendar year, but in no event later than the date required by the Investment's lenders (if any) or Ninety (90) days after the end of the calendar year, whichever is the earlier.

4. They shall retain, employ, and coordinate the services of all independent contractors, accountants, attorneys, and other persons necessary or appropriate to carry out the business affairs of Family Partnership Associates.

5. They shall pay or arrange for the payment of all insurance premiums, debts, and other obligations of the Property, including but not limited to premiums for property and casualty insurance in an amount at least equal to Ninety-Five percent (95%) of the fair market value of the Property.

6. They shall maintain all funds of Family Partnership Associates in a separate bank account or accounts designated by the Manager, who shall, in connection with others designated by the Manager, have the power to deposit and withdraw funds. However, no funds of the Property may be commingled with funds or accounts of any Co-Owner. No disbursement in an amount greater than Five Thousand Dollars ($5,000.00) shall be made without the approval of at least Fifty percent (50%) of the Co-Owners.

NOTE: Because the parents (grantor) own 70 percent of the interests (see Schedule B, below), they will have sufficient authority in the first year to make any payments. If the parents give away an additional 30 percent of the property (actually co-ownership interests) in the second year, they will then own 40 percent and will need the approval of one additional person for a major expenditure. While it is not essential to put this type of limitation on the parents (in their capacity as manager), it does demonstrate that the parents really have given up ownership control to the children.

---

7. They shall, subject to the provisions of this Agreement, operate, lease, maintain, repair, and otherwise manage the Property.

8. They shall generally maintain, manage, and operate the Property in a reasonable manner consistent with the objectives and goals of long-term investment for income.

E. If the Manager and a majority in interest of the Co-Owners agree that Family Partnership Associates requires additional capital for reasonable repairs or maintenance expenses, all Co-Owners shall make equal contributions to Family Partnership Associates. If any Co-Owner is unwilling or unable to lend the required amount, and the other Co-Owners lend Family Partnership Associates the additional amount necessary, interest shall accrue on this additional amount at the rate of Nine percent (9%) per annum. Should Family Partnership Associates, in the sole discretion of the Manager, not have sufficient funds to repay the principal or interest of such loan, then such loan shall continue to accrue interest until it is repaid out of the proceeds of any future sale of the Property. This provision shall not be interpreted to grant to any Party any right to force the sale of the Property.

NOTE: Provisions must always be made to deal with the possibility that additional money may be needed for an emergency. A tenant could move out leaving damage to repair; a boiler could break; and so forth. If the parent (grantor) merely pays for these items personally, it might make the independent status of the partnership somewhat questionable to the IRS. It is important to treat the affairs of the partnership as an independent business.

F. In the event that the Manager consents to execute or enter into or be bound by any lease, contract, or other agreement with any entity related to or affiliated with any Co-Owner, or with Family Partnership Associates, then Family Partnership Associates and such other contracting party shall be deemed to be independent and unrelated entities for the purpose of any such lease, contract, or agreement, and regarding the performance, implementation, and enforcement of any such lease, contract, or agreement. The terms of any such lease, contract, or other agreement shall not be less favorable to Family Partnership Associates than the comparable terms available from an arm's-length lease, contract, or other agreement obtainable with an unrelated party. Notwithstanding anything herein to the contrary, the Manager shall not be entitled to any salary or fee (other than reimbursement for reasonable and necessary, properly substantiated, out-of-pocket expenses) for serving as Manager.

NOTE: The preferred approach would be for the family partnership to pay the manager a management fee that is appropriate for the type of property involved, based on what is a typical fee in that area. When the parent, as manager, renders any significant services, it is important to have the transaction respected by the IRS. If substantial services are rendered and no fee is paid, the IRS may argue that the parent is attempting to transfer income to the children. The IRS may require that a management fee be paid, or may challenge the validity of the entire transaction.

For larger commercial projects, a percentage of rental income, say 4 percent to 6 percent, may be charged. For smaller properties, such as a one- or two-family house, it may be a flat annual fee. Call a few local brokerage and management firms for price quotes. Save the letters they send to prove that the fee you used is reasonable, in case the IRS ever questions it.

G. All revenues received shall be deposited into the bank account of Family Partnership Associates.

H. The expenses of Family Partnership Associates shall include only those ordinary, necessary, and reasonable expenses that are direct costs for the maintenance, insurance, operation, sale, or refinancing of the Property. Notwithstanding anything herein to the contrary, any Co-Owner may make reasonable repairs, or take reasonable protective measures of an emergency nature, without the consent of any other Co-Owners, up to Five Hundred Dollars ($500) in amount.

I. Notwithstanding anything in this Agreement to the contrary, should any provision of this Agreement, or any act of the Parties, result in a violation of the family partnership provisions of Internal Revenue Code Section 704(e) and the regulations and cases thereunder, the Manager may amend this Agreement, or take any other actions reasonably necessary to prevent such violation, or to correct such violation.

NOTE: This clause gives the manager the right to make changes necessary for the transaction to be respected for tax purposes. The relevant section of the tax law permits a child, for example, to receive a gift of a partnership interest and for this to be respected for tax purposes if certain requirements are met. The child must really own the interest in the partnership and capital must be a material income-producing factor. In a real estate partnership, the property (capital) will be the only income-producing factor unless the parent is providing substantial services. This rule also requires that the parent be paid reasonable compensation for services.

IV. ACCOUNTING, CONTRIBUTIONS, ADVANCES, DISTRIBUTIONS, AND ALLOCATIONS

A. The Co-Owners agree that they each shall have the respective interests in Family Partnership Associates and the Property as set forth in Exhibit A, attached hereto, as amended from time to time. Each Co-Owner shall share in the profits or losses from the sale or lease of the Property and in all distributions of assets of the Property, whether distributions of cash flow or capital or otherwise, in the proportions set forth in Exhibit B attached hereto, as amended from time to time. Each Co-Owner shall share in any deductions relating to the ownership of the Property in proportion to his or her ownership interest set forth in Exhibit B attached hereto, as amended from time to time, to the extent that such expenses were paid directly by Family Partnership Associates. However, should any Co-Owner be required to make a loan to Family Partnership Associates, such loan, including interest accrued at the rate provided in this Agreement, shall be repaid before any distributions are made to the other Co-Owners.

B. The interests of the Co-Owners in the operation of the Property, and all monies that may be derived and the obligations and liabilities of each of the Parties as between themselves in connection with these operations and with respect to liabilities and losses in connection with it, shall be in the proportions set forth in Exhibit B attached hereto, as amended.

C. Any Co-Owner shall have the right once in every Two (2) year period to appoint, at such Co-Owner's sole expense, an independent certified public accountant for the purpose of reviewing the financial results of the Property and Family Partnership Associates. Any such accountant shall be provided with reasonable access to all financial reports, receipts, canceled checks, accounting summaries, bank reports, and other documents relating to the affairs of the Property and Family Partnership Associates.

NOTE: This right to inspect the books with an independent accountant can be important if family disputes ever develop.

D. Family Partnership Associates shall distribute its available cash flow as and when the Manager shall reasonably determine. The Manager may make reasonable reserves of cash flow for expected business expenses and anticipated repairs, to maintain a reasonable emergency fund, for repayment of debts, and for other reasonable and necessary business needs.

E. No party shall have the right to borrow money on behalf of any other Party or to use the credit of the other Party for any purpose, except as specifically agreed to in a writing executed by such other Party and for the sole reason of accomplishing the objectives of the Investment as set forth in this Agreement.

F. All drafts or checks issued in connection with the Investment and Family Partnership Associates shall be signed by the Manager, unless the Manager authorizes otherwise, or when more than one signature is required for major expenses as described in Section III.D.6., above.

V.   TERM

A. The affairs of Family Partnership Associates commenced on the date of this Agreement and shall continue until the Property is sold, or in no event later than December 31, 2021.

VI.   TRANSFER, TERMINATION, SALE

General Requirements of Transfer:

A. No transfer, of any nature, shall be made of any interest in Family Partnership Associates, unless the provisions of this article are complied with.

B. No Co-Owner shall mortgage, pledge, sell, assign (by other than gift to another Co-Owner), hypothecate, or otherwise encumber, transfer, or permit to be transferred in any manner or by any means whatever, whether voluntarily or by operation of law, all or any part of their interests in Family Partnership Associates, except as provided for in this Agreement.

C. Any Co-Owner transferring an interest in Family Partnership Associates shall be responsible for any costs incurred in effecting such transfer, including but not limited to legal and accounting fees. No transfer may be completed until such time as the transferee has become a signatory to this Agreement and bound by its terms.

D. Should any Co-Owner wish to sell his or her interests in Family Partnership Associates (the "Selling Co-Owner"), he or she shall give Notice to Family Partnership Associates and the other Co-Owners and shall retain, at his or her sole expense, an appraiser to appraise the Property. The Selling Co-Owner shall give the other Co-Owners and Family Partnership Associates Notice of the valuation of the Property and a copy of the appraisal report. If neither the Manager nor a majority in interest of the Co-Owners (excluding the Selling Co-Owner) agrees with the appraisal, they shall retain a second appraiser, the expense of which shall be shared equally by all Co-Owners other than the Selling Co-Owner. If the two appraisers cannot agree on a value, they shall select a third appraiser whose valuation shall be binding. The cost of the third appraiser shall be borne one-half by the Selling Co-Owner and one-half by the other Co-Owners. The accountant for the Investment, as selected by the Manager, shall determine the adjustments to make to such valuation determined by the appraisers to reflect any other assets and liabilities. Such amount shall be considered to be the value of all interests in Family Partnership Associates (the "Appraised Value"). The Selling Co-Owner's interests shall be valued by multiplying that Co-Owner's percentage interest as set forth in Exhibit B, as amended, by the Appraised Value.

E. The Co-Owners, other than the Selling Partner, and the Manager (on behalf of Family Partnership Associates) shall provide Notice as to what portion of the Selling Co-Owner's interests they wish to purchase. They shall then each purchase the Selling Partner's interests in the proportion that the amount each indicated a willingness to purchase bears to the total interests they have hereby indicated a willingness to purchase. If all interests of the Selling Co-Owner are not purchased, the Selling Co-Owner shall have no recourse against the other Partners.

F. The Co-Owners, other than the Selling Co-Owner, and/or Family Partnership Associates, shall purchase to the extent provided for in the preceding section, and the Selling Co-Owner shall sell his or her interest in Family Partnership Associates on the following terms: (i) Ten percent (10%) down payment on the signing of the contract of sale which shall be not less than Sixty (60) days nor more than Ninety (90) days following the determination of the value of the Property as provided above; (ii) the balance over a period of Seventy-Two (72) months in equal monthly installments, beginning with the first day of the third full month following the signing of the contract to sell, with interest at Nine percent (9%).

G. No Co-Owner may deliver more than One (1) Sales Notice or Buy/Sell Notice to the Co-Ownership or any of the Co-Owners during any One (1) year period.

H. A transfer by gift to other Co-Owners shall not be required to comply with this article.

I. Should one of the Co-Owners die, his or her estate, beneficiaries, successors or assigns, may, but is not required to, sell his or her interest to the other Co-Owners or Family Partnership Associates as provided in this section.

NOTE: This buy-out provision is very different from the more elaborate provisions contained in the second "For Your Notebook" agreement for this chapter. This buy-out is designed for a family partnership, where there is less concern about being taken advantage of by other partners. Here the main concern is that each co-owner, particularly the children, can realize the fair value of their investment. This is necessary so that the IRS will respect the gift of the interest in the property (partnership) by the parents to the children. If the children cannot realize the value of their investment, the entire value of the property could be taxed in the parents' estate. The later buy-out agreement is designed for more complex commercial real estate transactions, where there may be a number of sophisticated, and unrelated, partners.

VII. DEFAULT

Default is where a Co-Owner is unable to pay his or her share of the costs of the Investment and the other Co-Owners are required to advance funds on behalf of such Co-Owner, for a period of more than Thirty-Six (36) months ("Defaulting Co-Owner"). The nondefaulting Co-Owners shall have the option to acquire all of the Defaulting Co-Owner's interests in Family Partnership Associates for an amount equal to the Appraised Value of the Defaulting Co-Owner's interests, less the amount of principal advanced and interest calculated at Nine percent (9%).

VIII. MISCELLANEOUS

A. This Agreement shall be construed and enforced in accordance with the laws of the State of STATE'S NAME. The Parties hereto, by executing this Agreement, consent to personal jurisdiction in any court of competent subject matter jurisdiction within the State of STATE'S NAME.

B. All pronouns used herein shall be deemed to refer to the masculine, feminine, neuter, singular, or plural as the identity of the Person or Persons may require in the context, and the singular form of nouns (including but not limited to Manager), pronouns, and verbs shall include the plural, and vice versa, whichever the context may require.

C. This Agreement may be executed in several counterparts, each of which shall be deemed to be an original copy, and all of which together shall constitute one agreement binding on all Parties hereto.

D. Each provision of this Agreement shall be considered severable, and if, for any reason, any provision that is not essential to the effectuation of the basic purposes of the Agreement is determined to be invalid and contrary to any then existing law, such invalidity shall not impair the operation of or affect those provisions of this Agreement that are valid.

E. All notices, demands, or requests provided for or permitted to be given pursuant to this Agreement must be in writing, by depositing the same in the United States mail, addressed to the Party, postpaid and registered, or certified, or be taken via personal delivery, or overnight courier, to the address set forth for each in the Preamble. Any party can change its address for purposes of notification by written notice to all interested parties ("Notice"). For any Notice to be valid, a copy of such Notice must in all instances be sent to Grantor.

F. This Agreement contains the entire agreement between the Parties hereto relative to the formation, ownership, and operation of the Property. No variations, modifications, or changes herein or hereof shall be binding upon any party hereto unless set forth in a document duly executed by or on behalf of such party.

G. Subject to the restrictions on transfers and encumbrances set forth herein, this Agreement shall issue to the benefit of and be binding upon the undersigned Co-Owners and their respective heirs, executors, legal representatives, successors, and assigns. However, notwithstanding anything herein to the contrary, any Co-Owner may transfer or assign its interests to a family member, or to a trust for the benefit of a family member.

H. Any and all disputes between the Co-Owners arising from, or out of, the terms and conditions of this Agreement, or the execution, breach, or enforcement thereof, shall be resolved by arbitration in the City of Los Angeles in accordance with the Rules and Regulations of the American Arbitration Association. Any award of Arbitrators shall be final and binding and may be entered as a judgment in any court of competent jurisdiction, whether state or federal.

IN WITNESS WHEREOF, this Agreement is executed effective as of the date first set forth above.

_____
GRANTOR'S NAME

_____
CHILD'S NAME

_____
SON-IN-LAW'S NAME

_____
CHILD'S NAME, as custodian for GRANDCHILD'S NAME
under the STATE'S NAME Uniform Transfers
to Minors Act

[EXHIBIT A—LEGAL DESCRIPTION OF PROPERTY, NOT ILLUSTRATED]

EXHIBIT B

CO-OWNERS OWNERSHIP OF FAMILY PARTNERSHIP ASSOCIATES

DATE: MONTH DAY, YEAR

NAME OF CO-OWNER	PERCENTAGE INTEREST
GRANTOR'S NAME	70.00%
CHILD'S NAME	10.00
SON-IN-LAW'S NAME	10.00
GRANDCHILD'S NAME	10.00
Total Interests	100.00%

ACKNOWLEDGED AND AGREED:

_____

GRANTOR'S NAME

_____

CHILD'S NAME

_____

SON-IN-LAW'S NAME

_____

CHILD'S NAME, as custodian for GRANDCHILD'S NAME
under the STATE'S NAME Uniform Transfers to
Minors Act

NOTE: This page shows how much of the property each family member owns through ownership of interests in the family partnership. Each year, after the parent or other grantor makes additional gifts, a new Exhibit A will be added to the agreement. Based on the percentages above, the property involved may have been worth $200,000. When both parents, as grantors, join in making a gift to their child, son-in-law, and grandchild, a total of $20,000 per year is given, or 10 percent of the value of the property to each. Assuming that the property doesn't increase in value, the parents could give the children the entire investment in about a three-year period. The gift to the grandchild is made under the Uniform Transfers to Minors Act because the child is a minor (see Chapter 11).

[NOTARY FORMS OMITTED]

EXHIBIT C

FAMILY PARTNERSHIP ASSOCIATES

ASSIGNMENT OF PARTNERSHIP INTEREST

The undersigned hereby assigns by gift to DONEE'S NAME, an individual who resides at DONEE'S ADDRESS (the "Assignee"), a current Co-Owner (as such term is defined in an Agreement, Family Partnership Associates, dated DATE OF FAMILY PARTNERSHIP AGREEMENT), a STATE'S NAME general partnership, a percentage interest in Family Partnership Associates. The percentage interest hereby assigned is ___ percent (___%) of the total interests in the partnership. The value of this partnership interest is $_____.

ASSIGNOR/DONOR:

_____   Date: MONTH DAY, YEAR

GRANTOR'S NAME

STATE OF STATE'S NAME   )
                         :   ss.:
COUNTY OF COUNTY'S NAME)

On this DAY of MONTH, YEAR, before me personally came, GRANTOR'S NAME, to me known and known to me to be the individual described in and who executed the foregoing instrument, and she duly acknowledged to me that she understood the meaning of the instrument and that she executed the same.

_____
Notary Public

[ATTACH APPRAISAL OF PROPERTY MADE NEAR DATE OF GIFT]

NOTE: This form is used by the parents to transfer interests in the property (partnership) to the children. One form would be filled out each year for each child to whom a gift is made. An appraisal should be obtained to prove the value of the interest transferred. It is also important to notarize the form to prove to the IRS that the transfer was in fact made when claimed. Check with an attorney in your area regarding any local requirements for this type of transaction.

For Your Notebook:

SAMPLE BUY-OUT PROVISIONS FOR REAL ESTATE PARTNERSHIP AGREEMENT
(WITH COMMENTS)

FOR DISCUSSION WITH YOUR LAWYER ONLY—DO NOT USE AS A PARTNERSHIP CLAUSE

I.   GENERAL REQUIREMENTS OF TRANSFER

A. No transfer, of any nature shall be made of any interest in this Partnership, unless the provisions of this Buy-Out are complied with.

B. No Partners, without the prior written consent of all of the other Partners, shall mortgage, pledge, sell, assign, hypothecate, or otherwise encumber, transfer, or permit to be transferred in any manner or by any means whatever, whether voluntarily or by operation of law, all or any part of their interests in the Partnership, except as provided for in this Agreement.

C. Any Partner acquiring an interest in this Partnership shall be responsible for any costs that the Partnership reasonably incurs in effecting such transfer, including but not limited to legal and accounting fees. No transfer of any Partnership interest shall be made unless the Partnership has first obtained opinion of counsel that such transfer will not: (i) result in the termination of the Partnership pursuant to Code Section 708; (ii) trigger the acceleration of any mortgage on the Partnership's Property; or (iii) violate the Securities Act of 1933 or the provisions of any state's blue sky statutes. No transfer may be completed until such time as the transferee has become a signatory to this Agreement and is bound by its terms.

II.   SALE TO THIRD PARTIES

Should any Partner wish to sell or transfer all or part of his or her interest in the Partnership (the "Selling Partner") to other than the other Partners or the Partnership as provided in Section III below, he or she shall do so only in accordance with the provisions of Section II.

A. The Selling Partner shall deliver to the Partnership and each other Partner written notice (the "Sale Notice"). Such Sale Notice shall constitute an irrevocable offer to sell said Partnership interest to the Partnership for a period of Thirty (30) calendar days (such 30-day period, and all other time periods provided for in this Buy-Out, shall begin on the day following the date that such Sale Notice was properly dispatched). The Partnership shall have a right for a period of Thirty (30) calendar days after receipt of such Sale Notice to accept the offer with respect to all or any part of the Partnership interest being sold by providing Notice of such acceptance prior to the close of such Thirty (30) day period.

B. If the Partnership does not accept such offer, or if the Partnership accepts the offer to the extent of less than the total Partnership interest being offered, each other Partner shall have the right, for a period of Fifteen (15) days following the expiration of the first Thirty (30) day period provided in Section II.A., to accept the offer to sell contained in the Sale Notice. Each Partner may accept any portion of the Partnership interests offered for sale up to the total amount of such interests remaining after the Partnership's exercise of its rights under Section II.A. The Partnership interests that each Partner shall be entitled to shall be determined by multiplying the Partnership interests, which such Partner has given Notice that he or she wishes to purchase, by a fraction in which the numerator is the Partnership interests that such Partner has given Notice that he or she wishes to purchase, and the denominator is the sum of all such Partnership interests that all Partners have given Notice that they wish to purchase.

C. If the Partnership or the nonselling Partners do not agree to purchase any part of the Partnership interests offered pursuant to the Sale Notice, then the Selling Partner may, after the expiration of the Fifteen (15) day period provided for in Section II.B. above, consummate a transfer to any third party of such remaining Partnership interests within a period of Sixty (60) days following the expiration of such Fifteen (15) day period. The Selling Partner may not, during such Sixty (60) day period, consummate any such sale or transfer to a third party on terms that are less onerous to the purchasing third party than the terms offered pursuant to the Sale Notice.

NOTE: When a partner has a legitimate offer from a potential investor who is not a partner, the other partners are first given an opportunity to buy the partnership interests involved. This is important when the partnership is owned by a small number of people. If the partnership interest being sold is a general partnership interest, general partners can have a say in how the property is managed, so keeping control over who the partners are is a substantial concern. If a limited partnership interest is being sold, limited partners cannot participate in the management of the partnership's real estate, so there is less concern.

III. RECIPROCAL BUY/SELL

Should any Partner (the "First Partner") wish to buy the interests of any other Partner or Partners in the Partnership, or alternatively sell his or her interests to the other Partners or the Partnership, he or she shall do so under the provisions of this Section III.

A. The First Partner shall initiate the reciprocal buy/sell procedures of Section III by providing Notice to the Partnership and any or all of the other Partners (the "Second Partner") that he or she wishes to engage in a reciprocal buy/sell transaction (the "Buy/Sell Notice"). The Buy/Sell Notice shall designate a price at which such First Partner is committed to purchase the entire interest of the Second Partner, or alternatively, to sell his or her interest in the Partnership to the Second Partner.

B. If the First Partner desires to acquire the Partnership interests of more than one Partner and desires that the Buy/Sell Notice be contingent on the acceptance of his or her offer by all of said other Partners, then the Buy/Sell Notice shall set forth this condition. In order for this contingency to be effective, the First Partner must give Notice of such contingency to all other Partners who are to be bound.

C. Upon receipt of the Buy/Sell Notice, the Second Partner shall have the right within Thirty (30) days to indicate by Notice to the First Partner whether or not the Second Partner shall agree to sell his or her interests in the Partnership to the First Partner pursuant to the terms contained in the Buy/Sell Notice. If the Second Partner agrees to sell, or does not otherwise provide Notice within such Thirty (30) day period that he or she rejects the offer to purchase the Partnership interests, then the First Partner must purchase, and the Second Partner must sell, the Second Partner's interest in the Partnership.

D. If the Second Partner shall provide Notice to the First Partner that he or she rejects the First Partner's offer to purchase the interests in the Partnership pursuant to the terms contained in the Buy/Sell Notice, then the Second Partner must purchase, and the First Partner must sell, the First Partner's interest in the Partnership.

NOTE: If you're selling a minority interest (an interest that cannot control the management of the partnership), it may be difficult or impossible to sell. Suppose, for example, you own 10 percent of a partnership that owns a shopping center, and two cousins own the remaining 90 percent in equal portions. It will be difficult to sell your 10 percent interest because the other partners will have total control over how the property is managed. To sell the 10 percent interest, you will probably have to give a big discount from what the fair value should be (a minority discount). This provision, which is often overlooked and left out of buy/sell agreements, attempts to address this disadvantage by giving each partner a right to be bought out, or to buy out all of the other partners. When the entire partnership is effectively put up for sale, the price is likely to be much closer to the true value.

IV.   DISABLED OR DECEASED PARTNER

The Parties hereto acknowledge that a widow or widower or other successor to a deceased Partner, or a Partner who has become disabled (the "Disadvantaged Partner"), may be at a disadvantage in negotiating the sale of his or her Partnership interests to the Partnership or the other Partners pursuant to the above provisions. Therefore, this Section IV provides a special method of determining the price and terms of a sale, should such Disadvantaged Partner elect to sell his or her Partnership interest pursuant to the terms of this Section IV.

A. Upon the death or permanent disability of any Partner, such disabled Partner, or the successor to such deceased Partner, shall have the option to sell any or all of his or her interest in the Partnership for an amount equal to the Appraised Value of such interests. The Appraised Value of the Disadvantaged Partner's interests shall be determined by having the Disadvantaged Partner select an independent appraiser at the Partnership's expense to value his or her interest in the Partnership. If the other Partners (the "Purchasing Partners") do not accept such appraised value, they shall select an independent appraiser at their sole expense, to value the Disadvantaged Partner's interest in the Partnership. If the two appraisers cannot agree on a value for such interest, they shall select a third independent appraiser, at the expense of the Partnership, and the appraisal of such appraiser shall control. The accountant for the Partnership shall determine the adjustments, if any, to make to such valuation to reflect other assets and liabilities of the Partnership and any amounts due to or from the Disadvantaged Partner (the "Appraised Value").

B. Any purchase under this section shall be made as follows: not less than Twenty percent (20%) down payment upon execution of the contract of sale, with the balance payable in equal monthly installments over a Five (5) year period with interest at the federal midterm rate determined under Code Section 1274(d) and the regulations thereunder as at the date of such contract.

NOTE: A disabled partner, or a surviving spouse who is not familiar with the real estate involved, risks being taken advantage of in the other types of buy-out arrangements contained in this agreement, since he or she won't have the negotiating clout of the other partners. To address this situation, a buy-out price set by independent professional appraisers can be used. This appraisal approach is not used under other circumstances, because many professional real estate investors believe that the value determined by appraisal is too often not a reflection of the real value of the property involved.

V.   TERMS

Any Sale Notice provided in Section II and any Buy/Sell Notice provided pursuant to Section III shall set forth the proposed terms of such transfer, including the offering price of the Partnership interest being sold, the terms of payment, and any other material terms. Such terms (when the sale is to a Partner, the Partnership, or the successor of a deceased Partner), as well as the terms for a sale pursuant to Section IV, must include, however, a period of at least Ninety (90) days to consummate the closing of said transaction. All closings shall take place at the office of the Partnership.

VI.   FREQUENCY

No Partner may deliver more than One (1) Sales Notice or Buy/Sell Notice to the Partnership or any of the Partners during any Six (6) calendar month period.

VII.   EXCEPTIONS

A transfer by will or intestate succession to a member of such Partner's immediate family, or an *inter vivos* transfer by gift to a trust for the benefit of members of a Partner's immediate family, shall not be required to comply with this Buy-Out.

NOTE: This final provision provides some flexibility for the partners to plan their estates by using a trust or other arrangement to hold their partnership interest for the benefit of family members.

---

16 FAMILY BUSINESS

A closely held business (for example, a medical, law, or other professional practice) and a family business present a number of unique problems. When such a business is organized as a corporation, it presents several differences from planning for stock in a public company. These conditions will dictate the planning techniques discussed in this chapter.

SPECIAL ISSUES IN PLANNING FOR A FAMILY BUSINESS

A family business faces issues of valuation, liquidity, and divisibility. If you own stock in a corporation that is traded on a major stock exchange or over the counter, you can value the shares simply by looking up the price in a newspaper. You can transfer almost any dollar value you want by giving away or selling the precise number of shares necessary, and this can be arranged through a phone call to your broker.

A closely held or family business is much more awkward to work with in implementing an estate plan. Valuation is likely to be difficult, imprecise, time consuming and costly; you may have to call in an appraiser, accountants, and other experts. Transferring ownership interests may be constrained by restrictions in a shareholder's agreement. (If the business is organized as an S corporation, the tax laws impose several constraints on who you can transfer stock to—see Chapter 17.) Mechanically, you'll have to prepare and sign stock powers and transfer forms and arrange to physically cancel some of your shares and reissue shares to the new owner (this process is not that difficult or time consuming, but it must be done properly for a transfer to be completed). Finally, to deal with divisibility, you may have to recapitalize the company, creating enough shares so that the value of each share is less than the annual $10,000 gift tax exclusion. This step may require amending the certificate of incorporation to authorize additional shares of stock.

If the family business is a partnership, some of the issues of transfer discussed in Chapter 15 will apply. If the business is operated as a sole proprietorship, transfer of interests in the business is especially difficult, and the business may have to be restructured into a partnership, corporation, or S corporation so that interests can be given to trusts, children, or other heirs.

STOCK PURCHASE ARRANGEMENTS FOR A BUY-OUT

It is critical to provide for the orderly transfer of ownership and payment of estate taxes in a closely held business. Apart from determining the method of establishing a buy-out price, such as by getting three appraisals, and so forth (see Chapter 15), consideration must be given to the overall structure of the transaction. Who will actually consummate the buy-out, and how should the buy-out be funded?

The two general approaches are: (1) the corporation redeems your interests (a redemption arrangement); or (2) the various shareholders purchase your interests (a cross-purchase arrangement). There are a number of tax consequences to this planning that should be considered.

Stock Redemption Arrangement

When a stock redemption approach is used, the corporation can obtain the necessary monies through an accumulation of cash flow or through the purchase of an insurance policy on the life of the shareholders. Accumulating cash flow is difficult because you will prefer to put available cash to use, rather than holding it in an investment account waiting for a shareholder to die. (Cash accumulations may also become subject to a special tax on accumulated earnings. Review this matter with your accountant.)

If insurance is used, the corporation will receive the death benefit on your death. This money will be applied toward the purchase of your shares. This insurance arrangement will have the following tax consequences:

- The corporation will not be entitled to a tax deduction for the payment of the insurance premiums.
- The shareholders will not have to recognize income on the corporation's payment of the premium.
- The proceeds received by the corporation on your death won't create taxable income.
- The proceeds, in excess of the premiums paid, will be included in calculating the corporation's earnings and profits, which can affect the tax consequences of dividends and other matters.
- If the redemption constitutes a complete termination of your interests in the corporation (as it will in most circumstances), or meets selected other requirements, your estate will report the excess of

the amount received in the redemption over your adjusted basis (cost) in the stock as a capital gain.

Cross-Purchase Arrangement

Since any cash accumulations or insurance policies will be subject to the general creditors of the corporation, if the perceived risks are material, a cross-purchase arrangement (the shareholders purchase the terminating interest) may be preferable.

EXAMPLE: Four doctors join forces in a new fertility practice. At the recommendation of their attorney, they organize as a professional corporation in order to minimize liability exposure. Although it is cumbersome and more costly to use a cross-purchase arrangement for their buy/sell provision, since so many shareholders are involved, the doctors unanimously choose this approach to avoid placing their permanent insurance at risk from potential malpractice claims. Individually, they review the use of irrevocable life insurance trusts to further protect the insurance policies from personal creditors and malpractice claimants.

Using a cross-purchase arrangement to buy out the terminated interest in a closely held corporation may be more costly than using a redemption arrangement, because the monies used by the shareholders to purchase the terminated interest will already have been subjected to two tiers of taxation—corporate and shareholder. However, if the corporation pays a bonus or increased salary to the shareholders, it may get a tax deduction, so there will effectively be only one tax. If the corporation is an S corporation, only the individual tax will have been incurred (see Chapter 17). (In this latter situation, the tax advantage of a corporate redemption over a shareholder cross-purchase arrangement will depend, in part, on the relative tax brackets of the corporation and the shareholders.)

A cross-purchase arrangement will have the following tax consequences:

- No tax deduction will be available for the payment of the insurance premium.
- The proceeds the other shareholders receive on your death will not be taxable.
- Your estate should not have to recognize any gain on the sale for income tax purposes, since the shares will have received a step-up in basis to their fair market value on either the date of your death or the alternate valuation date (see Chapter 6).
- The shareholders purchasing your shares will get an increase in tax basis, which will reduce their taxable gain on a later sale.

Whether the valuation used for the buy-out is realistic and made at arm's length will be a factor considered by the IRS in evaluating your interest in the business for estate tax purposes. When the buy/sell agreement is the result of a voluntary action by the stockholders and is binding during life as well as death, such agreement may, depending upon the circumstances of each case, fix the value for estate tax purposes. However, the agreement is not the only relevant factor. The IRS also considers the relationship of the parties, the relative number of shares held by the decedent, and other material facts in determining whether the agreement represents a bona fide business arrangement or is merely a device for passing your shares to your heirs at a discounted estate tax cost. The terms of the transaction must be comparable to buy-out agreements used by unrelated people.

SPECIAL USE VALUATION

Special rules exist that permit a more favorable method for valuing real estate used in a closely held business for estate tax purposes. These rules are addressed in Chapter 18.

STOCK REDEMPTION PROVISIONS PROVIDE FAVORED TREATMENT FOR ESTATES

When the stock in a closely held corporation comprises a substantial portion of your estate, sufficient liquidity to pay the estate taxes and administration expenses may be difficult to obtain. However, one potential source for the necessary cash may be the corporation in which you're a shareholder. The problem is that if the corporation distributes money or property to your estate, the corporation will not get a deduction, and your estate may be taxed on the full amount of any distribution for income (not estate) tax purposes.

There is an important exception to this treatment, designed for this very purpose. Internal Revenue Code Section 303 contains a special rule that may enable your estate or heirs to avoid any tax on a distribution of money in exchange for shares of your stock. If the requirements of this code section are met, the transaction will be characterized as a redemption. The tax consequences of a redemption are that capital gain will only be recognized to the extent that the money distributed exceeds the tax basis in the stock surrendered. This contrasts favorably with a dividend, the entire amount of which may be taxable. Since assets included in your estate are generally stepped up on your death (or the alternate valuation date) to a tax basis equal to the fair market value of the stock, your tax basis on the date of the distribution may already equal the fair value of the stock; hence, no tax cost.

To qualify for this treatment, the value of the stock in the closely held corporation must exceed 35 percent of your adjusted gross estate (the fair market value of all of the assets in the estate, reduced by funeral and administrative expenses, claims against the estate, certain mortgages and other debts and losses arising during the settlement of the estate).

The redemption must occur after your death but within approximately three years following the filing of your estate tax return. Distributions can only qualify up to the amount of death taxes and funeral and administrative expenses. The shareholder making the redemption (your estate or an heir) can claim this redemption benefit only to the extent that his or her interest in the corporation has been reduced. When a generation-skipping transfer or a distribution more than four years after your death are involved, special rules apply.

TIPS: Planning can help your estate qualify for this favorable tax treatment. Gifts of property that don't qualify for this treatment will increase the percentage of qualifying property in your estate and help your estate exceed the 35 percent threshold. If these gifts are made within the three years prior to your death, they will be included in your estate solely for the purpose of making the 35 percent calculation.

The comprehensive example in the "For Your Notebook" section following this chapter illustrates the calculation of the amount of stock that could qualify for this favorable redemption treatment. When both the favorable redemption privilege and the estate tax deferral can apply, as in the example, the period for making the distribution that qualifies for redemption treatment is extended for the period provided by the deferred-payment rule (14 years, see below).

DEFERRAL OF ESTATE TAX

Even if you take advantage of the stock redemption treatment provided in Code Section 303, you may have estate taxes due within a short time. The federal estate tax is generally payable within nine months of the date of death. When the estate consists mostly of nonliquid assets, a tremendous hardship can result, forcing sales when market conditions may not be appropriate, the undertaking of additional debt obligations, or the advance purchase of large amounts of insurance. Internal Revenue Code Section 6166 provides an alternative schedule for payment of the estate tax. The tax can be deferred entirely for four years (with only interest payments being made), and thereafter the tax is paid in installments over a 10-year period. In addition, the interest on the tax due on the first $1 million is charged at a low, 4 percent rate. Qualifying for this tax extension can mean the difference between keeping intact an estate that the decedent spent years building or having it ravaged to pay the estate taxes.

To qualify for Code Section 6166 deferral, the following requirement must be met: The interests in the closely held business must exceed 35 percent of your adjusted gross estate. A practical issue is that you may own interests in a number of different businesses, some directly, some indirectly through partnerships, S corporations, and closely held C corporations. The deferral provisions of Code Section 6166 allow for the aggregation of different interests in order to meet these tests. Specifically, interests in the following can be aggregated:

- Sole proprietorships (Schedule C on Form 1040)
- Partnerships having 15 or fewer partners, or in which the decedent owned 20 percent or more of the capital
- Stock in a closely held corporation having 15 or fewer shareholders, or in which you owned 20 percent or more of the voting stock
- Interests in certain qualifying holding companies.

Finally, if your estate qualifies for the deferral, your executor must make an election on or before the extended due date of the estate tax return, Form 706. If your executor disposes of interests in your closely held business prior to the payment of the tax, this action can trigger acceleration of the tax deferred.

TIP: As with the stock redemption planning, when the closely held business assets are close to meeting the 35 percent test, some advance planning can help ensure compliance. Nonqualifying business assets can be sold and the proceeds used to purchase greater interests in qualifying assets. Alternatively, a gift program can be used to reduce the proportion of nonqualifying assets in your estate, so that the qualifying assets will represent a larger portion of the estate.

An illustration of the planning for deferral on the estate tax for a closely held business is given in the "For Your Notebook" section following this chapter.

TRANSFERRING OWNERSHIP WHILE RETAINING CONTROL

If you want to transfer ownership of interests in your closely held or family business for estate tax purposes but want to avoid giving up control, one solution is to recapitalize the corporation (as long as it's not an S corporation) to have at least two classes of stock, one voting and one nonvoting. The nonvoting shares can be used for gifts. In a partnership, a limited partnership format can be used and limited partnership interests can be given away, while you retain the general partnership interests. Because only general partners are permitted to participate in management, this can accomplish your objective (see Chapter 15). Alternatively, the shareholders or partnership agreement can be used to provide some element of control, as long as the shares given away aren't sufficient for the recipients (perhaps your children) to combine their voting power to your detriment.

Some other techniques are worth considering. A sale of some of the interests in a closely held business to your children can occasionally be appropriate. The private annuity arrangement may be another method of structuring such a sale (see Chapter 20). A grantor-retained annuity trust (nicknamed a GRAT) may be appropriate for transferring stock in exchange for a specific amount of income each year in order to reduce the value of the gift made.

A GRAT works as follows. The owner of a closely held business can transfer a qualified interest in the business to family members. The business owner (the grantor) transfers the business interests to a trust and retains the right to receive a fixed payment at least annually and to control the trust. The value of the closely held business transferred to the family members as remaindermen under the trust will vary depending on the length of the trust and the size of the fixed payment the grantor reserves. Thus, if the trust is for a long period and the grantor reserves a large fixed payment, the gift to the children of a future interest in the business can be accomplished at a nominal gift tax cost. Similar planning can be done using an annuity arrangement (called a GRUT). These techniques are quite complicated and should only be pursued after thorough analysis with your tax adviser.

CONCLUSION

Closely held and family businesses can often present valuable investment and work opportunities. These assets, however, require special attention in any estate plan. The anti-freeze rules are very important and should be considered in all situations (see Chapter 7). If the business is organized as an S corporation, the special S corporation rules should also be evaluated (see Chapter 17).

For Your Notebook:

ILLUSTRATION OF PLANNING WITH ESTATE TAX DEFERRAL AND SECTION 303 STOCK REDEMPTION

FACTS AND COMMENTS

Tom Taxpayer is married to his second wife, Tammy Taxpayer. Tom has a number of children from his first marriage and no children from his second marriage. Tom's children are active in the family business, and, in setting up his estate plan, his goal was to turn over stock in the business to them as soon as possible. Tom's stock in the family business is worth $3.5 million. In addition, he has advanced $200,000 as a long-term loan to the business. Tom has only $500,000 in life insurance, but it is owned by an irrevocable insurance trust and properly excluded from his estate. The state in which Tom resides has no death or inheritance tax—only an estate tax to mop up the federal credit for state death taxes.

Tom's insistence on bequeathing stock in the family business to his children immediately upon his death will result in a substantial estate tax. If Tom had been willing to put all but the $600,000 unified credit amount into a Q-TIP trust for his wife's benefit, the estate tax could have been deferred until her death, and the children from his first marriage could then have received the stock. Tom also wanted to limit the bequest to his wife to $500,000, because he had made substantial gifts to her after their marriage. The estate tax deferral provisions and the stock redemption provisions are both available, however, minimizing the effect of the estate tax. Tom is confident that the business will generate more than adequate cash flow to make the necessary payments under the deferral arrangement. As a result, the amount listed below as the "Family Share" of assets to the children, is actually considerably larger, because the tax cost will be spread over a 14-year period.

It appears, at first, that Tom's estate will have a substantial liquidity problem, with a cash shortfall of $1,488,609 (or $988,609 when the $500,000 life insurance trust is considered). Not so. Actually, Tom's estate has liquid assets of $895,000 [$50,000 stocks and bonds + $345,000 of liquid notes, mortgage, and the like + $500,000 in the irrevocable life insurance trust]. The total expenses due in the current year are $833,962 [$183,575 funeral and administration expenses + $120,000 debts and losses + $267,548 state death taxes + $262,839 federal tax not deferred under Code Section 6166]. Therefore, Tom's estate has a net surplus of $61,038 liquidity [$895,000 − $833,962].

Tom and Tammy Taxpayer
Main Worksheet*

	Husband	Wife
Year of Death	1991	1999
Adjusted Gross Estate	4,376,435	1,176,320
Marital Deduction	500,000	0
Charitable Deduction	0	0
Taxable Estate	3,876,425	1,176,320
After 1976 Taxable Gifts	0	0
Federal Estate	3,876,425	1,176,320
Federal Tax per Schedule	1,772,834	418,091
Unified Credit	192,800	192,800
Federal Tax + Max Credit	1,580,034	225,291
State Death Tax—Max Credit	267,548	43,684
Federal Tax	1,312,486	181,607
Total Death Taxes	1,580,034	225,291
Family Share	2,261,391	951,029
Family Share Both Spouses	0	3,212,420

*Calculations and format have been prepared using the Estate Tax Spreadsheet, published by BNA Software, a division of the Bureau of National Affairs, Inc., Washington, DC

Tom and Tammy Taxpayer
Adjusted Gross Estate

	Husband	Wife
Separate Gross Estate	4,645,000	842,000
Mar. Ded. From Dec'd Spouse	0	500,000
Fam—FVal Increase in GE	0	0
Gross Estate	4,645,000	1,342,000
Funeral & Admin Exps in $	21,000	32,000
Plus Admin Exp—% of GE	3.5	4
Total Funeral & Admin Exps	183,575	85,680
Inc Tax—Elected Admin Exps	35,000	0
Schs K & L—Debts & Losses	120,000	80,000
Increased Estate Tax	0	0
Debts + Exp + Incr Est Tax	268,575	165,680
Adjusted Gross Estate	4,376,425	1,176,320

Figure 16.1. Illustration of Planning with Estate Tax Deferral and Section 303 Stock Redemption.

**Tom and Tammy Taxpayer
Gross Estate**

	Husband	Wife
Sch A—Real Estate	250,000	400,000
Sch B—Stocks & Bonds	3,500,000	0
Stocks & Bonds—Liquid	50,000	32,000
Sch C—Mtgs Notes & Cash	200,000	100,000
Mtgs Notes & Cash—Liquid	345,000	10,000
Sch D—Life Insur—Liquid	0	0
Sch E—Jointly Owned Property	300,000	300,000
Gross Estate	4,645,000	842,000

**Tom and Tammy Taxpayer
Marital Deduction**

	Husband	Wife
Specified Marital Bequests	500,000	0*
Total Marital Bequests	500,000	0

*Assumes no remarriage

**Tom and Tammy Taxpayer
Sec. 6166 Planning**

	Husband
Adjusted Gross Estate	4,341,425
35% Thereof	1,519,499
Value of Business	3,500,000
Qualify—1/Not Qualify—2	1
Interest % on Non—4% Amt	10.5
Federal Estate Tax	1,312,486
Tax Deferrable on Business	1,049,647
Tax Not Deferrable	262,839
Federal Tx on $1,000,000	345,800
Less: Unified Credit	192,800
4% Amt of Deferrable Tax	153,000
Amt-Deferrable Tax	896,647
Executor's Election	
No of Installments (2-10)	10
Amt of 1st Payment—1 Yr +	
9 Months After Death—1st Yr	105,497
Amt of 2d Payment—2d Year	105,947
Amt of 3d Payment—3d Year	105,947
Amt of 4th Payment—4th Yr	105,947
Principal Payment—5th Yr	104,965
Interest Payment	105,947
Principal Payment—6th Yr	104,965
Interest Payment	94,947

Figure 16.1. *Continued.*

Tom and Tammy Taxpayer, Sec. 6166 Planning, continued

Principal Payment—7th Yr	104,965
Interest Payment	84,398
Principal Payment—8th Yr	104,965
Interest Payment	73,848
Principal Payment—9th Yr	104,965
Interest Payment	63,298
Principal Payment—10th Yr	104,965
Interest Payment	52,748
Principal Payment—11th Yr	104,965
Interest Payment	42,199
Principal Payment—12th Yr	104,965
Interest Payment	31,649
Principal Payment—13th Yr	104,965
Interest Payment	21,099
Principal Payment—14th Yr	104,962
Interest Payment	10,550

**Tom and Tammy Taxpayer
Sec. 303 Planning**

	Husband
Adjusted Gross Estate	4,341,425
35% Thereof	1,519,499
Value of Stock	3,500,000
Qualify-1/Not Qualify-2	1
Amount of Protection for Sec. 303 Redemption	
Funeral & Admin Expenses	183,575
Federal Estate Taxes	1,312,486
State Death Taxes	267,548
Max Protected Redemption	1,763,609

Liquidity on Death of H & W

	Husband
Sch B Stocks & Bonds—Liquid	50,000
Sch C Mtgs Notes Cash—Liquid	345,000
Total Liquid Assets	395,000
Liquid Assets Given in Marital Deduction	0
Liq Assets After Mar. Deduction	395,000
Taxes on Death	1,580,034
Funderal & Admin Expenses	183,575
Debts & Losses	120,000
Decrease for Fut Liq Gifts	0
Total Cash Needs	1,883,609
Liquidity	−1,488,609
Nonincludable Life Ins. Trust	500,000
Liquidity With Nonincludable Property	− 988,609

Figure 16.1. *Continued.*

17 S CORPORATION

The S corporation is a very popular ownership structure for a closely held business. But an S corporation is, first of all, a corporation. The reason for organizing a business as a corporation under a state's laws is so that shareholders can limit their liability. In the event of a lawsuit, the corporation will be held liable, but you, as a shareholder, will only be at risk for the amount you've invested—not for your personal assets. Although the corporation structure is far from a fail-safe protection (you may have signed personal guarantees, accidentally transacted business in your name, and so forth), it's worth doing.

THE S

The "S" in an S corporation derives from the special tax treatment accorded under this election. With an ordinary (or C) corporation, there is a double-tax structure. The corporation pays tax on its income, and if it distributes a dividend to you, you pay a second tax on the income. A closely held business with an S structure generally can avoid double taxation, because the corporation can pay a reasonable salary to you and deduct this amount for tax purposes. (Actually, any corporation can use this approach to achieve only one level of tax. However, for reasons beyond the scope of this book, S corporations have become a common ownership entity. For example, many businesses elected S corporation status in response to the 1986 tax changes.)

In spite of the valuable benefits of an S structure, there are a number of traps, drawbacks, and caveats you should be aware of with regard to estate planning.

PASSIVE INCOME ISSUE

An S corporation that was formerly a C (regular) corporation can face a costly corporate-level tax if the S corporation has accumulated earnings and profits (analogous to financial statement retained earnings) from its former C corporation years and too much passive income. If the results of your financial and other planning are that real estate, stocks, or other investment assets are being held by your S corporation, be sure to review the passive income issue with your tax adviser.

ONE-CLASS-OF-STOCK REQUIREMENT

Estate Planning Considerations

A regular corporation can have nearly endless classes of stock—preferred, cumulative preferred, noncumulative preferred, class A common, class B common, and so forth—with each class having different rights. An S corporation, however, can have only one class of stock. The presence of a second class of stock, or even some forms of debt that could be recharacterized as stock, can result in a termination of the S corporation status and bring potentially costly tax consequences. Thus, flexibility in structuring the corporation for gifts to your children or other heirs is limited.

Your estate plan may call for the annual giving of S corporation stock to each of your children, perhaps using the $10,000 gift tax exclusion. Such giving has several benefits: (1) it can accomplish the general estate planning objective of removing assets from your estate; (2) it can foster greater interest by your children in your business; and (3) it can even begin the process of turning over some control of the business to the younger generation in anticipation of your retirement. However, the prospect of turning over control of a family business to children may raise concern about their ability to handle the increased responsibility and income. For this reason, some exceptions to the one-class-of-stock requirement can be useful in your planning.

Variations Within One Class of Stock That Are Allowed

Different voting rights won't necessarily create the prohibited second class of stock, as long as there is no difference in the income and assets to which any share of stock may be entitled. A solution to your concerns may be to give or sell your heirs stock that has no voting rights or lesser voting rights than the stock retained by you and the other principals. As the heirs prove their mettle, additional stock or increased voting rights can be transferred to them. Another technique is to set up a voting trust. This trust can hold the stock in the S corporation for the benefit of some or all of the shareholders. You can provide that you control the voting of all stock held in this voting trust.

If your children are employed by your S corporation, you may have an even greater incentive to give them stock. But what happens if you've transferred stock to one child and that child decides that he or she no longer wishes to be involved with the family business? You may prefer to have the stock sold back to the corporation, so that the children participating in the business will have the ownership. This can be arranged within the structure of an S corporation. The stock issued to your children can contain a requirement that it be resold to the company if they terminate their employment. Neither of these two restrictions—no voting rights and resale to the company when employment terminates—will violate the one-class-of-stock requirement.

How to Lend to the S Corporation and Not Violate the One-Class Requirement

You may be involved in lending money to an S corporation to help out the family business, particularly during the critical time when management and ownership are being transferred to a younger generation. When structuring an investment or loan transaction, the safest approach is to use a written, unconditional obligation to pay on demand (or on a specified date) a sum certain in money, with the obligation meeting the following criteria:

- The interest rate and dates are not contingent on company profits or the borrower's directions.
- The debt is not convertible into stock.
- The creditor is an individual or a qualifying estate or trust.

Watch Out for Fringe Benefits

The IRS has cracked down on what it saw as a significant abuse of S corporations, focusing particularly on violations of the one-stock requirement. The IRS has sought to expand this rule to cover (and prohibit) situations in which you or other shareholders use the corporation as a personal pocketbook, drawing cash as desired, paying personal expenses, and so forth. Thus, if your S corporation makes distributions that differ as to time or amount, you can inadvertently create a prohibited class of stock and jeopardize your S corporation status. About the only exceptions provided are when the differences are unintentional, or they are corrected within a three-month period. An exception is also provided for stock redemptions (see Chapter 16).

These rules are tough on a family business, because there is a tendency, particularly when some of the shareholders are minor children (or trusts for their benefit), to withdraw some funds as extra perks. You should carefully review all compensation, expenses, and similar payments with your accountant to avoid problems.

SHAREHOLDER QUALIFICATIONS

An S corporation can have up to but not more than 35 qualified shareholders. Qualified shareholders include only individuals (except for nonresident aliens) and certain types of trusts. Corporations cannot be shareholders.

Trust Qualifications

Only certain types of trusts may qualify as S corporation shareholders. A grantor trust, for example, can qualify (but it doesn't have to be a grant or trust). This is a trust set up by you and in which the income is fully taxable to you. An example is the living trust described in Chapter 4. On the other hand, the typical bypass trust used in many estate plans (see Chapters 6 and 9) can create serious problems because a trust to which S corporation stock is transferred pursuant to the terms of a will can only be an S corporation shareholder for 60 days, or the S corporation status will be lost.

Those trusts that can qualify for S corporation treatment are as follows:

- Grantor trust
- Qualified subchapter S trust (see the "For Your Notebook" section to this chapter)
- A trust to which stock was transferred by will (these qualify for 60 days)

Those trusts that do not qualify are as follows:

- Bypass trust
- Any trust that is not specifically qualifying

The special trust for holding S corporation stock, when properly used, can be a very useful estate planning technique.

EXAMPLE: Two brothers have a manufacturing business operated as an S corporation. They agree that it's time to start transferring stock to their children in order to reduce their estate taxes, so they set up qualified S corporation trusts for each of their minor children. They will gift $20,000 of stock (jointly with their respective spouses) each year to each child's trust. This approach will enable them to control the use of the assets for the benefit of each child, while insulating the stock from their creditors and their children's creditors.

To obtain the benefits illustrated in the above example, the trust must meet a number of strict requirements:

- During the life of the current income beneficiary (a child in the above example), the income can only go to one beneficiary. This means the trustee cannot have the power to sprinkle trust income to different beneficiaries (see Chapters 11 and 12). You can have only one current income beneficiary. But a different beneficiary can receive the remainder interest on the death of the first beneficiary.

- Any distributions of trust assets (corpus) during the life of the current income beneficiary can only be made to that beneficiary.

- The current income beneficiary's income interest in the trust must end at the earlier of his or her death, or the termination of the trust. If the trust ends during his or her life, the trust assets must all be distributed to the current income beneficiary.

All of these requirements are illustrated in the Sample S Corporation Trust in the "For Your Notebook" section following this chapter.

Be Careful

It is easy to violate these restrictions inadvertently—when raising capital or negotiating relationships with key suppliers or customers, or through common estate planning oversights. Therefore, it is incumbent on you to encourage a regular review of the corporation's capital structure, compensation programs, principal stock holdings, and so forth, to ensure compliance. Representations should probably be obtained in the shareholders' agreement that estate plans will be reviewed and changed if necessary.

CONCLUSION

S corporations are a very common form of doing business for smaller or closely held businesses seeking the corporate protection of limited liability and wanting to avoid double taxation. However, the various requirements of maintaining an S corporation status make it a tricky asset to use in planning for estate purposes.

For Your Notebook:

SAMPLE QUALIFIED SUBCHAPTER S TRUST
(WITH COMMENTS)

FOR DISCUSSION WITH YOUR LAWYER ONLY—DO NOT USE AS A TRUST

THIS AGREEMENT dated as of MONTH DAY, 1991, between GRANTOR'S NAME, who resides at GRANTOR'S ADDRESS (the "Grantor"), and TRUSTEE'S NAME, who resides at TRUSTEE'S ADDRESS (the "Trustee").

WHEREAS, the Grantor desires to create a trust, the terms of which are hereinafter set forth, and the Trustee has consented to accept and perform said trust in accordance with such terms,

NOW, THEREFORE, IN CONSIDERATION OF THE PREMISES AND MUTUAL COVENANTS HEREIN:

I. PROPERTY TRANSFERRED IN TRUST

In consideration of the premises and covenants set forth below, the Grantor assigns and transfers to the Trustee, and the Trustee, by the execution of this Trust, acknowledges receipt from the Grantor of the property described in Schedule "A," which may include certain stock in a corporation making an election to be taxed as an S corporation. This property, together with any other property acceptable to the Trustee that may after the date of this Trust be transferred to the Trustee by the Grantor, the legal representatives of the Grantor's estate pursuant to the provisions of the Grantor's last will and testament, or any other person, as well as the proceeds from such property, and the securities or other assets in which such proceeds may be invested and reinvested, shall be the "Trust Estate."

II. TRUSTEES SHALL HOLD TRUST ESTATE

A. The Trustee shall hold the Trust Estate for the following purposes and subject to the terms and conditions hereof.

B. During the life of the Grantor:

1. The Trustee shall hold the Trust Estate, with respect to portions of the Trust Estate other than stock in S corporations, in trust:

a. The Trustee shall hold the Trust Estate in trust, to pay or apply to or for the benefit of the following person: Grantor's child, NAME OF CHILD, ("Grantee"). The net income of the Trust shall be applied as the Trustee, in the exercise of his or her absolute discretion, may consider desirable for the comfort and welfare of any one of the Grantee.

b. The Trustee may accumulate any of the net income not paid or applied for the benefit of the Grantee, and add it to the principal of this Trust at least annually and thereafter to hold, administer, and dispose of it as a part of the Trust Estate.

2. The Trustee shall hold the Trust Estate, with respect to stock in S corporations included in the Trust Estate, in trust:

a. To pay or apply to or for the benefit of the Grantee all of the net income thereof; or

b. To accumulate any other amounts not paid or applied in II.B.2.a. above, and add the same to the principal of this Trust at least annually and thereafter to hold, administer, and dispose of same as a part of the Trust Estate.

NOTE: A qualified subchapter S trust may have assets other than S corporation stock. The above provisions permit the trustee to exercise discretion regarding whether to pay out, or accumulate, this non-S corporation income. However, income from the S corporation stock must be paid out currently in order for the trust to continue to qualify.

C. Upon the death of the Grantor, the Trustee shall collect and add to the Trust Estate any amounts payable under insurance policies on the life of the Grantor held in this Trust, or for which the Trustee was designated beneficiary, property payable to the Trustee by the legal representatives of the Grantor's estate pursuant to the provisions of the Grantor's last will, and property payable by any other person whether pursuant to the provisions of such person's last will or otherwise. The Trustee then shall deal with and dispose of these additions as part of the Trust Estate, as provided in Section B above.

NOTE: Although this trust is set up primarily to hold stock in an S corporation, broader provisions, such as this allowing the trustee to claim life insurance policies, are included for flexibility. You may not have set up another trust for insurance or other assets. The right to receive assets from the grantor's will is a pour-over trust provision (see Chapters 4 and 5).

D. Upon the death of the Grantee, if the Grantee shall be survived by issue, the Trustee shall divide the Trust Estate into such number of equal shares that there shall be one share set aside for each of the Grantee's children then living and one share set aside for the issue collectively then living of each of the Grantee's children who may then be deceased, and each such share so set aside for a child of the Grantee (hereinafter "Grandchild") or issue of a deceased child of the Grantee shall be dealt with and disposed of as follows:

1. The Trustee shall hold each share set aside for the beneficiary as a separate trust, in trust, to pay or apply the net income to or for the benefit of the Grandchild, in annual or more frequent installments. When the Grandchild attains the age of Twenty-Five (25) years, the Trustee shall transfer and pay over to the Grandchild One-Third (1/3) of the Trust Estate; when the Grandchild attains the age of Thirty (30) years, the Trustee shall transfer and pay over to the Grandchild One-Half (1/2) of the Trust Estate; and when the Grandchild attains the age of Thirty-Five (35) years, the Trustee shall transfer and pay over to the Grandchild the balance of the Trust Estate.

2. The Trustee shall transfer and pay over each share set aside for the issue of a deceased child in equal parts per stirpes to such issue.

3. Any trust created under Subsection 1. of this section shall terminate on the death of the Grandchild before having attained the age of Thirty-Five (35) years, and, thereupon, the Trustee shall transfer and pay over the Trust Estate in equal parts per stirpes to the Grandchild's then living issue, or if none, in equal parts per stirpes to the Grantee's then living issue (provided, however, that any principal or income distributable to any person for whose benefit there shall then be a trust in existence under this article shall be added to and form a part of the principal of such trust and be dealt with and disposed of accordingly).

E. The Trustee of any trust created hereunder is authorized and empowered, at any time and from time to time, with respect to any person then eligible to receive the net income thereof, to pay, distribute or apply to or for the benefit of such person so much of the principal of such trust, including the whole thereof, as the Trustee, in the exercise of his or her absolute discretion, may consider desirable for such person's comfort and welfare, without regard to such person's income or other resources, the duty of anyone to support such person, or any other funds that may be available for the purpose.

F. Notwithstanding anything to the contrary contained in this Agreement, if the Trustee shall determine that the aggregate value or the character of the assets of any trust created hereunder makes it inadvisable, inconvenient, or uneconomical to continue the administration of such trust, then the Trustee, in the exercise of his or her absolute discretion, may transfer and pay over the Trust Estate, equally or unequally, to or among one or more persons then eligible to receive the net income thereof.

G. For convenience in administration, the Trustee, in the exercise of his or her absolute discretion, may administer together the assets of any trust created hereunder and any property held pursuant to the provisions of Subsection D.1.a. However, the Trustee shall maintain a separate record of the transactions for any trust created hereunder and for property held pursuant to the provisions of such section.

H. The exercise by the Trustee of the discretionary powers herein granted with respect to the payment, distribution, or application of principal or income of any trust created hereunder shall be final and conclusive upon all persons interested hereunder. It is the Grantor's intention that the Trustee shall have reasonable latitude in exercising such discretionary powers, and that the person or persons entitled to receive the principal of any trust created hereunder shall upon the termination of such trust be entitled only to such principal as may remain after the last exercise of such continuing discretionary powers; provided, however, that under no circumstances shall any person who may be acting as a Trustee participate in the exercise of any power granted hereunder with respect to the discretionary payment, distribution, or application to him or her of principal or income of such trust.

III.   DISTRIBUTIONS TO A PERSON UNDER A DISABILITY

A. Whenever pursuant to the provisions of this Trust any property is to be distributed to a Person Under a Disability ("Donee Property"), title to that property shall vest in that Person Under a Disability, but the payment or transfer of the property may be deferred until the disability ceases. If the transfer of property is deferred under this section, that Donee Property shall be held by the Trustee, who shall apply the principal and income thereof, or so much of such principal and income as the Trustee, in the exercise of his or her absolute discretion, may determine, for the comfort and welfare of the Person Under a Disability. This determination by the Trustee shall be made without regard to the income or other resources of the Person Under a Disability, or of his or her parents or spouse.

B. When the disability ceases, the Trustee shall transfer to the person formerly under a disability the remaining Donee Property, and any accumulations of income or principal ("Remaining Property"). If the Person Under a Disability should die, the Trustee shall deliver the Remaining Property to the legal representatives of the estate of that person. Notwithstanding the foregoing provisions, the Trustee may at any time, in the exercise of his or her absolute discretion, deliver all or a portion of the Donee Property that shall then remain, together with any accumulations of income, to a parent, guardian, custodian under the Uniform Gifts (Transfers) to Minors Act of the State, committee, conservator of the property, or an individual with whom such Person Under a Disability resides, and the receipt by such person or entity shall constitute a full discharge of the Trustee for such payment or delivery. The powers granted to the Trustee shall be applicable to any donee property dealt with in this section and shall continue until the actual distribution of the Donee Property.

IV.   TRUSTEE'S COMPENSATION

Each Trustee acting hereunder, except for NAME OF TRUSTEE NOT ENTITLED TO COMPENSATION, shall be entitled to withdraw from the Trust Estate, without obtaining court or other approval, the compensation that is allowed to a trustee under the laws of the State that govern compensation to the trustee of a testamentary trust, computed in the manner and at the rates in effect at the time the compensation is payable.

V. ANNUAL DEMAND POWER

A. Immediately following any Addition to the Trust, the Beneficiaries (individually, the "Holder") shall have the right to withdraw up to the amount of such Addition. Notwithstanding anything herein to the contrary, the total withdrawals by any Beneficiary under this provision, for any calendar year, shall not exceed the lesser of (i) the maximum annual gift tax exclusion allowable under Internal Revenue Code Section 2503(b), as amended; or (ii) the proportion of the Addition during any year divided by the number of Beneficiaries during such year who may make a demand that would qualify a portion of such Addition as a gift of a present interest. This demand power shall take precedence over any other power or discretion granted to the Trustee. This demand power shall not be interpreted to limit the income distributions that may be made by the Trustee to the Beneficiaries.

B. With respect to this demand power, the following rules shall apply:

1. The Holder can exercise this demand power by a written request delivered to the Trustee.

2. If the Holder is unable to exercise this demand power because of a legal disability, including minority, his or her parent, guardian, or personal representative (including but not limited to committee or conservator) may make the demand on the Holder's behalf. However, in no event can the Grantor make the demand for the Holder, regardless of the Grantor's relationship to the Holder.

3. The Trustee must reasonably notify the person who would exercise the Holder's demand power of its existence, and that of any contributions made to the Trust that are subject to this demand power, not later than November 30 of each year.

4. The Holder's demand power is noncumulative and lapses on the earlier of (i) the last day of the calendar year in which the Addition was made; or (ii) Thirty (30) calendar days following the Trustee's sending the Holder notice of such contribution. No payment may be made in a subsequent year on account of the Holder's failure to demand a distribution in a prior year.

5. The Trustee may satisfy the Holder's demand for a distribution by distributing cash, other assets, or fractional interests in other assets, as the Trustee in his or her sole discretion deems appropriate.

C. Notwithstanding the foregoing, if upon the expiration of any right of withdrawal or any portion thereof, the Holder of such right would be deemed to have made a gift for federal gift tax purposes, such right shall continue in existence to the extent of the amount that would have been a taxable gift until and to the extent that its expiration shall not result in a taxable gift by the Holder thereof.

D. The Trustee shall give reasonable written notice to each Holder entitled to exercise the right of withdrawal of any additions to or for the benefit of the Trust Estate (other than accumulated income, if any) and the right to exercise the right of withdrawal.

NOTE: This is the Crummey power provision, which enables you to qualify for the annual $10,000 gift tax exclusion. This provision is discussed in detail in Chapter 11.

VI. ACCOUNTING

A. No Trustee acting under this Trust shall be under a duty to render a judicial accounting upon resignation or otherwise.

B. The Trustee may render an accounting upon termination of any trust created hereunder and at such other time or times as the Trustee, in the exercise of his or her absolute discretion, may deem necessary or advisable. The written approval or assent of all persons not subject to a legal disability then entitled to receive the net income of any trust created hereunder and also all persons not subject to a legal disability then presumptively entitled to the principal thereof, as to all matters and transactions shown in the account, shall be final, binding, and conclusive upon all persons who may then be or thereafter become entitled to all or any part of the income or the principal of any such trust, as the case may be. If the Trustee is accounting to another fiduciary, then the written approval or assent of such other fiduciary shall be final, binding, and conclusive upon all persons beneficially interested in the estate or trust estate represented by such other fiduciary. The written approval or assent of these persons shall have the same force and effect in discharging the Trustee as a decree of a court of competent jurisdiction. However, any such written approval or assent shall not enlarge or shift the beneficial interest of any beneficiary of any trust created hereunder. Notwithstanding anything herein contained to the contrary, the Trustee, in the exercise of his or her absolute discretion, may submit the account to a court for approval and settlement.

VII.   TRUSTEE'S POWERS

The Trustee shall have in addition to, and not in limitation of, the powers granted elsewhere in this Trust, or the powers allowed by law, the following powers:

A. To invest and reinvest any assets comprising the Trust Estate in any securities or other property, whether real or personal, of any class, kind, or nature (including an undivided interest in any one or more common trust funds), as the Trustee may deem advisable without regard to any restrictions of law on a trustee's investments.

B. To exercise voting rights in person or by proxy, rights of conversion or of exchange, or rights to purchase or subscribe for stocks, bonds, or other securities or obligations that may be offered to the holders of any asset, and to accept and retain any property that may be acquired by the exercise of any such right with respect to any stocks, bonds, or other securities or obligation included in the Trust Estate, in the Trustee's absolute discretion.

C. To employ or retain accountants, custodians, agents, legal counsel, investment advisers, and other experts as the Trustee shall deem advisable. To rely on the information and advice furnished by such persons. To fix the compensation of such persons, and in the case of legal counsel, who may also be acting as a Trustee hereunder, to take payments on account of legal fees in advance of the settlement of the Trustee's account without applying to or procuring the authority of any court.

D. To the extent permitted by the laws of the State, to hold securities in the name of a nominee without indicating the trust character of such holdings, and to hold unregistered securities, or securities in a form that will pass by delivery.

E. To retain and continue for any period deemed appropriate by the Trustee, in exercise of his or her absolute discretion, any asset, whether real or personal, tangible or intangible, included in the Trust Estate, constituting the Trust Estate.

F. To sell at public or private sale and to exchange or otherwise dispose of any stocks, bonds, securities, personal property, or other asset constituting the Trust Estate at the time, price, and terms as the Trustee deems advisable.

G. To grant options for the sale or exchange of any asset comprising the Trust Estate, at times, prices, and terms that the Trustee deems advisable, without applying to or procuring the authority of any court.

H. To sell, exchange, partition, convey, and mortgage, and to modify, extend, renew, or replace any mortgage that may be a lien on all, or any part, of any interest in real property included in the Trust Estate.

I. To lease any real or personal property, whether or not for a term beyond the period of time fixed by statute for leases by a trustee, and whether or not extending beyond the termination of any Trust, and upon such terms as the Trustee deems advisable, without obtaining the approval of any court.

J. To foreclose mortgages and bid in property under foreclosure and to take title by deed in lieu of foreclosure or otherwise.

K. To extend the time of payment of any bond, note, or other obligation or mortgage included in the Trust Estate, or of any installment of principal thereof, or of any interest due thereon. To hold such instrument after maturity, as a past due bond, note, or other obligation or mortgage, either with or without renewal or extension. To consent to the modification, alteration, and amendment of any terms or conditions of such instrument, including those regarding the rate of interest, and to waive any defaults in the performance of the terms and conditions of such instrument.

L. To compromise, adjust, settle, or submit to arbitration upon terms the Trustee deems advisable, in his or her absolute discretion, any claim in favor of or against the Trust Estate. To release with, or without, consideration any claim in favor of the Trust Estate.

M. To participate in any refunding; readjustment of stocks, bonds, or other securities or obligations; enforcement of obligations or securities by foreclosure or otherwise; corporate consolidation by merger or otherwise; or reorganization that shall affect any stock, bond, or other security or obligation included in the Trust Estate. To participate in any plan or proceeding for protection of the interests of the holders of such instruments. To deposit any property under any plan or proceeding with any protective or reorganization committee and to delegate to such a committee the discretionary power with respect thereto. To pay a proportionate part of the expenses of a committee. To pay any assessments levied under such a plan, and to accept and retain any property that may be received pursuant to any such plan.

N. To borrow money for the purpose of raising funds to pay taxes or for any other purpose deemed by the Trustee, in his or her absolute discretion, beneficial to the Trust Estate, and upon such terms as the Trustee may determine. To pledge as security for the repayment of any loan any assets included in the Trust Estate.

O. To make any distribution under any Trust, in cash or in property, or in any combination of cash and property. To make non-pro rata distributions of cash and property then included in the Trust Estate.

P. To exercise for the benefit of the Trust Estate, and for any property included in the Trust Estate, all rights, powers, and privileges of every nature that might or could be exercised by any person owning similar property absolutely and in his or her own right, in connection with the exercise of any or all of such rights, powers, and privileges, even when such right, power, or privilege may not have been specifically mentioned in this Trust. To negotiate, draft, enter into, renegotiate, or otherwise modify any contracts or other written instruments that the Trustee deems advisable, and to include in them the covenants, terms, and conditions as the Trustee deems proper, in the exercise of his or her absolute discretion.

NOTE: See the comments in the trust in the "For Your Notebook" section of Chapter 11.

VIII. TRUSTEE'S EXERCISE OF AUTHORITY

Any authority, discretion, or power granted to or conferred upon the Trustee by this Trust may be (i) exercised by such of them as shall be, or the one of them who shall be, acting hereunder from time to time, and (ii) by such one of them who shall be so designated by an instrument in writing delivered to such one Trustee by the Trustee.

IX.   THIRD-PARTY RELIANCE

No bank or trust company, corporation, partnership, association, firm, or other person dealing with the Trustee or keeping any assets, whether funds, securities, or other property of the Trust Estate, shall be required to investigate the authority of the Trustee for entering into any transaction involving assets of the Trust Estate. Nor shall such person be required to see to the application of the proceeds of any transaction with the Trustee, or to inquire into the appropriateness, validity, expediency, or propriety thereof, or be under any obligation or liability whatsoever, except to the Trustee; and any such person, bank or trust company, corporation, partnership, association, or firm shall be fully protected in making disposition of any assets of the Trust Estate in accordance with the directions of the Trustee.

X.   TRUSTEE'S LIABILITY

A. The Trustee shall not be individually liable for any loss to or depreciation in the value of the Trust Estate occurring by reason of (i) the exercise or nonexercise of the powers granted to the Trustee under this Trust; or (ii) a mistake in, or error of, judgment in the purchase or sale of any investment or the retention of any investment, so long as the Trustee shall have been acting in good faith.

B. Every act done, power exercised, or obligation assumed by the Trustee, pursuant to the provisions of this Trust, shall be held to be done, exercised, or assumed, as the case may be, by the Trustee acting in the Trustee's fiduciary capacity and not otherwise, and every person, firm, or corporation contracting or otherwise dealing with the Trustee shall look only to the funds and property of the Trust Estate for payment under such contract or payment of any money that may become due or payable under any obligation arising under this Trust, in whole or in part, and the Trustee shall not be individually liable therefor even though the Trustee did not exempt itself from individual liability when entering into any contract, obligation, or transaction in connection with or growing out of the Trust Estate.

XI.   TRUSTEE'S CONSULTATION WITH COUNSEL

The Trustee may consult with legal counsel (who may be counsel to the Grantor) concerning any question that may arise with reference to the Trustee's duties or obligations under this Trust, and the opinion of such counsel shall be full and complete authorization and protection in respect of any action taken or suffered by the Trustee in good faith and in accordance with the opinion of such counsel.

XII.   RESIGNATION OF TRUSTEES

A. Any Trustee hereunder may resign at any time without obtaining prior judicial approval. Such resignation shall be deemed complete upon the delivery of an instrument in writing declaring such resignation to the Grantor, or if the Grantor shall then be deceased, to the remaining Trustee hereunder, or if there be no remaining Trustee, to the successor Trustee hereunder. Such resigning Trustee shall promptly deliver the assets of the Trust Estate to the remaining or successor Trustee hereunder.

B. The resigning Trustee shall, at the request of the remaining or successor Trustee hereunder, promptly deliver such assignments, transfers, and other instruments as may be reasonably required for fully vesting in such remaining or successor Trustee all right, title, and interest in the Trust Estate.

C. Each Trustee acting hereunder shall be entitled to withdraw from the Trust Estate, without obtaining judicial authorization, the compensation that is allowed to a trustee under the laws of the State governing compensation to the trustee of a testamentary trust, computed in the manner and at the rates in effect at the time such compensation shall be payable.

XIII.   ADDITIONAL OR SUCCESSOR TRUSTEES

A. The Trustee may appoint an additional or successor Trustee, which may be an individual (other than the Grantor), or a bank or trust company. This appointment shall be by an instrument in writing delivered to the Trustee. It shall become effective on the date or condition specified in the instrument. Prior to the specified date or condition, however, the appointment may be withdrawn by an instrument in writing delivered to the Trustee. In the event that there shall be no Trustee acting hereunder for a period of Thirty (30) days, the Grantor appoints as a successor Trustee the individual (other than the Grantor) or the bank or trust company to be designated by an instrument in writing signed by the law firm of NAME OF GRANTOR'S LAWYER, or any successor firm, and delivered to the Grantor and Trustee, or if the Grantor shall then be decreased, to the legal representatives of the estate of the Grantor.

NOTE: In an irrevocable trust, the best approach is for you to name in the trust as many alternates as you believe would properly fulfill the role of trustee, in the event that the initial trustee can no longer serve.

B. The acceptance of trusteeship by any Trustee who is not a party to this Trust shall be evidenced by an instrument in writing delivered to the remaining Trustee hereunder, or if there be no remaining Trustee, to the Grantor, or if he or she shall then be deceased, to the legal representatives of the estate of the Grantor, or to such person as designated by a court of competent jurisdiction.

XIV. NO BOND REQUIRED

No bond or security of any kind shall be required of any Trustee acting hereunder.

XV. TRANSACTIONS WITH GRANTOR'S ESTATE

The Trustee is authorized and empowered, at any time and from time to time, (i) to purchase at fair market value from the legal representatives of the Grantor's estate any property constituting a part, or all, of the Grantor's estate, and (ii) to lend for adequate consideration to the legal representatives of the Grantor's estate such part, or all, of the Trust Estate, upon such terms and conditions as the Trustee, in the exercise of his or her absolute discretion deems advisable.

XVI. ADDITIONAL ASSETS

The Grantor, or any other person, may assign or transfer to the Trustee securities or other property, whether real or personal, tangible or intangible, reasonably acceptable to the Trustee ("Addition"). All Additions shall be added to the Trust Estate, and the Trustee shall hold and dispose of any Addition as part of the Trust Estate subject to the terms and provisions of this Trust.

XVII. S CORPORATION ELECTION

A. With respect to any part of the Trust Estate that is stock in a corporation electing under the provisions of Section 1362 of the Internal Revenue Code of 1986, as amended (the "Code") to be taxed as an S corporation ("S corporation Assets"), this Trust is intended to be a Qualified Subchapter S Trust, as such term is defined under Section 1361(d) of the Code. Notwithstanding any provision to the contrary in this Trust, the Trustee shall, with respect to such stock, operate the Trust in a manner consistent with such requirements. All provisions of this Trust shall be construed consistently with the requirements of a Qualified Subchapter S Trust.

B. Notwithstanding anything herein to the contrary, regarding the S corporation Assets, the Trustee shall do the following:

1. During the life of the Beneficiary, there shall be only One (1) current income beneficiary of this Trust, who shall be the Grantee designated above.

2. All of the income, as defined in Code Section 643(b), of the S corporation Assets shall be distributed currently to the current income beneficiary.

3. Any corpus distributed during the life of such current income beneficiary, pursuant to the provisions elsewhere in this Trust, may be distributed only to such beneficiary.

4. The income interest of the current income beneficiary in this Trust shall terminate on the earlier of such beneficiary's death or the termination of this Trust.

5. If this Trust terminates during the life of the current income beneficiary, the Trustee shall distribute all S corporation Assets to such beneficiary.

6. If upon the death of the Grantee this Trust will not meet the requirements of a Qualified Subchapter S Trust, the Trustee shall distribute the S corporation Assets to the person or persons then constituting income beneficiaries of this Trust if, and only if,

such distribution will enable the S corporation Assets to continue to meet the requirements of an S corporation in their hands. Any such distribution shall be made within the time periods required by the Code to prevent disqualification of the S corporation elections of the S corporation Assets.

7. The Trustee is authorized to make any minor technical corrections necessary to the terms of this Trust to ensure that, with respect to the S corporation Assets, this Trust shall continue to meet the requirements of a Qualified Subchapter S Trust.

8. The Trustee may pay to the current income beneficiary, in addition to all other payments provided under this Trust, an amount approximately equal to the federal, state, and local income taxes imposed on the current income beneficiary with respect to the S corporation Assets, on account of any income or gain allocated to trust principal, according to applicable accounting principles. The Trustee's decision on the amount to be distributed shall be final.

NOTE: This provision lists the requirements for this trust to be a qualified S corporation trust.

XVIII. IRREVOCABLE TRUST

A. The Grantor has been advised with respect to the difference between revocable and irrevocable trusts and hereby declares that this Trust and the Trust Estate created hereby are to be irrevocable. The Grantor has no power to alter, amend, revoke, or terminate any Trust provision or interest, whether under this Trust or any rule of law. The Grantor shall not have any reversionary interest in this Trust or the Trust Estate.

B. The Trustee shall not have the power to use any of the Trust Estate for the benefit of the Grantor's estate, as such term is defined in Regulation Section 20.2042-1(b). The Trustee, however, may modify or amend this Trust to facilitate the administration of the Trust Estate or to conform this Trust to laws or regulations affecting *inter vivos* trusts, or the requirements of qualifying as a Qualified Subchapter S Trust, as the same may be amended from time to time. No such modification or amendment shall affect the possession or enjoyment of the Trust Estate.

XIX. NOT A GRANTOR TRUST

Notwithstanding anything herein to the contrary, none of the rights or powers given to the Trustee shall be interpreted to enable the Grantor, the Trustee, or anyone else to buy, exchange, or otherwise deal with trust principal or income for less than adequate and full consideration in money or money's worth, or to enable the Grantor, the Trustee, or any entity in which the Grantor, the Trust, or the Trustee, has a substantial interest, to borrow any of the principal of the Trust, directly or indirectly, without adequate interest, terms, and security. Only the Trustee may vote or direct the voting of any corporate shares or other securities of the Trust, control the Trust's investments or reinvestments by direction or veto, or reacquire or exchange Trust property by substitution for other property of equal value. The Trustee shall not use any of the Trust's funds or assets to pay the premiums on policies of insurance on the life of the Grantor. The Trustee is not required to surrender Trust assets upon being tendered substitute assets, regardless of the relative values of the assets involved.

NOTE: This section is a saving clause to help prevent the trust from being treated as a grantor's trust, which would result in your being taxed on the trust's income instead of your child.

XX. DEFINITIONS

The following terms when used in this Trust are defined as follows:

A. "Child" is an issue in the first degree.

B. "Addition" means any cash or other assets transferred to the Trust to be held as part of the Trust Estate. The amount of any contribution is its federal gift tax value, as determined by the Trustee at the time of the transfer.

C. "Issue" is a descendant in any degree, whether natural or adopted.

D. "Per stirpes" is a disposition of property whereby issue take a portion thereof in representation of their deceased parent, with division to be made into such number of equal shares at each succeeding degree of relationship from the common ancestor that there shall be one share for each person of such degree living at the time of such division and one share for the issue collectively then living of each person of such degree who is then deceased; such division to be made although there may not then be any person living within such degree.

NOTE: See the "For Your Notebook" section of Chapter 19 for an application of per stirpes.

E. "Trustee" is the trustee named in this Trust or appointed by a court or pursuant to the terms of this Trust and any and all successors, and may be masculine, feminine, or neuter, and singular or plural, as the sense requires.

F. "Donee Property" is any net income of any trust created hereunder or all or any part of the Trust Estate distributable to a Person Under a Disability to be held by the donee of a power to manage during disability.

G. A "Person Under a Disability" is either a person who has not attained the age of Twenty-One (21) years or a person who, for such period as the Trustee shall determine, is deemed by the Trustee in the exercise of his or her absolute discretion to be physically or mentally incapable of managing his or her affairs, although a judicial declaration may not have been made with respect to such disability.

H. To hold "in Trust" is to manage, invest, and reinvest the principal of a trust and to collect the income thereof.

I. "Trust Estate" is the then remaining principal of any trust, as then constituted, and upon the termination of such trust, any accrued and undistributed income.

J. "Income" and "Principal" are defined as follows: All cash dividends, other than those described hereafter, shall be income. Principal shall be all corporate distributions in shares of stock (whether denominated as dividends, stock splits, or otherwise, and cash proceeds representing fractions thereof) of any class of any corporation (whether the corporation declaring or authorizing such distributions or otherwise). Dividends on investment company shares attributed to capital gains also shall be principal, whether declared payable at the option of the shareholders in cash or in shares or otherwise. Liquidating dividends, rights to subscribe to stock and the proceeds of the sale thereof, and the proceeds of unproductive or underproductive property shall be principal. There shall be no apportionment of the proceeds of the sale of any asset of the Trust Estate (whether real or personal, tangible or intangible) between principal and income because such asset may be or may have been wholly or partially unproductive of income during any period of time. Notwithstanding anything in this definition to the contrary, all income, as defined under applicable provisions of the Internal Revenue Code of 1986 and Treasury Regulations, attributable to S corporation stock shall be distributed as required for the trust to retain its status as a Qualified S Corporation Trust.

K. "State" means STATE'S NAME.

XXI. CONSTRUCTION

A. The validity, construction, and effect of the provisions of this Trust shall be governed by the laws of the State. This Trust may be executed in more than one counterpart, each of which is an original, but all taken together shall be deemed one and the same instrument. Headings have been inserted for convenience only and shall not serve to limit or broaden the terms of any provision.

B. Any provision of this Trust to the contrary notwithstanding, this Trust, and any other trusts created under this document, shall be interpreted so as not to violate the rule against perpetuities. Notwithstanding anything herein to the contrary, this Trust shall terminate upon the expiration of Twenty-One (21) years after the death of the grantee, and if any trust created hereunder has not sooner terminated, the Trustee shall at said time pay over, convey, and deliver the trust fund or funds then in their possession to the persons then entitled to receive the income therefrom in the same shares or portions in which such income is then being paid or payable to them.

XXII. BINDING AGREEMENT

This Agreement shall extend to and be binding upon the executors, administrators, heirs, successors, and assigns of the Grantor and the Trustee.

IN WITNESS WHEREOF, the undersigned Grantor and Trustee have executed this Agreement as of the date first-above written.

_____ (L.S.)
GRANTOR'S NAME, Grantor

_____ (L.S.)
TRUSTEE'S NAME, Trustee

[NOTARY FORMS - OMITTED]

[SCHEDULE A — PROPERTY TRANSFERRED - OMITTED]

18 FARM OR RANCH

The estate planning dilemma faced by farmers and ranchers, and certain others with substantial investments in land, buildings, and equipment, is how to pay the estate tax without forcing the liquidation of the business—in other words, how to pass the business on, intact, to children or other heirs. There are a few special tax provisions, and a number of tax planning steps, that can help you achieve this goal. There are also special charitable contribution rules if you decide not to pass the business on to heirs.

SPECIAL USE VALUATION OF FARM PROPERTY

The tax laws contain a provision that permits real estate used in a farming, ranching, or closely held business to be valued in a special, more favorable way for estate tax purposes than the regular method. An exception is made from the general rule that property must be listed in your gross estate at its fair market value (price for highest and best use), so that qualifying farm property can be valued according to its current business or farming use. The maximum reduction in your gross estate permitted by using the special valuation rules is $750,000. Therefore, the maximum savings is $412,500, at the current 55 percent estate tax rate.

Requirements to Qualify for Special Use Valuation

The requirements to qualify a property for special use are so strict that the usefulness of this provision is severely limited—but when they can be met the benefits are tremendous. They don't go into effect until you die, but the planning must be done while you're alive. They are the following:

1. The real estate must be in use as a farm (or ranch) in a qualified farming activity, or in a closely held active trade or business other than farming, at the time of the owner's death. This activity includes cultivating the soil or raising or harvesting any agricultural or horticultural commodity on a farm. The mere passive

rental of real estate subject to a net lease, in which you are not subject to risk of loss (can't lose money on the deal) does not constitute a qualifying closely held trade or business use. If the property is being leased to a related party who conducts a qualified farming or closely held trade or business use on the property, this use is considered to meet the test, even though you aren't directly involved.

2. You must be a citizen or resident of the United States.

3. The property must be in the United States.

4. The combined value of the real and personal property used in the farming, ranching, or closely held business activity must equal at least 50 percent of your adjusted gross estate (gross estate reduced by mortgages, other debt, and certain expenses). Personal property includes only that property which is used in the same business as the qualifying real estate. For purposes of this 50 percent test (and the 25 percent test below), the farm, ranch, or closely held business property is valued at its fair market value, not at the special use valuation. Multiple properties—for example, real estate used in a farm and a closely held retail furniture store—can be aggregated to meet these tests.

5. The value of the real property used in the farming or closely held business activity must equal at least 25 percent of the adjusted value of your gross estate.

6. The qualified real property must pass from you to a qualified heir. (A qualified heir is a member of your family—spouse, parents, siblings, children, stepchildren, and their lineal descendants.) This requirement includes property received by a qualified heir as a result of a qualified disclaimer. (A qualified disclaimer is when a beneficiary refuses to accept a bequest and the bequest is then distributed in accordance with other provisions of the will, or state law if the will is silent.) If the business is operated in corporate form, a redemption of stock by the corporation that results indirectly in an increase in interests of the other shareholders who are qualified heirs is also acceptable (see Chapter 16). Property can pass to a trust in which a qualified heir has a present interest and still meet this requirement. A small amount of property can pass to someone other than a qualified heir.

7. You, or a member of your family must have participated materially in the operation of the farm, ranch, or closely held business for five of the eight years prior to your death or disability. This requires active management, which means making business decisions other than those relating to daily operations.

8. You or your family had to have owned and used the property in the farming, ranching, or closely held business for five of the last eight years.

9. Your executor must file a special election agreement with the estate tax return, Form 706, agreeing to be bound by all of the requirements to qualify for this benefit (see Chapter 6).

Determining the Value under the Special Rules

If all of the above requirements are met, the real estate can be valued based on an average annual gross cash rental for comparable land, less real estate taxes. This amount is then capitalized (divided) by an interest rate. If you can't find a comparable property, the valuation is based on consideration of a number of factors, such as assessed value, capitalization of income, and so forth.

If the property that qualified for this benefit is transferred to a nonqualified person, or if the property is no longer used in a qualified business, the tax benefits your estate received will have to be recaptured (given up).

This special valuation procedure can be used in conjunction with the alternate valuation date discussed in Chapter 6.

DEFERRAL

Another important estate tax benefit can help you keep your farm in the family. When more than 35 percent of your adjusted gross estate consists of assets used in your farming (or closely held) business, you may qualify to defer the payment of the estate tax attributable to the business for approximately 14 years (see Chapters 15 and 16).

EXAMPLE: You operated a farm and earned income based on crop production (not based on a return as a fixed rental income). The IRS should agree that you were engaged in a trade or business, so that the estate tax attributable to the farm should qualify to be paid out over the 14-year deferral period. If, on the other hand, you maintained an office, collected rents on farm properties, negotiated leases, and contracted for maintenance services, the IRS might say that you were merely an owner managing investment properties, and your assets would not qualify for a tax deferral.

DONATING A REMAINDER INTEREST IN YOUR HOUSE OR FARM

You can donate a remainder interest in a personal residence or farm and qualify for a charitable deduction (see Chapter 14). The way it works is that you make a gift today of a future interest in your farm or house, obtain a current tax deduction, and still live in your house or farm for the rest of your life, or for some specified number of years. The amount of the charitable deduction will depend on a number of factors, including your life expectancy, the value of the property, the estimated life and residual value of the depreciable property, interest rates, and so forth. On your death, or at the specified time, the charity will obtain full use and ownership of the property. The value of the property, even if included in your gross estate, will be offset by an estate tax charitable deduction. In addition, you can accomplish all of this without having to go through the legal complications and expense of setting up a trust. The gift, however, must be irrevocable. You can use these rules to gift a house, cooperative apartment, or even vacation home.

The "For Your Notebook" section following this chapter contains an illustration of this planning opportunity.

OTHER CONSIDERATIONS

Techniques described elsewhere in this book should also be considered. For example, the best use of your unified credit and marital deduction should be made. Many of the real estate planning techniques described in Chapter 15 may be applicable to you. You might give equipment to your children under the annual $10,000 per person gift tax exclusion to remove it from your estate. You could continue to use the equipment by leasing it back from your children. Alternatively, these assets could be contributed to a family corporation, with stock given to your children annually.

CONCLUSION

Farmers and ranchers face unique estate tax problems. However, with careful planning to make the most use of the special tax benefits designed for these businesses, and to take the most advantage of the estate planning opportunities available to all taxpayers, these problems can be minimized.

For Your Notebook:

ILLUSTRATION OF DONATING A CHARITABLE REMAINDER INTEREST IN A HOME OR FARM

FACTS AND COMMENTS

The following two examples assume that you're age 57 years old, your farm land is worth $235,600, and that the depreciable property (house, barn, fencing, and so forth) is worth $124,567.

In the first example, it is assumed that the property has a useful life of 20 years, after which its value is estimated to be $23,000. Your charitable deduction of $61,491 will have a value of approximately $24,600, assuming a combined federal and state tax rate of 40 percent.

If the assumptions are changed slightly, so that the estimated useful life of the property is 25 years, the value at that time will only be $15,000, your contribution deduction increases slightly to approximately $62,400.

```
┌──────────────────────────────────────────────────────────────────────┐
│   C H A R I T A B L E   R E M A I N D E R :   R E S I D E N C E / F A R M │
├──────────────────────────────────────────────────────────────────────┤
│ Single Life                          Wednesday February 13, 1991       │
├──────────────────────────────────────────────────────────────────────┤
│     Transfer Date: 2/1991   10.2%   9.8%   9.6%  Table Rate: 9.60%      │
│                                                                        │
│   Land Value:    $235,600.00   Depreciable Property Value:  $124,567.00│
│                                                                        │
│     Depreciable Property Value at End of Useful Life:    $23,000.00     │
│                                                                        │
│       Estimated Useful Life in Years:20    Beneficiary's Age: 57        │
├─────────────────────── Calculation Results ═══════════════════════════┤
│ Total Value of Property ..................................... $360,167.00│
│ Depreciable Part = $124,567.00 - $23,000.00  .............. $101,567.00 │
│ Nondepreciable Part = $235,600.00 + $23,000.00  ........... $258,600.00 │
│ Adjustment Factor = (1,221.6071 - 141.530070) / (20 x 466.4364)        │
│                   = ........................................     0.11578 │
│ Remainder Factor ...........................................     0.20338 │
│ Remainder = ($101,567.00(0.20338 - 0.11578))+(0.20338 x $258,600.00)   │
│ Charitable Deduction for Remainder Interest ............... $61,491.34  │
└──────────────────────────────────────────────────────────────────────┘
```

```
┌──────────────────────────────────────────────────────────────────────┐
│   C H A R I T A B L E   R E M A I N D E R :   R E S I D E N C E / F A R M │
├──────────────────────────────────────────────────────────────────────┤
│ Single Life                          Wednesday February 13, 1991       │
├──────────────────────────────────────────────────────────────────────┤
│     Transfer Date: 2/1991   10.2%   9.8%   9.6%  Table Rate: 9.60%      │
│                                                                        │
│   Land Value:    $235,600.00   Depreciable Property Value:  $124,567.00│
│                                                                        │
│     Depreciable Property Value at End of Useful Life:    $15,000.00     │
│                                                                        │
│       Estimated Useful Life in Years:25    Beneficiary's Age: 57        │
├─────────────────────── Calculation Results ═══════════════════════════┤
│ Total Value of Property ..................................... $360,167.00│
│ Depreciable Part = $124,567.00 - $15,000.00  .............. $109,567.00 │
│ Nondepreciable Part = $235,600.00 + $15,000.00  ........... $250,600.00 │
│ Adjustment Factor = (1,221.6071 - 60.058628) / (25 x 466.4364)         │
│                   = ........................................     0.09961 │
│ Remainder Factor ...........................................     0.20338 │
│ Remainder = ($109,567.00(0.20338 - 0.09961))+(0.20338 x $250,600.00)   │
│ Charitable Deduction for Remainder Interest ............... $62,336.80  │
└──────────────────────────────────────────────────────────────────────┘
```

Note: These two examples were calculated with the Charitable Financial Planner software, published by Commerce Clearing House, Inc., Chicago, Illinois.

Figure 18.1.   Illustration of donating a charitable remainder interest in a home or farm.

19 LIFE INSURANCE

If properly planned, insurance can be one of your estate's most valuable and flexible assets. Insurance can be used in many ways—as an investment vehicle, to provide funds for your children's education, to provide living expenses for your spouse and children in the event of your untimely death, and to meet substantial estate tax costs. This latter use is particularly important. Without adequate insurance coverage, real estate, business interests, or other assets may have to be sold at an inopportune time to raise funds to meet estate taxes. A proper insurance plan can give your estate the necessary liquidity to pay the tax, so that the assets can be passed on to your heirs intact.

HOW MUCH INSURANCE AND WHAT KIND?

Amount

Too many people assess their insurance needs based on rules of thumb. This may provide an appropriate answer, but only coincidentally. The proper analysis of your insurance needs can only be made as part of your overall estate objectives, in consultation with your insurance agent, accountant, and financial planner.

If your sole objective is to pay the estate tax, then an estimate of that expected tax should serve as the benchmark of your insurance needs. However, when making the assessment, the likely effects of the following techniques should be taken into account: your gift program, the possibility of qualifying for the deferred payment of estate taxes, the special valuation methods that may reduce the estate tax cost, the unified credit, and the marital deduction. Such an analysis may show that there is no need for insurance at all. Your estate may have sufficient liquidity. For example, when your estate includes substantial real estate (which is generally considered to be a nonliquid asset), depending on the type and nature of the property and the current debt load, it might be quite easy to obtain mortgage financing to meet estate tax costs.

When the objective is to provide income for family members after your death, a couple of approaches to estimating your insurance needs are possible. The more detailed approach is to estimate family living expenses after your death and offset that amount by the other sources of income your heirs will have. The shortfall can be made up by insurance. The amount needed will be the present value of the income stream under various assumptions of taxes and rates of return. A simpler and more conservative approach, for those who can afford it, is simply to determine the minimum income you want your family to have and to estimate the insurance necessary to provide that income under conservative assumptions.

CAUTION: When insurance is important to meet your estate planning objectives, as it is for many people, deciding on the necessary coverage should be a methodical and deliberate process involving a number of your estate planning experts. It is far too important to leave to a simple rule of thumb.

Kind—The Second-to-Die Policy

An analysis of the various types of insurance policy—for example, term, whole life, universal life, and so forth—is well beyond the scope of this book. There are many options to evaluate in the context of your overall estate plan, and the best decisions will be made when you integrate your insurance agent into an overall estate planning team with your attorney, accountant, financial planner, pension consultant, and other experts. Your present ability to pay premiums and your insurance needs (see above) all must be factored into the analysis.

NOTE: The related issues of the options to choose under any insurance policy are vitally important. Should dividends be reinvested in the purchase of additional insurance, or used to reduce premiums? The answer depends on the cost of the additional purchases, your present insurance needs and how they are likely to change over time, and your ability to pay larger premiums. Payout options are important. In some instances, it may be advisable to delay the payment of some portion of insurance proceeds to provide the surviving spouse some time to address the new circumstances before the responsibility of investing a substantial insurance recovery is added to other burdens. In other instances a payout may be necessary to pay for living expenses, estate taxes, and so forth. Also consider the likely payout under a company pension plan, other insurance policies, death benefit from a pension plan or employer, and so forth. These issues should be discussed and analyzed in detail with your insurance agent, financial planner, estate planning attorney, and accountant.

However, one type of insurance policy warrants specific mention—the second-to-die policy. This policy was designed specifically to address the basic problem in planning for many estates. This is the problem: On the death of the first spouse, the entire estate can be given to the surviving spouse under the marital deduction without any estate tax being incurred; however, if the estate of the surviving spouse exceeds $600,000, at his or her death, an estate tax will be due (see Chapters 9 and 10). With a second-to-die insurance policy, the death benefit is paid only on the death of the *second* of two lives—typically, the last to die of a husband and wife. The result is that the cost of the insurance is reduced as compared with a policy on just one life. The insurance paid on the second death is used to meet any estate tax costs. Thus, a simple estate plan may call for all assets to go to the surviving spouse, with a second-to-die life insurance policy, established to cover any estate tax cost on the death of the second spouse.

This approach can be simplistic, however, and result in throwing away valuable tax benefits. At the minimum, consideration should be given to setting up a bypass trust to use the first-to-die spouse's unified credit, keeping $600,000 of assets out of the estate of the surviving spouse (see Chapter 9). When this approach is combined with the second-to-die insurance policy, an effective estate plan is created. The second-to-die policy pays the estate tax only on assets in excess of $1.2 million, because full use is being made of both unified credits.

WHO SHOULD OWN YOUR INSURANCE POLICIES?

For estate planning, who owns the policy is one of the most important issues. There is a fundamental estate tax planning point for ownership of life insurance.

> **EXAMPLE:** Your estate is worth $3 million without insurance and you purchase a $1 million insurance policy. Your estate is now worth $4 million, and the tax cost on the $1 million insurance proceeds on your death will exceed $500,000. Effectively, you've paid for a $1 million policy, but your estate and heirs will see less than half that amount. Planning for the proper ownership of the policy to avoid this result is vital to an estate plan.

Self

As illustrated, you can own an insurance policy yourself. This approach provides you with the maximum flexibility and control, so that you can change beneficiaries or borrow from your policy as you desire. The drawback is that there can be a tremendous tax cost if your estate, when combined with the insurance proceeds, exceeds your $600,000 lifetime exemption (unified credit). If you're married and the proceeds pass under your will to your spouse, they will escape tax in your estate as a result of the unlimited marital deduction. However, this will bunch assets in your spouse's estate, as explained below.

Spouse

Instead, your spouse could own the policy. This would keep the proceeds from being included in your estate on your death. However, it would expose the policy money to your spouse's creditors, or to equitable distribution in the event that you and your spouse divorce. Further, if significant assets are to be transferred to your spouse if you die first, the result could be a costly bunching of assets in your spouse's estate, which would push that estate into a higher marginal tax bracket. In such an event, there can be no guarantee that your spouse will apply the insurance proceeds to purchase assets from your estate and provide the liquidity that was one of the reasons for acquiring the policy.

Children—Directly

Another alternative is to have your children, who are often the primary persons for whom the insurance protection is purchased, be the beneficiaries and owners of the policy. Cash can be given to the children, and they can then purchase the insurance on your life directly. This approach is not without its shortcomings. The children may use the funds for other purposes, borrow excessively against the policy, or cash in the policy. Also, their ownership will cause the death benefit under the policy to be included in their estates. However, when the amount of the policy is small, direct ownership by the children may be appropriate.

CAUTION: When children are named as beneficiaries, be careful how you list the children's names. If you presently have two children, Dick and Jane, and list them as beneficiaries, any children born at a later date will be left out unless you formally change the beneficiary designation. A better approach is to name as beneficiary "my children Dick and Jane, and any later-born or adopted children of mine."

Children (or Others)—In Trust

The most practical and secure answer in many instances, avoiding the problems described above, will be to have an irrevocable life insurance trust established to own the insurance on your life. This can offer a host of advantages. It can remove the insurance proceeds from the estate of both you and your spouse, and it can protect your family by providing flexibility to distribute money to those most in need. Because of its great usefulness, the irrevocable life insurance trust is examined in greater detail below.

There is an intermediate approach between the use of an irrevocable insurance trust and having family members own the policy. Using a revocable insurance trust may remove the insurance proceeds from your probate estate, which may simplify the administration of your estate and, if trustee fees are less than probate fees, produce some savings for your heirs. With a revocable trust, you retain all the rights of ownership to borrow against the policy, and so forth. But this comes at a price—the insurance will be included in your estate. If your estate is less than the $600,000 lifetime exclusion, this will not create any tax cost. In fact, it can be an affirmative tax planning technique for using your lifetime exclusion. The trust, however, should not qualify for the marital deduction for this result to be achieved (see Chapters 6 and 9).

Business Partners or Corporation

When closely held business interests are involved, buy-out agreements may contain cross-purchase or redemption arrangements. In these cases, the tax and financial planning for the business may govern who should own the insurance policies (see Chapter 16).

GIFT TAX ADVANTAGES AND ISSUES OF GIVING AWAY LIFE INSURANCE

A basic objective in planning any gift is to select property to give that is likely to appreciate substantially in value after the date of the gift. This results in the lowest possible value at the date of the gift, and hence, hopefully little, if any, gift tax. It also results in the removal of the future appreciation from the donor's estate, providing the maximum estate planning benefit. One asset that often meets these objectives and criteria is life insurance. Term insurance, for example, has a relatively modest current value for gift tax purposes. However, on the death of the insured, the face value of the policy is often significant.

It has been stated that life insurance can be one of the most advantageous assets to give away, because the entire death benefit, which is often substantial, can be removed from the donor's estate and tremendous savings in estate taxes can result. Be careful, however, to address the potential gift tax issues. Your insurance agent should be able to provide you with a calculation of the value of the insurance given, in accordance with a prescribed IRS formula. If the value exceeds the $10,000 per year exclusion ($20,000 for a joint gift), either a gift tax will be triggered or a portion of your lifetime $600,000 exclusion will be used.

When the insurance is given to a trust, this $10,000 annual exclusion may not be available (and the entire gift may be taxable), depending on whether the transfer of the insurance policy (or later cash contributions to pay premiums) to the trust will qualify as a gift of a present interest. In general, for the transfer to qualify, a provision in the trust must give the beneficiary a right to withdraw up to the $10,000 value of the insurance policy in the year the gift to the trust is made. The use of this arrangement, called a Crummey power, is discussed in Chapter 11, and illustrated in the For Your Notebook section on page 260.

HOW TO GET INSURANCE POLICIES TO THE DESIRED OWNER—TRANSFER OF INCIDENTS OF OWNERSHIP

In light of the foregoing, you may be convinced to transfer insurance policies owned in your name to another owner—perhaps a trust. To successfully accomplish this objective, the policy, and all incidents of ownership in the policy, must be given away. That is, estate tax won't be due on insurance proceeds that are paid to a beneficiary other than your estate, if you (the insured) had no incidents of ownership in the insurance policy at the time of your death. But note that only if you are able to transfer all incidents of ownership more than three years prior to your death, can the estate tax be avoided.

An "incident of ownership" means the right to borrow the cash value, change the name of the beneficiary, assign the policy to another person, borrow against the policy, and so forth. Determining whether you have effectively transferred all incidents of ownership in a policy becomes quite difficult, especially if you wind up as a trustee of the trust owning the policy. Similar complications can arise if you are a partner or shareholder in a partnership or corporation that owns insurance policies on your life. This incidents-of-ownership test is vitally important and, unfortunately, broad and complex.

For example, if you transferred an insurance policy to your spouse five years before death, but you retained the right to borrow against the policy in the event of a business emergency, this single right could result in the inclusion of the entire policy proceeds in your estate. *All* incidents of ownership must be surrendered more than three years prior to death. If you make a commitment to make the premium payments in the policy application and then die in less than three years, the IRS may argue that the proceeds should be included in your estate. The courts, however, have held that the mere payment of premiums should not result in the inclusion of the policy proceeds in your estate.

To eliminate all incidents of ownership, and remove the proceeds of an insurance policy from your estate, you must assign the policy a new owner and surrender every power over the policy and all of the benefits the policy can provide. You must irrevocably give up all these rights. When you transfer insurance to a trust, you should not have a reversionary interest equal to more than 5 percent of the value of the policy (there cannot be more than a 5 percent possibility that the insurance policy or the proceeds of the policy may return to you).

In all, the best option is for policies to be owned by someone other than the insured, such as an insurance trust, from inception, and for the insured to have no interests in or control over the trust.

USING AN IRREVOCABLE LIFE INSURANCE TRUST

An irrevocable life insurance trust is a common estate planning technique, and it can be one of the most powerful.

Advantages

If properly established, an irrevocable life insurance trust can have the following benefits:

- It can enable both your estate and your spouse's estate to avoid tax on insurance proceeds—potentially a huge savings.

- It may provide a measure of protection from creditors and from divorce implications, depending on state law.
- Liquidity for estate needs can be provided if the trustee is authorized to purchase assets from your estate.
- For those concerned about publicity, the insurance proceeds included in the trust are not included in your probate estate. So, unless there is a legal challenge to the trust, the insurance proceeds, other assets, and the terms of their disposition will not be made available for public knowledge.
- The insurance proceeds can not only avoid taxation in your estate, but they can also avoid taxation in the estate of your spouse, even though the surviving spouse benefits from the insurance monies held in trust.
- The surviving spouse can receive some or all of the annual income from the insurance trust, distributions of the principal in the trust, and even a right to demand up to $5,000 or 5 percent of the trust principal in any year. This right, however, must be noncumulative—use it or lose it.
- Another important benefit of using a trust is to provide children, and perhaps your surviving spouse, more formal or professional management of what is likely to be a substantial sum of money. Your surviving spouse, however, cannot hold a general power of appointment over the insurance proceeds if they are to be excluded from his or her estate.

Drawbacks

There are some drawbacks to the use of an irrevocable life insurance trust, but for most taxpayers they are not significant in comparison with the potential benefits.

- When a trust is set up to hold life insurance policies, it will generally be irrevocable in order to accomplish the desired tax savings objective. This means that once it is established, it cannot be changed or revoked. There is a way around this, however, by providing substantial flexibility to the trustee to allocate income and principal of the trust according to the beneficiaries' need. (See below under "Provisions to Include.")
- There will be legal fees required to set up the trust and annual tax return filings that will require preparation fees and tax payments.

Provisions to Include in Your Insurance Trust

- The trust must be irrevocable. This means you cannot reserve any rights to receive the assets transferred to the trust, or to change the provisions of the trust. If the trust terms meet this requirement, no additional steps are necessary to realize the tax benefits of removing life insurance proceeds from your estate. However, it has become customary to add a clause to the trust stating that you specifically intend that the trust is irrevocable.

- The trust should permit the trustee to receive additional contributions of property, proceeds from additional life insurance policies on your life, and other assets from your will.

- A Crummey demand power, as described above and in Chapter 11, should be included.

- If you die within three years of transferring the insurance to your trust, the insurance proceeds will be included in your estate. There is a backup approach that can salvage an estate tax benefit. If you are married, transfers to your spouse can qualify for the unlimited marital tax deduction. Thus, your life insurance trust can provide that if the insurance is to be included in your estate as a result of your dying within three years of making the transfer, the proceeds will be transferred into a trust that qualifies for the marital deduction. This will typically be a qualified terminal interest property trust, more commonly called a Q-TIP. For the trust to qualify, a number of requirements will have to be met, the most important being that your spouse will be entitled to all of the income from the trust, at least annually, for her life.

- The life insurance trust should also provide the trustee with the authority to purchase assets from your estate. For example, if your estate includes expensive equipment or valuable property, the trust could use insurance proceeds to purchase these nonliquid assets, thus providing your estate with the cash necessary to meet expenses and estate taxes. When the trustee is granted this right, it is generally advisable to have the trust document give the trustee broad powers for the management, lease, improvement, and so forth, of the property.

- Consideration should be given to the possible consequences of divorce, remarriage, and other personal events, so that the trust can proﬁde the flexibility to address the disposition of assets under different scenarios. For example, the trustee can be directed to sprinkle trust income and assets among a group of beneficiaries, typically your spouse and children, based on their needs. This flexibility can ensure that a child with special needs or one who pursues lengthier academic studies than your other children, will be provided for.

- The trustee should be authorized, but not required, to purchase insurance and take any steps necessary to maintain the desired insurance in force. This should include the right to use income or principal to pay for premiums and the right to purchase additional policies. However, the trustee should not be required to pay any debt or expense of your estate.

Other Considerations

There are a number of ancillary considerations when using a life insurance trust:

- It is preferable that you not be a trustee. This is true even though you can serve as a trustee in certain very limited circumstances, when your powers over the trust are solely as a fiduciary and cannot be exercised for your benefit, and when your becoming a trustee was not part of a prearranged plan. When a second-to-die policy is used, your spouse also should not be a trustee. A statement should be added to the trust document prohibiting either you or your spouse from being a trustee.
- The grantor of the trust (whoever sets it up) should not be given the right to change the trustee.
- It is preferable that the trust, and not the insured, pay the premiums to the insurance company. Further, if money is transferred each year to the insurance trust to pay for the insurance premiums, the transfers should not be exactly equal to the insurance premiums.
- When setting up an insurance trust with existing policies, care should be taken in deciding which policies will be given to the trust. Since you will lose all rights to borrow against the policy, it is best to give policies with little or no cash value. This will also minimize any possible gift tax implications.
- For income tax purposes, the life insurance trust could be characterized as a grantor trust, which means that the grantor will be taxable on any income earned by the trust. This income should not be significant, because most monies that a life insurance trust earns will be applied toward the purchase of insurance.

CONCLUSION

Substantial tax savings can be achieved by properly planning the ownership of your life insurance policies. However, care must be taken to ensure that the gift ends all incidents of ownership so that the insurance will be removed from your estate. If a trust is used, attention must be given to the trust terms to ensure that your personal objectives will be met.

For Your Notebook:

SAMPLE IRREVOCABLE
LIFE INSURANCE TRUST
(WITH COMMENTS)

**FOR DISCUSSION WITH YOUR LAWYER
ONLY—DO NOT USE AS A TRUST**

THIS TRUST dated as of MONTH DAY, 1991, between, GRANTOR'S NAME, who resides at GRANTOR'S ADDRESS (the "Grantor"), and TRUSTEE'S NAME, who resides at TRUSTEE'S ADDRESS (the "Trustee").

NOTE: You should not be the trustee of a trust holding insurance on your life. When second-to-die insurance is used on the life of you and your spouse, neither of you should be trustees.

WITNESSETH:

WHEREAS, the Grantor desires to create a trust, the terms of which are hereinafter set forth, and the Trustee has consented to accept and perform said trust in accordance with such terms;

NOW, THEREFORE, in consideration of the premises and mutual covenants herein:

I. TRANSFER OF PROPERTY TO TRUST

In consideration of the premises and covenants set forth below, the Grantor assigns and transfers to the Trustee, and the Trustee, by the execution of this Trust, acknowledges receipt from the Grantor of, the property described in Schedule "A." This property, together with any other property acceptable to the Trustee that may, after the date of this Trust, be transferred to the Trustee by the Grantor, the legal representatives of the Grantor's estate pursuant to the provisions of the Grantor's last will and testament, or any other person, as well as the proceeds from such property, and the securities or other assets in which such proceeds may be invested and reinvested, shall be the "Trust Estate."

II. TRUSTEE SHALL HOLD TRUST ESTATE

A. The Trustee shall hold the Trust Estate for the following purposes and subject to the terms and conditions of this Trust.

B. During the life of the Grantor:

1. The Trustee shall hold the Trust Estate, in trust, to pay or apply to or for the benefit of any one or more of the following persons: Grantor's spouse, NAME OF SPOUSE ("the Spouse"), and Grantor's children, to include NAMES OF CHILDREN, and any children born or legally adopted after the execution of this Trust ("Children"), as shall be living during Grantor's life. The net income of the Trust shall be applied in amounts, whether equal or unequal, as the Trustee, in the exercise of his or her absolute discretion, may consider desirable for the comfort and welfare of any one of the Spouse and Children.

NOTE: You can name any beneficiaries you wish but use language that will be flexible enough to address future changes (additional children), because you will not be able to change the trust at a later date.

---

    2. The Trustee may accumulate any of the net income not paid or applied for the benefit of the Spouse and Children, and add it to the principal of this Trust at least annually and thereafter to hold, administer, and dispose of it as a part of the Trust Estate.

    C. Upon the death of the Grantor:

    1. The Trustee shall collect and add to the Trust Estate the following: (i) amounts payable under insurance policies on the life of the Grantor held in this Trust; (ii) amounts payable under insurance on the life of the Grantor in which the Trustee has been designated beneficiary; (iii) amounts payable under the Grantor's employee benefit plans in which the Trustee has been designated as beneficiary; (iv) property payable to the Trustee by the legal representatives of the Grantor's estate pursuant to the provisions of the Grantor's last will; and (v) property payable by any other person, whether pursuant to the provisions of such person's last will or otherwise. The Trustee shall then deal with and dispose of these additions as part of the Trust Estate as provided in this Trust.

    2. The Trustee shall hold the Trust Estate, in trust, for the following purposes: (i) to pay to, or apply for the benefit of, any one or more of the Beneficiaries then living the net income, in equal or unequal portions, that the Trustee in the exercise of his or her absolute discretion considers desirable for their comfort and welfare; or (ii) to accumulate any net income that is not paid or applied and add it to the principal of the Trust Estate, at least annually, and thereafter to hold, administer, and dispose of it as a part of the Trust Estate.

    3. Upon the last to occur of (i) the death of both the Grantor and the Grantor's Spouse, and (ii) the Grantor's youngest child reaching Twenty-One (21) years of age (or the death of all of the Grantor's Children), the Trustee shall divide the Trust Estate into a number of parts equal to the number of Children and the surviving issue, per stirpes, of any deceased child of the Grantor ("Beneficiary").

NOTE: Although the above paragraph suggests an equal distribution, this is not always appropriate. If one child has special needs due to a greater academic pursuit than his or her siblings, or to a disability, or for any other reason, this should be considered in setting up the allocation of the trust following the death of both the grantor and spouse.

---

    a. The Trustee shall hold each share set aside for any Beneficiary as a separate trust, in trust, to pay to, or apply for the benefit of, the Beneficiary the net income of that trust, in annual or more frequent installments. When the Beneficiary reaches Twenty-Five (25) years, the Trustee shall transfer to the Beneficiary One-Third (1/3) of the trust estate of that trust. When the Beneficiary reaches Thirty (30) years, the Trustee shall transfer to the Beneficiary One-Half (1/2) of the trust estate of that trust. When the Beneficiary reaches Thirty-Five (35) years, the Trustee shall transfer to the Beneficiary the balance of the trust estate of that trust.

    b. If any trust under the preceding section shall terminate as a result of the death of the Beneficiary of such trust prior to reaching Thirty-Five (35) years, the Trustee shall transfer the trust estate of such trust, in equal parts per stirpes, to that Beneficiary's then living issue. If there are no living issue, then in equal parts per stirpes to the Grantor's then living issue. If any of Grantor's living issue is a beneficiary of a trust under the preceding section, then the amount such person is entitled to shall be added to the trust estate of that trust and shall be dealt with accordingly. If there are no living issue of the Grantor, then the Trustee shall divide the trust estate of that trust into the same number of equal parts as there are points in the following provisions, and transfer that trust estate to the following:

(1) One (1) part to ALTERNATE ONE, or his or her issue, per stirpes if he or she is deceased.

(2) Two (2) parts to ALTERNATE TWO, or his or her issue, per stirpes if he or she is deceased.

(3) Four (4) parts to ALTERNATE THREE, or his or her issue, per stirpes if he or she is deceased.

III. ALTERNATE DISPOSITION FOR INSURANCE PROCEEDS INCLUDED IN GRANTOR'S ESTATE

A. Notwithstanding anything herein to the contrary, if the amounts payable under insurance policies on the life of the Grantor held in this Trust or the amounts payable under insurance on the life of the Grantor for which the Trustee has been designated Beneficiary (collectively, the "Proceeds") are includable in the Grantor's gross estate for purposes of the federal estate tax, and the Grantor's Spouse is then living, then the Trustee shall hold such Proceeds, in trust, and shall manage, invest, and reinvest the same, to collect the income thereof, and to pay over the net income to the Grantor's Spouse, or to apply the same for the benefit of such Spouse, in convenient installments but at least annually, and so much of the principal as may be necessary or appropriate for the support, maintenance, and medical care of such Spouse, during such Spouse's life.

B. Upon the death of the Grantor's Spouse, the principal of the trust, as it shall then be constituted, shall be transferred to the Grantor's living descendants as provided in Section II.C.3., above.

C. When the Proceeds are includable in the Grantor's estate, and when the Grantor's Spouse survives the Grantor, this section is intended to qualify the Proceeds as a qualified terminable interest property ("Q-TIP") trust under Internal Revenue Code Section 2056(b)(7), and this section should be interpreted in such manner.

NOTE: This provides a backstop (if you are married) in case your efforts to remove the insurance proceeds from your estate fail. If the insurance becomes taxable, perhaps because you didn't live three years after the transfer, or because you inadvertently failed to rid yourself of all incidence of ownership, this section qualifies that insurance for the unlimited marital deduction. Care should be exercised, because this approach, while it can save substantial taxes, may deprive your children (or other beneficiaries) of an inheritance.

IV. STANDARD FOR PAYMENT OF PRINCIPAL

The Trustee of any trust created under this Trust is authorized, at any time, with respect to any person then eligible to receive the net income from such trust, to pay to, or apply for the benefit of, such person as much, or all, of the principal of such trust as the Trustee, in the exercise of his or her absolute discretion, may consider desirable for such person's comfort and welfare, without consideration to such person's income, assets, or other resources, the duty of anyone to support such person, or any other funds that may be available.

V. ADMINISTRATION OF TRUST; TERMINATION OF TRUST

For the Trustee's convenience in administering the trusts created under this Trust, the Trustee, in the exercise of his or her absolute discretion, may administer as a unified account the assets of any trust created under this Trust and any property held under the provisions concerning Donee Property held for a Person Under a Disability. However, the Trustee shall keep a separate record of all transactions. Notwithstanding anything to the contrary contained in this Trust, if the Trustee shall determine that the aggregate value or the character of the assets of any trust created under this Trust, or the aggregate value or the character of the assets being held for a donee under a disability, makes it inadvisable, inconvenient, or uneconomical to continue the administration of such trust or assets, then the Trustee, in the exercise of his or her absolute discretion, may transfer the Trust Estate or property, equally or unequally, to or among one or more persons then eligible to receive the net income thereof.

VI.   DISTRIBUTIONS TO A PERSON UNDER A DISABILITY

A. Whenever pursuant to the provisions of this Trust, any property is to be distributed to a Person Under a Disability ("Donee Property"), title to that property shall vest in that Person Under a Disability, but the payment or transfer of the property may be deferred until the disability ceases. If the transfer of property is deferred under this section, that Donee Property shall be held by the Trustee, who shall apply the principal and income thereof, or so much of such principal and income as the Trustee, in the exercise of his or her absolute discretion, may determine, for the comfort and welfare of the Person Under a Disability. This determination by the Trustee shall be made without regard to the income or other resources of the Person Under a Disability, or of his or her parents or spouse.

B. When the disability ceases, the Trustee shall transfer to the person formerly under a disability the remaining Donee Property, and any accumulations of income or principal ("Remaining Property"). If the Person Under a Disability should die, the Trustee shall deliver the Remaining Property to the legal representatives of the estate of that person. Notwithstanding the foregoing provisions, the Trustee may at any time, in the exercise of his or her absolute discretion, deliver all or a portion of the Donee Property that shall then remain, together with any accumulations of income, to a parent, guardian, custodian under the Uniform Gifts (Transfers) to Minors Act of the State, committee, conservator of the property, or an individual with whom such Person Under a Disability resides, and the receipt by such person or entity shall constitute a full discharge of the Trustee for such payment or delivery. The powers granted to the Trustee shall be applicable to any Donee Property dealt with in this section and shall continue until the actual distribution of the Donee Property.

VII.   TRUSTEE COMPENSATION

Each Trustee acting hereunder, except for NAME OF TRUSTEE NOT ENTITLED TO COMPENSATION, shall be entitled to withdraw from the Trust Estate, without obtaining court or other approval, the compensation that is allowed to a trustee under the laws of the State that govern compensation to the trustee of a testamentary trust, computed in the manner and at the rates in effect at the time the compensation is payable.

NOTE: If a friend or close family member is named the Trustee, he or she may agree to waive any fees. This section should then state that it applies to all trustees other than those specifically named as serving without fees.

VIII.   TRUSTEE'S DETERMINATIONS FINAL

The exercise by the Trustee of the discretionary powers herein granted with respect to the payment, distribution, or application of principal or income of any trust created under thisTrust is final and conclusive upon all persons and shall not be subject to any review whatsoever. Grantor intends that the Trustee shall have the greatest latitude in exercising such discretionary powers, and that the persons entitled to receive the principal of any trust created under this Trust shall upon the termination of such trust be entitled only to such principal as may remain after the last exercise of the Trustee's continuing discretionary powers. However, under no circumstances shall any person who may be acting as a Trustee participate in the exercise of any power granted under this Trust with respect to the discretionary payment, distribution, or application to him or her of principal or income of any trust.

IX.   ANNUAL DEMAND POWER

A. Immediately following any Addition to the Trust, the Beneficiaries (individually, the "Holder") shall have the right to withdraw up to the amount of such Addition. Notwithstanding anything herein to the contrary, the total withdrawals by any Beneficiary under this provision, for any calendar year, shall not exceed the lesser of (i) the maximum annual gift tax exclusion allowable under Internal Revenue Code Section 2503(b), as amended; or (ii) the proportion of the Addition during any year divided by the number of Beneficiaries during such year who may make a demand that would qualify a portion of such Addition as a gift of a present interest. This demand power shall take precedence over any other power or discretion granted to the Trustee. This demand power shall not be interpreted to limit the income distributions that may be made by the Trustee to the Beneficiaries.

B. With respect to this demand power, the following rules shall apply:

1. The Holder can exercise this demand power by a written request delivered to the Trustee.

2. If the Holder is unable to exercise this demand power because of a legal disability, including minority, his or her parent, guardian, or personal representative (including but not limited to his or her committee or conservator) may make the demand on the Holder's behalf. However, in no event can the Grantor make the demand for the Holder, regardless of the Grantor's relationship to the Holder.

3. The Trustee must reasonably notify the person who would exercise the Holder's demand power of such right not later than November 30 of each year and of the existence of any contributions made to the Trust that are subject to this demand power.

4. The Holder's demand power is noncumulative and lapses on the earlier of (i) the last day of the calendar year in which the Addition was made; or (ii) Thirty (30) calendar days following the Trustee's sending the Holder notice of such contribution. No payment may be made in a subsequent year on account of the Holder's failure to demand a distribution in a prior year.

5. The Trustee may satisfy the Holder's demand for a distribution by distributing cash, other assets, or fractional interests in other assets, as the Trustee in his or her sole discretion, deems appropriate.

C. Notwithstanding the foregoing, if upon the expiration of any right of withdrawal or any portion thereof the Holder of such right would be deemed to have made a gift for federal gift tax purposes, such right shall continue in existence to the extent of the amount that would have been a taxable gift until and to the extent that its expiration shall not result in a taxable gift by the holder thereof.

D. The Trustee shall give reasonable written notice to each Holder entitled to exercise the right of withdrawal of any additions to or for the benefit of the Trust Estate (other than accumulated income, if any) and the right to exercise the right of withdrawal.

NOTE: This is the Crummey power provision to enable you to qualify for the annual $10,000 gift tax exclusion. This is discussed in detail in Chapter 11.

X.   ACCOUNTING

A. No Trustee acting under this Trust is under a duty to render a judicial accounting upon resignation or otherwise. Notwithstanding anything herein contained to the contrary, the Trustee, in the exercise of his or her absolute discretion, may submit any account to a court for approval and settlement.

B. The Trustee may render an accounting upon the termination of any trust created under this Trust, and at any other times that the Trustee, in the exercise of his or her absolute discretion, may deem necessary or advisable. The written approval of all persons who are not subject to a legal disability, and who are entitled to receive the net income of any trust created under thisTrust, and all persons not subject to a legal disability then presumptively entitled to the principal of any trust, as to all matters and transactions shown in the account, shall be final, binding, and conclusive upon all such persons who may then be, or thereafter become, entitled to any income or principal of any trust. The written approval or assent of the persons mentioned in this section shall have the same force and effect in discharging the Trustee as a decree by a court of competent jurisdiction. However, any such written approval shall not enlarge or shift the beneficial interest of any beneficiary of any trust created under this Trust.

C. If the Trustee is accounting to another fiduciary, then the written approval of the other fiduciary shall be final, binding, and conclusive upon all persons beneficially interested in the estate or trust estate represented by such other fiduciary.

XI. POWERS OF THE TRUSTEE

The Trustee shall have in addition to, and not in limitation of, the powers granted elsewhere in this Trust, or the powers allowed by law, the following powers:

A. To invest and reinvest any assets comprising the Trust Estate in any securities or other property, whether real or personal, of any class, kind, or nature (including an undivided interest in any one or more common trust funds), as the Trustee may deem advisable without regard to any restrictions of law on a trustee's investments.

B. To exercise voting rights in person or by proxy, rights of conversion or of exchange, or rights to purchase or subscribe for stocks, bonds, or other securities or obligations that may be offered to the holders of any asset, and to accept and retain any property that may be acquired by the exercise of any such right with respect to any stocks, bonds, or other securities or obligation included in the Trust Estate, in the Trustee's absolute discretion.

C. To employ or retain accountants, custodians, agents, legal counsel, investment advisers, and other experts as the Trustee shall deem advisable. To rely on the information and advice furnished by such persons. To fix the compensation of such persons, and in the case of legal counsel, who also may be acting as a Trustee hereunder, to take payments on account of legal fees in advance of the settlement of the Trustee's account without applying to or procuring the authority of any court.

D. To the extent permitted by the laws of the State, to hold securities in the name of a nominee without indicating the trust character of such holdings, and to hold unregistered securities, or securities in a form that will pass by delivery.

E. To retain and continue for any period deemed appropriate by the Trustee, in exercise of his or her absolute discretion, any asset, whether real or personal, tangible or intangible, included in the Trust Estate.

F. To sell at public or private sale and to exchange or otherwise dispose of any stocks, bonds, securities, personal property, or other assets constituting the Trust Estate at the time, price, and terms as the Trustee deems advisable.

G. To grant options for the sale or exchange of any asset comprising the Trust Estate at times, prices, and terms that the Trustee deems advisable, without applying to or procuring the authority of any court.

H. To sell, exchange, partition, convey, and mortgage, and to modify, extend, renew, or replace any mortgage that may be a lien on all, or any part, of any interest in real property included in the Trust Estate.

I. To lease any real or personal property, whether or not for a term beyond the period of time fixed by statute for leases by a trustee, and whether or not extending beyond the termination of any Trust, and upon such terms as the Trustee deems advisable, without obtaining the approval of any court.

J. To foreclose mortgages and bid in property under foreclosure and to take title by deed in lieu of foreclosure or otherwise.

K. To extend the time of payment of any bond, note, or other obligation or mortgage included in the Trust Estate, or of any installment of principal thereof, or of any interest due thereon. To hold such instrument after maturity, as a past due bond, note, or other obligation or mortgage, either with our without renewal or extension. To consent to the modification, alteration, and amendment of any terms or conditions of such instrument, including those regarding the rate of interest, and to waive any defaults in the performance of the terms and conditions of such instrument.

L. To compromise, adjust, settle, or submit to arbitration upon terms the Trustee deems advisable, in his or her absolute discretion, any claim in favor of or against the Trust Estate. To release, with or without consideration, any claim in favor of the Trust Estate.

M. To participate in any refunding; readjustment of stocks, bonds, or other securities or obligations; enforcement of obligations or securities by foreclosure or otherwise; corporate consolidation by merger or otherwise; or reorganization that shall affect any stock, bond, or other security or obligation included in the Trust Estate. To participate in any plan or proceeding for protection of the interests of the holders of such instruments. To deposit any property under any plan or proceeding with any protective or reorganization committee and to delegate to such a committee the discretionary power with respect thereto. To pay a proportionate part of the expenses of a committee. To pay any assessments levied under such a plan, and to accept and retain any property that may be received pursuant to any such plan.

N. To borrow money for the purpose of raising funds to pay taxes or for any other purpose deemed by the Trustee, in his or her absolute discretion, to be beneficial to the Trust Estate, and upon such terms as the Trustee may determine. To pledge as security for the repayment of any loan any assets included in the Trust Estate.

O. To make any distribution under any Trust, in cash or in property, or in any combination of cash and property. To make non-pro rata distributions of cash and property then included in the Trust Estate.

P. To exercise for the benefit of the Trust Estate, and for any property included in the Trust Estate, all rights, powers, and privileges of every nature that might or could be exercised by any person owning similar property absolutely and in his or her own right in connection with the exercise of any or all of such rights, powers, and privileges, even when such right, power, or privilege may not have been specifically mentioned in this Trust. To negotiate, draft, enter into, renegotiate, or otherwise modify any contracts or other written instruments that the Trustee deems advisable, and to include in them the covenants, terms, and conditions as the Trustee deems proper, in the exercise of his or her absolute discretion.

NOTE: See the comments on this section in the trust in the "For Your Notebook" section of Chapter 11.

XII. TRUSTEE'S EXERCISE OF AUTHORITY

Any authority, discretion, or power granted to or conferred upon the Trustee by this Trust may be (i) exercised by such of them as shall be, or the one of them who shall be, acting hereunder from time to time, and (ii) by such one of them who shall be so designated by an instrument in writing delivered to such one Trustee by the Trustee.

XIII. THIRD-PARTY RELIANCE

No bank or trust company, corporation, partnership, association, firm, or other person dealing with the Trustee, or keeping any assets, whether funds, securities or other property of the Trust Estate, shall be required to investigate the authority of the Trustee for entering into any transaction involving assets of the Trust Estate. Nor shall such persons be required to see to the application of the proceeds of any transaction with the Trustee, or to inquire into the appropriateness, validity, expediency, or propriety thereof, or be under any obligation or liability whatsoever, except to the Trustee; and any such person, bank or trust company, corporation, partnership, association, or firm shall be fully protected in making disposition of any assets of the Trust Estate in accordance with the directions of the Trustee.

XIV. TRUSTEE'S LIABILITY

A. The Trustee shall not be individually liable for any loss to or depreciation in the value of the Trust Estate occurring by reason of (i) the exercise or nonexercise of the powers granted to the Trustee under this Trust; or (ii) a mistake in, or error of, judgment in the purchase or sale of any investment or the retention of any investment, as long as the Trustee shall have been acting in good faith.

B. Every act done, power exercised, or obligation assumed by the Trustee, pursuant to the provisions of this Trust, shall be held to be done, exercised, or assumed, as the case may be, by the Trustee acting in the Trustee's fiduciary capacity and not otherwise, and every person, firm, or corporation contracting or otherwise dealing with the Trustee shall look only to the funds and property of the Trust Estate for payment under such contract or payment of any money that may become due or payable under any obligation arising under this Trust, in whole or in part, and the Trustee shall not be individually liable therefor even though the Trustee did not exempt itself from individual liability when entering into any contract, obligation, or transaction in connection with or growing out of the Trust Estate.

XV. TRUSTEE'S CONSULTATION WITH COUNSEL

The Trustee may consult with legal counsel (who may be counsel to the Grantor) concerning any question that may arise with reference to the Trustee's duties or obligations under this Trust, and the opinion of such counsel shall be considered full and complete authorization and protection in respect of any action taken or suffered by the Trustee in good faith and in accordance with the opinion of such counsel.

XVI. RESIGNATION OF TRUSTEE

A. Any Trustee hereunder may resign at any time without obtaining prior judicial approval. Such resignation shall be deemed complete upon the delivery of an instrument in writing declaring such resignation to the Grantor, or if the Grantor shall then be deceased, to the remaining Trustee hereunder, or shall there be no remaining Trustee, to the successor Trustee hereunder. Such resigning Trustee shall promptly deliver the assets of the Trust Estate to the remaining or successor Trustee hereunder.

B. The resigning Trustee shall, at the request of the remaining or successor Trustee hereunder, promptly deliver such assignments, transfers, and other instruments as may be reasonably required for fully vesting in such remaining or successor Trustee all right, title, and interest in the Trust Estate.

C. Each Trustee acting hereunder shall be entitled to withdraw from the Trust Estate, without obtaining judicial authorization, the compensation that is allowed to a trustee under the laws of the State governing compensation to the trustee of a testamentary trust, computed in the manner and at the rates in effect at the time such compensation shall be payable.

XVII. ADDITIONAL OR SUCCESSOR TRUSTEE

A. The Trustee may appoint an additional or successor Trustee that may be an individual (other than the Grantor), or a bank or trust company. This appointment shall be by an instrument in writing delivered to the Trustee. It shall become effective on the date or condition specified in the instrument. Prior to the specified date or condition, however, the appointment may be withdrawn by an instrument in writing delivered to the Trustee. In the event that there shall be no Trustee acting hereunder for a period of Thirty (30) days, the Grantor appoints as a successor Trustee the individual (other than the Grantor) or the bank or trust company to be designated by an instrument in writing signed by the law firm of NAME OF GRANTOR'S LAWYER, or any successor firm, and delivered to the Grantor and Trustee, or if the Grantor shall then be deceased, to the legal representatives of the estate of the Grantor.

B. The acceptance of trusteeship by any Trustee who is not a party to this Trust shall be evidenced by an instrument in writing delivered to the remaining Trustee hereunder. Shall there be no remaining Trustee, to the Grantor, or if he or she shall then be deceased, to the legal representatives of the estate of the Grantor, or to such person as designated by a court of competent jurisdiction.

NOTE: The Trust should not give the grantor the right to terminate one trustee and appoint a new one, because this control over the trust could result in the insurance proceeds being taxed in the grantor's estate.

XVIII.   NO BOND REQUIRED

No bond or security of any kind shall be required of any Trustee acting hereunder.

XIX.   TRANSACTIONS WITH GRANTOR'S ESTATE

The Trustee is authorized and empowered, at any time and from time to time, (i) to purchase at fair market value from the legal representatives of the Grantor's estate any property constituting a part, or all, of the Grantor's estate, and (ii) to lend for adequate consideration to the legal representatives of the Grantor's estate such part, or all, of the Trust Estate, upon such terms and conditions as the Trustee, in the exercise of his or her absolute discretion deems advisable.

XX.   INSURANCE

A. The Trustee shall accept and hold all policies of insurance upon the life of the Grantor that shall be assigned by the Grantor, or any other person, to the Trustee. The Grantor intends to assign all right, title, and interest, and every incident of ownership, in the policies of insurance listed in Schedule A (the "Policies"). On signing this Trust, the Grantor shall deliver to the Trustee all of the Policies. During the life of the Grantor, the Trustee shall take any action concerning the Policies that the Trustee considers appropriate for the benefit of the Trust Estate, and that are not inconsistent with the terms of this Trust. These actions can include, but are not limited to, (i) the modification, exchange, or surrender of any Policies or other insurance policies; (ii) the receipt and collection, at maturity or otherwise, of amounts payable under an insurance policy, or in settlement of, or upon the surrender of, any insurance policy; (iii) the receipt and collection of dividends or other increments on any insurance policies; and (iv) the distribution of any insurance policies and dividends or other increments.

B. The Trustee shall not be under any obligation to make payments of any premiums, dues, assessments, or other charges that may become due and payable on any insurance policy held under this Trust or for which the Trustee is designated a Beneficiary. The Trustee is not obligated to see that the above payments are made or to notify the insured or any other person that such payments are or will become due. The Trustee shall not have any liability if the above payments are not made, or are not made on a timely basis.

C. Notwithstanding anything in this Trust to the contrary, any form executed by the Grantor to assign any insurance policy to the Trustee or this Trust, or any form designating the Trustee or the Trust as a beneficiary under any insurance policy on the Grantor's life, the Grantor shall not be deemed to have entered into any covenant or agreement with the Trustee requiring that the Trustee maintain the Policies, or any other insurance policies, in full force.

D. The Trustee shall take appropriate action to collect amounts payable under, or in settlement of, any insurance policy, whether at maturity or otherwise, to which the

Trustee is or may become entitled. The Trustee is not responsible for his or her inability to enforce the collection of any proceeds or amounts payable under any insurance policies.

E. The Trustee, may, but is not required to, engage in any litigation to enforce the payment of any insurance policy until the Trustee shall have been indemnified against all expenses and liabilities that the Trustee, in the exercise of his or her absolute discretion, believes could relate to such litigation. The Trustee may utilize any property comprising the Trust Estate to meet expenses reasonably incurred in connection with enforcing the payment of any insurance policies.

F. When the net proceeds of any insurance policies, or other net amounts receivable under this Trust, shall be collected by the Trustee, the Trustee shall deal with and dispose of the same as set forth in this Trust. The terms "net proceeds" or "net amount" mean the proceeds, or the amounts of any policies, after reduction for any loans, advances, interest, or other indebtedness relating to such policies.

G. With respect to any policies of insurance held under this Trust, the Trustee, in the exercise of his or her absolute discretion, may make payment of the premiums thereon out of income or principal of this trust and may exercise any and all options, rights, and privileges in such policies including, without limitation, the right to obtain and receive from the insurance companies issuing such policies advances and loans on such policies, to direct the disposition of dividends or surplus, to convert such policies, or to surrender them and receive the proceeds.

XXI. TRUSTEE'S APPLICATION FOR INSURANCE ON GRANTOR'S LIFE

Should the Trustee, in the exercise of his or her absolute discretion, apply for any insurance policy on the Grantor's life, the Grantor agrees to submit to reasonable medical examinations upon reasonable notice.

XXII. ADDITIONAL ASSETS

The Grantor, or any other person, may assign or transfer to the Trustee securities or other property, whether real or personal, tangible or intangible, reasonably acceptable to the Trustee ("Addition"). All Additions shall be added to the Trust Estate, and the Trustee shall hold and dispose of any Addition as part of the Trust Estate, subject to the terms and provisions of this Trust.

XXIII. FURTHER ASSURANCES

The Grantor agrees to execute any documents reasonably necessary for the Trustee to implement his or her duties under this Trust, including but not limited to completing and executing any forms necessary to the purchase of insurance, when such acts will not result in the inclusion in the Grantor's estate of any such insurance.

XXIV. IRREVOCABLE TRUST

A. The Grantor has been advised with respect to the difference between revocable and irrevocable trusts and hereby declares that this Trust and the Trust Estate created hereby are to be irrevocable. The Grantor has no power to alter, amend, revoke, or terminate any Trust provision or interest, whether under this Trust, or any rule of law. The Grantor shall not have any reversionary interest in this Trust or the Trust Estate.

B. The Trustee shall not have the power to use any of the Trust Estate for the benefit of the Grantor's estate, as such term is defined in Regulation Section 20.2042-1(b). The Trustee, however, may modify or amend this Trust to facilitate the administration of the Trust Estate or to conform this Trust to laws or regulations affecting inter vivos trusts, or the requirements of qualifying as a Qualified Subchapter S Trust, as the same may be amended from time to time. No such modification or amendment shall affect the possession or enjoyment of the Trust Estate.

XXV. SPENDTHRIFT CLAUSE

To the extent permitted by law, the interests of the Spouse and the Children shall not be subject to their liabilities or creditor claims, or to assignment or anticipation.

XXVI. DEFINITIONS

The following terms when used in this Trust are defined as follows:

A. "Child" is an issue in the first degree.

B. "Addition" means any cash or other assets transferred to the Trust to be held as part of the Trust Estate. The amount of any contribution is its federal gift tax value, as determined by the Trustee at the time of the transfer.

C. "Issue" is a descendant in any degree, whether natural or adopted.

D. "Per stirpes" is a disposition of property whereby the issue take a portion thereof in representation of their deceased parent, with division to be made into such number of equal shares at each succeeding degree of relationship from the common ancestor that there shall be one share for each person of such degree living at the time of such division and one share for the issue collectively then living of each person of such degree who is then deceased; such division is to be made although there may not then be any person living within such degree.

NOTE: *Per stirpes* is a method of dividing assets among heirs. It can best be explained with a simple example. Parents have two children, Tom and Jane. Tom dies leaving two children. Jane dies leaving three children. On Parents death, if their $1 million estate is divided *per capita* (equally), each grandchild will receive $200,000 [$1 million/5]. The result is that Tom's family receives a total of $400,000, and Jane's family a total of $600,000. However, if it is divided *per stirpes*, Tom's survivors will share in their share of Tom's portion, and Jane's children will share in their share of her portion. Assume that Tom and Jane would have split the $1 million estate equally, so each would have been entitled to $500,000. Under this per stirpes division, Tom's children each receive $250,000 [$500,000/2], and Jane's children each receive $166,667 [$500,000/3]. Each family group receives the same total.

E. "Trustee" is the trustee named in this Trust or appointed by a court or pursuant to the terms of this Trust and any and all successors, and may be masculine, feminine, or neuter and singular or plural, as the sense requires.

F. "Donee Property" is any net income of any trust created hereunder or all or any part of the Trust Estate distributable to a Person Under a Disability to be held by the donee of a power to manage during disability.

G. A "Person Under a Disability" is either a person who has not attained the age of Twenty-One (21) years or a person who, for such period as the Trustee shall determine, is deemed by the Trustee, in the exercise of his or her absolute discretion, to be physically or mentally incapable of managing his or her affairs, although a judicial declaration may not have been made with respect to such disability.

H. To hold "In trust" is to manage, invest, and reinvest the principal of a trust and to collect the income thereof.

I. "Trust Estate" is the then remaining principal of any trust, as then constituted, and upon the termination of such trust any accrued and undistributed income.

J. "Income" and "principal" are defined as follows. All cash dividends, other than those described hereafter, shall be income. All corporate distributions in shares of stock (whether denominated as dividends, stock splits, or otherwise, and cash proceeds representing fractions thereof) of any class of any corporation (whether the corporation declaring or authorizing such distributions or otherwise) shall be principal. Dividends on investment company shares attributed to capital gains shall be principal whether declared payable at the option of the shareholders in cash or in shares or otherwise. Liquidating dividends, rights to subscribe to stock and the proceeds of the sale thereof, and the proceeds of unproductive or underproductive property shall be principal.

There shall be no apportionment of the proceeds of the sale of any asset of the Trust Estate (whether real or personal, tangible or intangible) between principal and income because such asset may be or may have been wholly or partially unproductive of income during any period of time. Notwithstanding anything in this definition to the contrary, all income attributable to S corporation stock shall be distributed as required for the trust to retain its status as a qualified S corporation trust.

K. "State" means STATE'S NAME.

XXVII. CONSTRUCTION

A. The validity, construction, and effect of the provisions of this Trust shall be governed by the laws of the State. This Trust may be executed in more than one counterpart, each of which is an original, but all taken together shall be deemed one and the same instrument. Headings have been inserted for convenience only and shall not serve to limit or broaden the terms of any provision.

B. Any provision of this Trust to the contrary notwithstanding, this Trust, and any other trusts created under this document, shall be interpreted so as not to violate the rule against perpetuities. Notwithstanding anything herein to the contrary, this Trust shall terminate upon the expiration of Twenty-One (21) years after the death of the Grantee, and if any trust created hereunder has not sooner terminated, the Trustee shall at said time pay over, convey, and deliver the trust fund or funds then in their possession to the persons then entitled to receive the income therefrom in the same shares or portions in which such income is then being paid or payable to them.

XXVIII. BINDING AGREEMENT

This Trust shall extend to and be binding upon the executors, administrators, heirs, successors, and assigns of the Grantor and the Trustee.

IN WITNESS WHEREOF, the undersigned Grantor and Trustee have executed this Trust as of the date first-above written.

_____ (L.S.)
Grantor
_____ (L.S.)
Trustee

[NOTARY FORMS OMITTED]

SCHEDULE A

PROPERTY TRANSFERRED TO TRUST

1. Cash in the amount of $_____.00.
2. Life Insurance policy insuring the life of NAME OF GRANTOR, with the NAME OF INSURANCE COMPANY. Policy Number: _____, issued DATE POLICY ISSUED.

For Your Notebook:

SELECTING A FINANCIAL ADVISER

When evaluating insurance needs for your estate, it should be done in the context of your overall estate, financial and insurance needs. To help you make the proper decision, you must first make the proper decision on selecting the adviser to guide you. The following checklists, adapted and excerpted from a brochure published by The National Association of Personal Financial Advisors, based in Buffalo Grove, Illinois, provides an excellent starting point for selecting the right adviser.

BACKGROUND & EXPERIENCE*

The backgrounds of financial planners can vary as much as the services offered. The planner's education and experience should demonstrate a solid foundation in financial planning and a commitment to keeping current. In addition to the following questions, ask the planner to describe his or her specific financial planning work experience.

1. What is your educational background?
_____College degree
Area of study: _____
_____Graduate degree
Area of study: _____

Financial planning education & designations:
_____Certified Financial Planner (CFP)
_____Chartered Financial Consultant (ChFC)
_____Registry of Financial Planning Practitioners
Other: _____

2. How long have you been offering financial planning services?
_____Less than 2 years
_____2-5 years
_____More than 5 years

3. What continuing education in financial planning do you pursue?

_____1-14 hours of professional education each year
_____15-30 hours of professional education each year
_____At least 30 hours of professional education each year

4. Are you a member of any professional financial planning associations?

_____Institute of Certified Financial Planners (ICFP)
_____National Association of Personal Financial Advisors (NAPFA)
_____International Association for Financial Planning (IAFP)
_____Registry of Financial Planning Practitioners
Other: _____

5. Will you provide me with references from clients?
_____Yes _____No

6. Have your ever been cited by a professional or regulatory governing body for disciplinary reasons?
_____Yes _____No

*This form was created by the National Association of Personal Financial Advisors (NAPFA) to assist consumers in selecting a personal financial planner. It can be used as a checklist during an interview or sent to prospective planners as a part of a preliminary screening. NAPFA recommends that individuals from at least two different firms be interviewed.

COMPENSATION

Financial planning costs include what a consumer pays in fees and commissions. Comparison between planners requires full information about potential <u>total</u> costs. It is important to have this information before entering into any agreement.

1. How is your firm compensated ?

_____Fee Only
_____Commission only
_____Fee and Commissions
_____Fee offset

How is your compensation calculated?

_____Fee only (as calculated below)

    Based on hourly rate of $ _____
    Flat fee or fee range of _____
    Percentage (____%) of _____
    Are fees capped? ____Yes ____No

_____Commission only (from securities, insurance, etc.) that clients buy from a firm with which you are associated.
_____Fee and commission ("Fee based")
_____Fee offset. You charge a flat fee against which commissions are offset. If the commissions exceed the fee, is the balance credited to me?
    ____Yes ____No

[Note: the Securities and Exchange Commission (SEC) requires that this information be disclosed.]

2. If you earn commissions, approximately what percentage of your firm's <u>commission income</u> comes from:

_____% Insurance products
_____% Annuities
_____% Mutual funds
_____% Limited partnerships
_____% Stocks and bonds
_____% Coins, tangibles, collectibles
_____% Other (explain) _____
100%

3. Does any member of your firm act as a general partner, participate in or receive compensation from investments you may recommend to me?
    ____Yes ____No

20 EXECUTIVE AND OTHER ASSETS

There is almost an unlimited number of assets that people can own. The previous chapters reviewed in considerable detail many of the more complicated assets and planning issues. This chapter will cover several of the other common assets, including those an executive is likely to encounter through his or her corporation (stock options, pension plans, and employer-provided insurance), plus annuities, bank and securities accounts, jointly held and community property, and personal effects.

These assets could be of major or minor significance with regard to your estate, but regardless of their size, they should not be overlooked in your estate planning.

AN EXECUTIVE'S ASSETS

While many of the estate issues common to all taxpayers will apply to executives, they are also likely to have assets and issues not noted elsewhere. These are discussed below. In general, however, the planning techniques and rules discussed throughout this book can be applied effectively to accomplish the executive's estate planning goals.

Deferred Compensation

Deferred compensations are often entered into with hopes of realizing income at a later date, when tax rates may be lower. When properly structured, deferred compensation will not be taxable until you actually receive the income. This can occur, for example, when the corporation has merely made an unsecured commitment to pay you. If you die before receiving the deferred compensation, the amount due you on your death will be included in your estate and be subject to the estate tax. You need to plan for this.

Stock Option

Another common asset you may have is an option to acquire stock in your employer. There are different types of option. An incentive stock option (ISO) generally does not trigger any taxable gain when granted or exercised. Among other requirements, you must not sell the stock before the later of one year from exercise of the option or two years from the date the option was granted. In addition, there are these requirements: The ISO must be granted under a plan that states the maximum shares to be issued; the plan must be approved by shareholders; the option must be exercised within 10 years of the grant; and so on. If an option is not exercised at the date of your death, the value of the option will be included in your estate. The option will then be disposed of as provided in your will, or it may be exercised by your executor. Special rules applicable to decedents eliminate some of the holding-period requirements.

Other options are classified as nonqualified stock options. The income taxation of these options will depend on whether they have an ascertainable fair market value, are subject to a substantial risk of forfeiture, and other factors.

Pension Plan

A qualified pension plan can be a substantial asset. When your distributions began under the plan before your death, they will generally continue following death at the same rate. When distributions did not start prior to your death, they may be required to be paid within a statutory period, or if payable to your surviving spouse, deferred until he or she reaches age 70 1/2. The retirement benefits to be received by your estate, or your beneficiary, are included in your gross estate. One planning technique is to have your will include your pension amounts in a credit shelter or bypass trust (see Chapters 6 and 9).

Employer-Provided Insurance

Insurance provided by your employer in the form of group term or split-dollar coverage is also common. Employers can provide up to $50,000 of group term life insurance as a nontaxable fringe benefit. This insurance often can be assigned to a life insurance trust or to another owner (see Chapter 19). However, the master policy must permit the assignment. You can give away a group term policy, subject to the general gift tax rules, but it is unlikely that a term policy will have any significant value that could trigger a gift tax. If you die within three years of transferring the policy, or retain any incidents of ownership on your death, the policy will be included in your estate.

Under a split-dollar insurance arrangement, you and your employer split the cost of insurance coverage. Your employer pays the portion of each year's annual insurance premium equal to the increase in the cash surrender value. You pay the rest. On your death, your employer receives the cash surrender value, and your named beneficiary receives any remaining policy proceeds. If you had any incidents of ownership, the policy will be included in your estate. You can transfer the insurance policy to remove it from your estate, subject to the general rules concerning the transfer of all of the incidents of ownership of an insurance policy (see Chapter 19). However, when you are a major shareholder in the corporation that is purchasing the policy as employer, the IRS is more likely to question the effectiveness of your assignment.

ANNUITIES

An annuity is a type of insurance product in which you contract with the insurance company to receive fixed monthly payments for a specified period (a number of years or for life) for yourself or another designated beneficiary. An annuity arrangement is useful for providing regular funds over time when you don't trust the beneficiary (perhaps yourself) to hold onto a large lump sum.

For example, if you're concerned that either you or your spouse don't have the discipline to save and invest, an annuity is a controlled alternative.

Before considering an annuity arrangement, however, compare the cost and benefit implications with the various trust arrangements available (see Chapter 4). The commission costs inherent in an annuity arrangement may exceed the costs of establishing and running a trust. Further, a trust has complete flexibility to respond to changes in circumstances, while an annuity contract is fixed once it is purchased.

Types of Annuities and Tax Implications

There are a host of types available. A variable annuity can pay a return based on the investment return to the insurance company. The annuity could be deferred so that it will only start at some future date. An annuity may pay for life, or for a fixed number of years. A hybrid approach may also be available having payments for life but not for less than some minimum number of years.

Some charitable organizations have arrangements in which you transfer cash or property to the charity and receive an annuity for part of the value and a charitable contribution for the balance. If the property transferred has appreciated, you will have to recognize the gain. This is far less favorable than the result under the charitable lead or remainder trust (see Chapter 14).

If you set up an annuity arrangement for both you and another beneficiary, there will be a gift to that person based on the value of the annuity he or she receives. The annual $10,000 gift tax exclusion is not available. However, if the second beneficiary is your spouse, the unlimited marital deduction will be available. For income taxes, a portion of each annuity payment you receive will be taxed as interest income, and a portion will be treated as a return of your investment.

When amounts are receivable by any beneficiary under the annuity arrangement as a result of your death, the value of the annuity to be included in your estate is based on the value of the payments to be made following your death. If your estate receives a refund under the annuity arrangement, this amount also will be taxable in your estate.

Private Annuity

Instead of structuring an annuity through an insurance company, you can set one up privately to use as an estate planning tool.

EXAMPLE: Mother holds an appreciated building. Son, who is not in the business of selling annuities, purchases the building from Mother, paying her with an annuity that, based on Mother's life expectancy and other required assumptions, has a value equal to the value of the building. Because the values are equal, Mother should not incur a gift tax.

Alternatively, Mother could accept an annuity worth less than the value of the property transferred so that part of the transaction would be treated as a gift. In that case, Mother would have to recognize gain on the appreciation of her building; however, this gain should be recognized over the period the annuity payments are to be received. Thus, a portion of each payment received by Mother would be a return of her investment in the building, interest, and gain on the sale of the building.

If properly structured, this technique can provide several benefits: (1) The mother's estate will not have any asset to be taxed on her death. (2) If the value of the annuity equals the value of the property transferred, no gift tax will be due. (3) The gain on the sale will be deferred. (4) The mother will be entitled to a fixed income for her life (assuming that the daughter is prudent and responsible).

There are some obvious drawbacks: (1) The transaction is complicated, and some costs will be incurred to set it up. (2) If the daughter is not reliable, the mother may have lost her primary, or even only, asset with little recourse. (3) If the mother outlives the actuarial life assumed by the IRS tables, the daughter may be required to pay much more than the building is actually worth. (4) Cash flow requirements to meet the payments.

The private annuity technique can be useful as a planning tool for closely held business and real estate assets (see Chapters 15 and 16). Private annuity arrangements are subject to a host of tax complications, which must be carefully reviewed with your tax adviser.

BANK, SECURITY, AND OTHER ACCOUNTS

Bank and security accounts, and safe-deposit boxes, are common assets, yet their simplicity can become a trap—careless planning can result in having these assets included in both your probate and tax estates. For example, a bank account is an asset that almost everyone owns. However, the title to your account—the name in which the account is placed—affects when a gift may occur for gift tax purposes, who may draw funds from the account, and in whose estate the funds will be taxed.

NOTE: The implications of the title on any bank account will be controlled both by the terms of the account agreement with the bank or other institution where the account is kept and by state law.

The following discussion highlights some of the implications of title (or ownership) on these everyday assets.

One Name

If yours is the only name on the account, the funds are yours, and on your death, they will be included in both your probate and taxable estate. No one else will be able to draw from the account until the estate is probated. Under a one-name arrangement, it is advisable that each family member has an account in his or her own name. In the event of a death, there will be another account immediately available for use.

Two Names, as Joint Tenants with Rights of Survivorship (JTWROS)

When you and another person, such as your spouse, own an account as joint tenants with rights of survivorship, on the death of the first of you, the funds will belong solely to the second joint tenant. The funds will not be part of the probate estate of the first to die, and the survivor can withdraw any of the funds in the account. This may not be an ideal method of transferring funds to a designated person after your death. A smarter way is to list a specific pecuniary bequest (a dollar amount) to the desired person in your will. If the amount is large, however, you should limit it to a specified percentage of your estate. This way, if your estate declines in value this pecuniary bequest won't become unreasonably large.

If the terms of the account, or local law, make the other account holder the immediate vested owner of one-half of the deposited amount, there will be a completed gift immediately to the extent of one-half (your half) of the balance in the account. If that money is added to all other gifts you've made to that person during the year and the total exceeds $10,000, the gift will be taxable (or will deplete your unified credit) (see Chapter 7). Opening a joint bank account may not trigger a taxable transfer for purposes of the gift tax if the mere opening of the account won't determine whether the recipient (the other name on the account) will get the funds—for example, if the terms say that you may withdraw all of the money first.

The estate tax implications of a joint bank or securities account can be severe. The IRS may argue that the entire account must be included in the estate of the first to die unless the executor can prove that some of the assets belonged to the surviving joint tenant (see below).

Safe-Deposit Box in Joint Names

Jointly owned safe-deposit boxes present different issues. While joint title will permit you and the other joint owner access, the title does not necessarily imply who owns the assets in the box. If the assets (for example, gold coins or jewelry) don't have their own title documents, the IRS is likely to try to tax them in the estate of the first to die. Also, the box may be sealed on the death of the first joint owner.

TIP: A way to avoid these problems is to open a safe-deposit box in the name of a family corporation and name yourself and other designees as officers of the corporation and signatories on the box.

One Name, as Trustee for the Benefit of Another Name

This type of account, often called a "totten trust," will provide you with sole control over the account. On your death, the proceeds will avoid probate and be transferred directly to the named beneficiary. The entire balance in the account, however, will be included in your taxable estate. If your bank permits, you may even be able to name more than one beneficiary under a totten trust. However, this approach has all of the shortcomings, and more, of gifts made under the Uniform Gifts to Minors Act (see Chapter 11). You have no control over the disposition of the funds after your death. If the beneficiary is a minor child, other approaches can be safer.

CAUTION: Totten trust accounts are affected by state law. There may be notice and other requirements to comply with. Even if you're separated at the time of your death, your spouse may have a claim against the account under a state's elective-share statute (see Chapter 13).

JOINTLY HELD PROPERTY

Joint tenancy with rights of survivorship, when two parties own a property together, should be distinguished from tenancy in common, when each person owns an undivided interest in the property. Although in both cases you and a second person can own equal interests in property, the legal consequences are substantially different. On the death of a joint tenant, the survivor obtains ownership of the entire property. On the death of a tenant in common, the deceased person's will governs where ownership of his or her interest in the property will go. Still another term is joint tenancy by the entirety, when property is owned jointly by a husband and wife.

When property is owned jointly, for example, "Sam Smith and Joe Jones, as joint tenants with rights of survivorship," on the death of the first joint tenant, the asset automatically becomes owned by the second. The advantage of the automatic transfer is that you don't need to specify it in a will. However, this approach is never an adequate substitute for a will. The reason is the same as with a living trust (see Chapter 4)—you can't be sure you've dealt with every asset.

A more important issue is that if you own property jointly with another person, it never goes through probate—your will has no effect on who gets this property. This eliminates any control or flexibility you may have. On your death, the property will automatically go to the joint owner. Joint ownership can also create some notable tax problems. Therefore, it is important to be aware of the tax implications before you title any significant assets in joint name.

NOTE: The first step is to ascertain the title of your assets. This should be done as part of developing your personal financial statement (see Chapter 1). Check the actual ownership documents to be sure.

Estate Tax Impact

The general estate tax rule is that the entire value of the joint property is included in the estate of the first joint tenant to die. (When the joint tenants are husband and wife, the presumption is that one-half of the value of the jointly held property is included in the estate of the first to die.) However, if the executor can prove that the surviving joint tenant contributed some portion to the property, some portion of the value can be excluded from the estate of the first joint tenant.

EXAMPLE: Sam Smith and Joe Jones purchased a beach house years ago for $55,000, as joint tenants with the right of survivorship. On Sam's death, the entire $400,000 fair value of the beach house presumably will be included in his estate. However, if Sam's executor can demonstrate that Joe contributed $30,000 of the original purchase price, a proportional amount of the current value of the beach house, $218,182, should be excluded from Sam's estate [$30,000/$55,000 × $400,000].

Gift Tax Impact

A joint tenancy can also have important gift tax consequences. If the joint tenants each own half of the property but only one joint tenant contributed to the purchase of the property, the joint tenancy will create a gift from the contributing joint tenant to the noncontributing joint tenant equal to one-half of the value of the property. The unlimited marital deduction, the $10,000 annual gift tax exclusion, or the $600,000 unified credit may eliminate any tax (see Chapters 7 and 10). Joint owners generally will report equal amounts of income on their respective tax returns. If one joint tenant is a minor under age 14, the kiddie tax may apply (see Chapter 11).

Termination

The decision may be made that it would be preferable to terminate a joint tenancy. There could be tax consequences to this move if you and the other joint tenant receive different percentages from those you own. For example, if you and a friend owned real estate equally but on the division of the joint tenancy you let the friend take a 75 percent ownership interest, this could constitute a gift by you to him or her equal to 25 percent of the value of the property. A similar result could obtain if the joint tenants have very different ages. If you're 85 and your joint tenant is 25, there could be a tax cost to making an equal division of the property, because your life expectancy is so much less.

NOTE: It is important to review the laws of the state where you are a permanent resident to learn of any special rules affecting joint ownership. If you own real estate in another state, that state's laws should be consulted, too. See below for the rules for community property states.

COMMUNITY PROPERTY

Eight states have special rules governing the ownership of property, called community property rules. These states are Arizona, California, Idaho, Nevada, New Mexico, Texas, Washington, and Wisconsin. If you've lived in any of these states during your marriage, it's important to be aware that these rules exist and that they will affect your estate planning. Any property acquired either by you or by your spouse while you were married and living in one of these sates is community property. This means that you and your spouse own equal shares in the property.

The community property rules are quite broad in their application. You and your spouse are also entitled to share equally in the income earned from your properties and from services you've each provided (wages). The fact that you move to a non-community-property state later will not automatically convert community property into non-community property. Applying these rules can become quite complicated, because you and your spouse can have separate property (for example, property acquired prior to marriage or a settlement from a personal injury award), joint property (property purchased as joint tenants before moving to a community property state), and community property.

For estate tax purposes, community property is treated like jointly held property—one-half is included in the estate of the first spouse to die. However, unlike jointly held property, community property does go through your probate estate, and it has an important tax advantage over jointly held property. When half the value of community property is included in the estate of the first spouse to die, the entire property obtains a step-up in its tax basis. This can eliminate any income tax on the later sale of the property. Joint property will only qualify for a step-up to the extent that it is included in the estate of the first joint tenant to die.

There is a second important tax advantage of community property as compared with jointly held property. When a spouse dies leaving community property, that spouse's one-half share can be placed in a marital trust for the surviving spouse so that the surviving spouse can obtain all of the income from the property. Also, only half the value of the asset will be included in the estate of the surviving spouse when that spouse dies. With joint property, the entire value of the property is included in the estate of the second joint tenant to die. This could result in half the property being subject to tax in both estates.

PERSONAL EFFECTS

Personal effects can include an art collection, jewelry, expensive crystal, antiques, a coin collection, and the like. These items may be of modest value—or substantial value. But no matter the economic value, these assets often require special attention in estate planning because of sentimental importance.

Your failure to provide for the distribution of these assets can result in unnecessary aggravation for your executor or, worse, intrafamily disputes and a will challenge. Generally, if you're married, your surviving spouse will be given any household effects. You may prefer to leave other items, such as a gun or coin collection, or musical instruments, to a specific beneficiary to whom they would be meaningful.

There are a few approaches that can be used to address the distribution of personal effects.

Provisions in Your Will

You can provide for the disposition of items in your will. A clause illustrating how this can be done appears in the sample will following Chapter 3. This clause gives all personal effects to the surviving spouse, or if the spouse doesn't survive, to the children at the discretion of the executor. It also says the estate will pay for all shipping and other costs. These can be significant, so it is appropriate to provide for their payment. You could add another clause to your will stating that a specific personal item should be given to a specific person—for example: "I give, devise, and bequeath my stamp and coin collections, located at [safe where maintained], to my cousin Sam Smith, who resides at [Sam's address]. If he does not survive me, then said coin and stamp collections shall be distributed as part of my other tangible personal property." This last sentence will result in the property's being distributed under a general clause of your will covering personal property, like the one referred to in the sample will. Be sure this general clause states clearly that it does not apply to any property that is transferred under a specific bequest made elsewhere in your will.

What if you're not sure how to divide your personal assets? Another approach can be a lottery-type system: "I give, devise, and bequeath all my tangible personal property to my children, in equal shares. My Executor shall assign an estimated fair market value to each item of personal property. My children shall then draw lots to determine an order for a rotational selection of items of my tangible personal property. They shall select one item each in a rotational order until each has selected the approximate value of personal property each is entitled to."

You may choose to label each item of personal property by writing a child's name on the back, to indicate your preference for distribution. If so, you should provide instructions to your executor that this distribution should be followed.

There is also a tax implication to your stating that a specific item of property should be distributed to a named beneficiary. It avoids having any income earned by your estate distributed as if it related to the property distribution.

Consider the affect of the tax allocation clause of your will if there is valuable personal property.

Letter of Instruction

You could provide in an informal letter of instruction how your personal effects should be distributed. The advantage of this approach is that it enables you to easily revise your bequests without the cost, formality, and effort of preparing a codicil to your will. State laws differ as to the validity of such letters, so check with your attorney.

Living Trust

If you use a revocable living trust to dispose of some or most of your assets, the distribution of your tangible personal property also can be achieved through this living trust. (See Chapter 4.)

NOTE: If you make a gift of personal property to a child or another person, be certain to change the insurance and any other evidence of ownership to the recipient's name, so that all of the facts will support that person's ownership of the property.

GLOSSARY

Alternate Valuation Date. A date of valuing assets six months later than death. Generally, assets included in an estate are taxed based on their fair value as of the decedent's date of death. Instead, an executor may elect to have the assets (except those already distributed or disposed of) valued as of a date six months later, which is useful when important assets have declined in value.

Annual Exclusion. An amount up to $10,000 per year every person is permitted to give away to any other person without incurring any gift tax. There is no limit on the number of people to whom these gifts can be made in a year. To qualify for this exclusion, the gift must be of a present interest, meaning that the recipient can enjoy the gift immediately. This can present problems in making a gift to a trust. This exclusion can be doubled to $20,000 per person annually if a married couple joins in making the gift. This is called *gift splitting.*

Beneficiary. A person who receives the benefits of a trust or of transfers made under a will.

Bequest. Property transferred under a will.

Buy-Sell Agreement. A contractual arrangement governing the transfer of ownership (stock or partnership interests) in a closely held business. This arrangement often relies on insurance to provide the necessary funds.

Bypass Trust. See *Credit Shelter Trust.*

Charitable Remainder Trust. The donation of property or money to a charity, when the donor reserves the right to use the property or to receive income from it for a specified time (a number of years, for the donor's life, or for the donor's life and the life of a second person, such as his or her spouse). When the agreed-upon period is over, the property belongs to the charitable organization. The trust can be an annuity trust (pays a fixed amount to a beneficiary each year) or a unitrust (pays an amount based on a percentage of asset values held by the charity).

Community Property. A way of owning property under some state's laws, such that when either partner in a married couple acquires any asset, each spouse will be considered to own a one-half interest in the asset.

Credit Shelter Trust. A trust designed not to qualify for the unlimited estate tax marital deduction, so that it will use up the lifetime $600,000 exclusion (unified credit). Often, it is the same as a bypass trust (because such a trust bypasses, is not included in, the surviving spouse's estate).

Decedent. The person who died.

Deferral of Estate Tax. Permission for an estate to pay the estate tax attributable to qualifying assets in a closely held and active business over a 14-year period instead of in the regular time, which is within nine months of death.

Disclaimer. The refusal by a beneficiary to accept receipt of property he or she is entitled to under a will. The property will then be transferred to the person next in line under the will and as provided under the laws of the particular state. The disclaimer often must be completed within nine months of death. Also called *renunciation.*

Donee. A person who receives a gift.

Donor. A person who makes a gift.

Estate Tax. The transfer tax that the federal government assesses on a person's right to transfer assets at the time of death. The tax generally applies to estates worth more than $600,000.

Executor. A person designated to manage an estate (marshalling assets, paying expenses and taxes, and making distributions to beneficiaries). *Executrix* is the feminine form. *Administrator* or *personal administrator* are sometimes used instead.

Fiduciary. A person in a position of trust and responsibility, such as the executor of a will or the trustee of a trust.

Generation-Skipping Transfer Tax (GSTT). A transfer tax generally assessed on gifts in excess of $1 million to grandchildren, great-grandchildren, and others at least two generations below the donor.

Gift. A transfer of property without receiving something of equal value in return. The federal government will assess a transfer tax when the value of the gift exceeds both the annual exclusion and the unified credit.

Gift-Leaseback. A gift of property a person presently owns and uses to his or her children, or to a trust for their benefit, which is then leased back from them. When properly structured, this approach will remove the property from an estate.

Grantor. The person who establishes a trust and transfers assets to it.

Gross Estate. The total value of the assets owned at death, or that are included in an estate. The value is determined at the date of the decedent's death or as of the alternate valuation date.

Guardian. The person designated as responsible for minor children or others who require special care. The term is also used in connection with a person appointed as guardian for assets.

Guardianship. The court appointment of a person to be responsible for a disabled person or minor.

Heir. A person who would be entitled to receive assets of the decedent where the decedent left no will.

Inheritance Tax. A tax imposed by a number of states based on the value of property that taxpayers inherit.

Installment Sale. A sale in which taxable gain is recognized over a number of years, as the payment for the property sold is received.

Insurance Trust. A trust established to own insurance policies in order to prevent them from being included in an estate.

Inter Vivos Trust. A trust created during a person's lifetime. Also called a *living trust.*

Irrevocable. Cannot be changed, as applied to a trust. This is an essential criterion in having the assets given to the trust removed from an estate.

Joint Tenancy. A way of owning property, in which a husband and wife, or any two people, each have automatic ownership rights to the property after the death of the owner. This approach is too often used as a means of avoiding probate, even though it may not be the optimal tax strategy.

Legacy. A piece of property transferred by a will. The person receiving it is called the *legatee.*

Living Will. A document that specifies which life-saving measures a person does, or does not, want to have taken on his or her behalf in the event of extreme illness. Also referred to as a *health care power of attorney.*

Marital Deduction. The assets (unlimited in amount) that can be transferred from one spouse to another at the death of the first without incurring any gift or estate tax cost. This is too often used simplistically as a way to eliminate the entire estate tax on the death of the first spouse without considering the consequences for the estate of the second spouse.

Marshalling Assets. The process by which the executor or administrator collects the assets of the estate.

Notary. A public officer or clerk who attests or certifies a document.

Pour-Over Will or Trust. A structure in which certain assets, often the remainder, are transferred (poured over into) a trust. This will is said to contain a *pour-over clause,* and the trust is said to be a *pour-over trust.*

Power of Appointment. The right and authority to transfer or dispose of property that a person does not own. Depending on the nature of the power, this can cause the value of the asset to be included in the estate of the person who holds the power of appointment.

Power of Attorney. A document in which one person grants certain other people the authority to handle his or her financial matters. When a power of attorney is *durable,* it will remain valid even if the person become disabled. When a power of attorney is *springing,* it only comes into effect once the person becomes disabled.

Present Interest. As applied to a gift, able to be enjoyed immediately. A gift must have this characteristic in order to qualify for the annual $10,000 gift tax exclusion.

Qualified Domestic Trust (Q-DOT). A special trust to which assets are transferred so that a spouse who is not a United States citizen will be entitled to claim the benefit of the unlimited marital deduction.

Qualified Terminable Interest Property Trust (Q-TIP). A trust that qualifies for the unlimited marital tax deduction. There will be no estate tax on the value of the property transferred to the surviving spouse in a Q-TIP trust on the first spouse's death, as long as the surviving spouse receives all income at least annually. The purpose of a Q-TIP is to enable an estate to avoid tax, while the grantor still designates who will receive the property remaining in the trust on the second spouse's death.

Residuary. The assets remaining in an estate after all specific transfers of property are made and all expenses paid.

Reversionary Interest. The possibility that property will return to the donor after it has been given away.

S Corporation. A corporation whose income is generally taxed to its shareholders, thus avoiding a corporate-level tax.

Second-to-Die Insurance. A type of insurance policy for a couple that pays a death benefit only on the death of the last spouse to die. This insurance is designed for an estate plan in which, on the death of the first spouse, all assets are given tax free to the surviving spouse using the unlimited marital deduction. On the death of the second spouse, the insurance benefit is paid and provides the cash to pay the estate tax. Also called *survivor's insurance.*

Section 303 Redemption. A rule in the tax code covering a distribution to redeem, or buy back, a shareholder's terminating interest. Generally, when a corporation distributes money or property, that distribution will be taxed in full as a dividend to the recipient shareholder. When the requirements of Code Section 303 are met, a distribution to redeem stock in the corporation can be treated as a sale, so that only the amount that exceeds the basis in (cost of) the stock will be taxed. Also, the amount taxed will qualify as a capital gain and thus receive a somewhat more favorable tax rate.

Section 2053(c) Trust. A special trust established for minor children that permits gifts to qualify for the annual $10,000 gift tax exclusion even though they are not gifts of a present interest.

Section 6166 Deferral. See *Deferral of Estate Tax.*

Sprinkling Power. The right granted to a trustee of a trust established for more than one beneficiary to pay income to the beneficiary (child) most in need, rather than to pay equally to all of the children.

Taxable Estate. The gross estate reduced by expenses, debts, and charitable contributions.

Tenancy by the Entirety. A special type of joint ownership for the case when husband and wife are joint tenants.

Trust. Property held and managed by a person (trustee) for the benefit of another (the beneficiary). The terms of the trust are generally governed by a contract that the grantor has prepared when establishing the trust.

Trustee. The person (fiduciary) who manages and administers a trust.

Unified Credit. An amount up to $600,000 in assets that every taxpayer is allowed to exclude from the estate and gift tax.

Uniform Gifts (Transfers) to Minors Act (UGMA or UTMA). A method of holding property for the benefit of another person, such as a child, which is similar to a trust but which is governed by state law. It is simpler and much cheaper to establish and administer than a trust, but it is far less flexible.

Will. A legal document completed in accordance with state law that specifies how assets will be distributed on a person's death, appoints an executor for the estate, may establish trusts for children and name a trustee for those trusts, names guardians for the children, and so forth.

INDEX